Work-Related Teaching and Learning

In the current economic climate, it is more important than ever that young people engage with the world of work and gain the knowledge, skills and experience they will need to prepare them for their future careers. This book provides an overarching framework for understanding all the separate parts of the work-related learning curriculum and constructs a research-based pedagogy with practical steps for students, teachers and practitioners.

Work-Related Teaching and Learning deepens our understanding of work-related learning and provides an overview of the programmes and recent initiatives designed to make learning more relevant and better connected to work. Drawing on contemporary research and innovative practice, it offers guidance to support teachers and practitioners in the delivery of the work-related learning curriculum.

Covering all aspects of work-related learning from enterprise education and economic wellbeing to careers education, work experience and the Diplomas, features include:

- an overarching conceptualisation of work-related learning
- an exploration of the benefits of work-related learning
- an examination of the key issues and challenges faced
- a detailed look at how teaching and learning activities have been used in various contexts and with what effects
- an assessment of the strengths and weaknesses of different curriculum models
- case studies and examples of good practice
- discussion questions for reflective practice.

This book is essential reading for current teachers and practitioners involved in work-related learning, as well as students and trainee teachers who wish to improve or develop their practice in the light of recent initiatives.

Prue Huddleston is Professorial Fellow at the Centre for Education and Industry at the University of Warwick; she has taught in further education and on community and outreach programmes and is a teacher trainer. Her research interests focus on 14–19 vocational qualifications and work-rela.......

Julian Stanley is Head of the C...... t the University of Warwick. He has taught extensiv...... g to the design and evaluation of work-related learni...... ent.

042975

Work-Related Teaching and Learning

A guide for teachers and practitioners

Edited by Prue Huddleston and Julian Stanley

Routledge
Taylor & Francis Group

LONDON AND NEW YORK

First published 2012
by Routledge
2 Park Square, Milton Park, Abingdon, Oxon OX14 4RN

Simultaneously published in the USA and Canada
by Routledge
711 Third Avenue, New York, NY 10017

Routledge is an imprint of the Taylor & Francis Group, an informa business

British Library Cataloguing in Publication Data
A catalogue record for this book is available from the British Library

Library of Congress Cataloging in Publication Data
Huddleston, Prue.
Work-related teaching and learning: a guide for teachers and practitioners/by Prue
Huddleston and Julian Stanley. – 1st ed.
p. cm.
1. Business education. 2. Economics—Study and teaching (Secondary) 3. Business
teachers—Training of. 4. Curriculum planning. 5. Curriculum evaluation. I. Stanley,
Julian C. II. Title.
HF1141.H84 2011
650.071'2—dc22
2011009974

ISBN: 978-0-415-57816-5 (hbk)
ISBN: 978-0-415-57817-2 (pbk)
ISBN: 978-0-203-80485-8 (ebk)

Typeset in Bembo
by Prepress Projects Ltd, Perth, UK

MIX
Paper from
responsible sources
FSC FSC® C004839
www.fsc.org

Printed and bound in Great Britain by
TJ International Ltd, Padstow, Cornwall

Contents

Figures

Tables

Contributors

Prue Huddleston is Professorial Fellow and formerly Director, Centre for Education and Industry, University of Warwick. Before joining the University of Warwick, she worked for many years within the further education (FE) sector and on community and outreach programmes. Prue has a particular interest in the 14–19 curriculum, particularly vocational qualifications and work-related learning. A chief research interest has been the use of alternative approaches to the schooling of those identified as underachieving. She has been involved in postgraduate teacher training (secondary and post-compulsory) for the past 20 years. She has completed research and evaluation contracts for the Department for Children, Schools and Families (DCSF), Learning and Skills Council, Qualifications and Curriculum Development Agency (QCDA), Economic and Social Research Council (ESRC), European Commission, British Council, Soros Foundation, companies, colleges, schools and local authorities.

Julian Stanley is Centre Head, Centre for Education and Industry, University of Warwick. Julian taught in a number of secondary schools for 18 years, during which time he was involved in work-related learning as Head of Business Education, Co-ordinator of Vocational Education and Work Experience Organiser. He is currently Head of the Centre for Education and Industry at the University of Warwick. He has carried out research into many kinds of work-related learning and he has been involved in the development of new vocational qualifications and of resources to support the teaching of work-related learning. He has worked as a consultant and adviser to the Qualifications and Curriculum Authority (QCA) and the DCSF.

Trisha Fettes is Principal Research Fellow, Centre for Education and Industry, University of Warwick. Trisha has held a particular interest in the development and recognition of generic skills for over 30 years, both as a researcher and as a facilitator of learning in school, college, work-based and community contexts. Whilst at the National Council for Vocational Qualifications (NCVQ) and the QCA she was responsible for developing the national standards for key skills. As Principal Research Fellow at the Centre for Education and Industry, University of Warwick, she has managed evaluations of enterprise education and Extended Projects, and researched the design of the Diploma's generic component and associated pedagogy.

Malcolm Hoare is Regional Director, Centre for Education and Industry, University of Warwick. Malcolm worked in secondary schools for 23 years before moving into higher education, initially at Durham University Business School (DUBS) before joining the University of Warwick as a Regional Director at the Centre for Education and Industry. He has worked as a consultant for a range of government agencies in Denmark, Finland, Italy, Norway, Spain and the UK. His research interests focus upon entrepreneurial teaching and learning and he is the co-author of the National Standard for Enterprise Education.

Marian Morris is Associate Director of SQW, formerly Principal Research Officer at the National Foundation for Educational Research (NFER). Prior to moving to SQW in May 2010, Marian worked for more than 20 years at the NFER, which she joined following an 11-year career teaching in secondary schools. She developed and directed the NFER's portfolios of work in careers education and guidance, widening participation and environmental education for government departments, regional and local authority organisations, funding councils, charitable foundations and a range of environmental organisations. Marian has also presented research and expert witness papers at national and international conferences and seminars and has been a member of a number of national advisory bodies, including the Nuffield 14–19 Review and the Royal Society Advisory Group for the State of the Nation Reports.

Faith Muir is Regional Director, Centre for Education and Industry, University of Warwick. Following 16 years' experience of secondary teaching, during which time she led an Arts Faculty, co-ordinated Technical and Vocational Education Initiative provision and was teacher-tutor for Postgraduate Certificate of Education (PGCE) Music at Goldsmiths College, Faith worked in and subsequently managed a London Education Business Partnership. Since joining the Centre for Education and Industry at the University of Warwick she has written practitioner guidance on work-related learning and financial capability for organisations including QCA/QCDA and the Personal Finance Education Group (pfeg). Recent contracts have covered research into work-related learning for disaffected learners, young apprenticeships and enterprise education. She is particularly interested in investigating the impact of the Extended Project Qualification.

Acknowledgements

We should like to thank all the teachers and learners who have shared their exemplary practice in work-related learning with us and who have enriched our understanding and provided inspiration for this book. We should particularly like to extend our appreciation to Postgraduate Teacher Trainees (Business Education) at the University of Warwick, who have given us hope that the future of creative teaching and learning within work-related learning is in safe hands.

Abbreviations

CBI	Confederation of British Industry
CEI	Centre for Education and Industry
CPD	continuing professional development
DCSF	Department for Children, Schools and Families
DfE	Department for Education
DfEE	Department for Education and Employment
DfES	Department for Education and Skills
DTI	Department for Trade and Industry
EBLO	education–business link organisation
EBP	education–business partnership
ECM	Every Child Matters
EWFC	Economic Wellbeing and Financial Capability
FE	further education
HE	higher education
IAG	careers information, advice and guidance
IEBE	Institute for Education Business Excellence
KS	Key Stage
LSIS	Learning Skills Improvement Service
Ofsted	Office for Standards in Schools, Children's Services and Skills
PLTS	personal learning and thinking skills
PSHE(E)	Personal, Social, Health and Economic (Education)
PW	Personal Wellbeing
QCA	Qualifications and Curriculum Authority
QCDA	Qualifications and Curriculum Development Agency
SSAT	Specialist Schools and Academies Trust
STEM	science, technology, engineering and mathematics
TVEI	Technical and Vocational Education Initiative
UKCES	United Kingdom Commission for Employment and Skills

Introduction

Julian Stanley

This book is aimed at those who want to both understand and practise work-related learning. It aims to do *more* than offer a description of activities, a checklist for planning, some exemplars and a few useful reminders. It aims to do *less* than provide a generalised explanation of how work-related learning has come about and how it fits into the rest of the educational system. It seeks to help those who teach, support or manage work-related learning develop a sufficient understanding of this diverse and complex collection of educational activities. Collectively the contributors to this volume want to explore what practitioners can hope to achieve through work-related learning and what alternative strategies they might make use of. It is our contention that teachers of work-related learning have to make judgements in their teaching which take account of what they, their students and partners want to achieve and which are appropriate to the contexts in which they are working. In order to make these judgements they will need a broad and critical understanding of work-related learning.

Getting a grip on work-related learning is made difficult by the fact that work-related learning is not a conventional subject. It is not supported by a longstanding community of subject teachers, ready to initiate young practitioners and to recognise their practice in school and college departments. It is not backed up by textbooks and university departments which define content and train its specialists. Of course, there are networks and organisations that are dedicated to advancing and supporting work-related learning and, since 2004, work-related learning has gained statutory recognition as a part of the secondary school curriculum in England. Nevertheless, although work-related learning has gained formal recognition in curriculum and institutional terms, it retains a contested, diverse and challenging character. Indeed, as this book goes to press, the status of work-related learning has been put into question by the new policies of the coalition government that came to power in May 2010.

Work-related learning represents a challenge to education because it directly addresses the relationship between education and work. It challenges the implicit assumption that a traditional subject-based curriculum will equip young people with the skills and knowledge that they are likely to need in work, that traditional schooling will enable young people to make successful decisions in relation to their entry into the workforce or support their socio-economic success. Work-related learning is not, as we shall see, the same as vocational learning. Although work-related learning owes much to vocational learning, and it does claim to prepare young people to be workers, it has wider ambitions: it aspires to be a curriculum for all young people, it claims relevance in relation to all kinds of work and it proposes distinctive processes for learning and distinctive environments for learning.

This ambition makes it more difficult to define the boundaries of work-related learning and so to define the scope of this book. Work-related learning does not just deal with work as a topic of learning. Work-related learning can play a part in subject teaching; for example, an English teacher or a maths teacher may make use of a work context to develop communication or numeracy skills. However, work is such a widely used category in our society, encompassing so much of what people do, that it might seem difficult to see what does not count as work-related learning. In order to try to pin down work-related learning it is helpful to recognise that there are several different ways of looking at it and discussing it.

The Education Act 2002 defines work-related learning as: 'planned activity designed to use the context of work to develop knowledge, skills and understanding useful in work, including learning through the experience of work, learning about work and working practices and learning the skills for work.'

This rather compressed definition is usually unpacked in terms of the three specified strands of work-related learning:

- learning through work by providing opportunities for young people to learn from direct experiences of work
- learning about work by providing opportunities to develop knowledge and understanding of work and enterprise
- learning for work by developing skills for enterprise and employability.

(QCA 2008, p. 2)

The notion of three strands suggests that, at the very least, we need to give attention to the character of the learning activities (learning through work), to what is learnt (learning about work) and to the purpose of the learning (learning for work).

Work-related learning activities

We can distinguish between the main types of teaching and learning activity that go on under the name of work-related learning. These learning activities constitute a family: they share some characteristics, but not all characteristics. Work experience, careers education and guidance, work shadowing and mock job interviews are pretty much always recognised as part of work-related learning. Enterprise education, vocational courses, industry days, role plays and visits to enterprises would usually be recognised as work-related learning. Mentoring, part-time work, personal financial education, visits to business organisations and functional skills lessons might or might not be seen as work-related learning, depending on the context, the purpose and the perspective. Some of these activities make use of workplaces, some of workers, some of work situations and tasks, some of work goals and some of more than one of these features.

In this book, we try to use the concept of work-related learning as a way of exploring what this family of educational activities have in common but also how they differ. By exploring what they share, we hope that it will be easier for teachers to make these kinds of learning complementary. However, we need to be able to understand how these activities differ as well. As the contributions to this book show, these different activities have distinctive histories, values and practices. Careers education, enterprise education and work experience, just to take the best-known, not only have different origins but even today, in many institutions, may be delivered by different teachers, working in different departments with different approaches.

The work-related learning curriculum

Despite the diversity of practice described above, we can also describe a formal work-related learning entitlement as set out in official documents. This curriculum has been gradually developed in order to make work-related learning more coherent and to support a more consistent and universal delivery. The language of the educational documents is varied, sometimes setting out requirements in terms of learning activities or experiences, sometimes in terms of learning outcomes such as knowledge, understanding and skills. Guidance, content and learning outcomes have been published both for elements of work-related learning, such as careers education and enterprise education, and also for work-related learning as a whole. The Department for Education (DfE), the Qualifications and Curriculum Development Authority[1] (QCDA), the Office for Standards in Schools, Children's Services and Skills (Ofsted), awarding bodies, support agencies and local educational agencies have produced a number of statements over the last 20 or so years. Broadly speaking these agencies work closely together so that usually they offer a consistent and converging account of the scope and meaning of work-related learning. However, the official work-related learning curriculum, like the rest of the curriculum, is subject to development and policy change. As we shall see, policy and curriculum have developed further for some Key Stages and for some elements of work-related learning than for others, so requirements are clearly defined in some respects, but more loosely spelled out for others.

Official statements on work-related learning offer variations in relation to scope, meaning and purpose – which gives some discretion to practitioners to decide just what is important for their students. The Qualifications and Curriculum Authority (QCA)'s most recent framework, 'Career, work-related learning and enterprise 11–19' (Figure 0.1), aims to make clear what is required for *all* learners aged 11–19. Rather than defining either the learning activities or the outcomes required for all learners, it provides a framework of broadly defined elements of learning together with guidance to what the minimum requirement might be and what kinds of learning outcomes might result.

It is expressly recognised that:

Schools will be able to choose the most appropriate work-related activities according to students' individual needs and local capacity. The experiences of students will differ as work-related learning is acquired in various ways for different students . . . For some students, work-related learning is built into their subject learning, supplemented by careers education and work experience. For others, it is provided largely through a course leading to a vocational qualification. Some students follow an extended work-related learning programme with an FE college, training provider or employer.

(DCSF 2007, p. 10)

However, this is by no means the only authoritative document relating to work-related learning; the national curriculum sets out programmes of study for economic wellbeing, financial capability, careers education, enterprise education and work-related learning which vary by Key Stage. Other educational agencies, such as the DfE, the National Taskforce for Education and Employers and the Learning and Skills Improvement Service (LSIS) have produced their own statements on work-related learning (or elements thereof). The documents emphasise the different ways in which work-related learning can be interpreted and realised, and this pluralism leaves space for teachers and learners to find their own ways of doing work-related learning.

Purposes

Evidently it is a distinctive feature of work-related learning that it does, in some sense, prepare young people for work. We have seen already that for many this is the key rationale for work-related learning: *learning for earning*. Work-related learning has been 'sold' to learners and employers on the basis of its use value in the world of work. However, different purposes have been associated with different types of work-related learning or indeed with one kind of work-related learning by different stakeholders or even the same stakeholders at different times. For example, work experience has been advocated as a means to develop awareness of alternative careers, or to develop social or intellectual capabilities that will be used in employment or as a way of actually gaining full- or part-time employment.

- recognise, develop and apply their skills for enterprise and employability;
- use their experience of work, including work experience and part-time jobs, to extend their understanding of work;
- learn about the way business enterprises operate, working roles and conditions, and rights and responsibilities in the work place;
- develop awareness of the extent and diversity of local and national employment opportunities;
- relate their own abilities, attributes and achievements to career intentions and make informed choices based on an understanding of the alternatives;
- undertake tasks and activities set in work contexts;
- learn from contact with personnel from different employment sectors;
- have experience (direct or indirect) of working practices and environments;
- engage with ideas, challenges and applications from the business world.

FIGURE 0.1 Career, work-related learning and enterprise 11–19: a framework to support economic wellbeing (QCA 2008, p. 20).

Moreover, to characterise work-related learning as serving to prepare young people for work still leaves a lot to be contested. Many have argued that preparing young people as workers is only a part of what work-related learning should do, particularly as entry into the workforce may be some way into the future for the vast majority of 11- to 16-year-olds. Furthermore, preparation for work is a complex process that admits of different perspectives and goals. From the point of view of the learner, for example, preparation may focus on career exploration, job evaluation and decision making, whereas from the point of view of the employer the acquisition of job-specific or generic employment skills may seem more important.

Claims about the purpose of work-related learning have been proposed and disputed in government policy papers and in the publications of employers' groups, trades unions, professional bodies, research centres, political parties and educational bodies.

The Department for Children, Schools and Families's review of work-related learning, *Building on the Best* (2007), defined the purposes extensively:

- raising standards of achievement;
- increasing the commitment to learning, motivation and self confidence of students;
- improving the retention of young people in learning after the end of compulsory schooling;
- developing career awareness and the ability to benefit from impartial and informed information and guidance;
- supporting active citizenship;
- developing key skills and broader personal aptitudes;
- developing the ability to make conscious applications of knowledge, understanding and skills;
- improving understanding of the economy, enterprise, personal finance and the structure of business organisations and how they work;
- encouraging positive attitudes to lifelong learning.

(DCSF 2007)

In practice, different types of work-related learning are likely to give greater scope to some purposes than others and some work-related learning, such as work experience or enterprise education, can be tailored to serve different purposes. More recently, the personalisation agenda has demanded that the curriculum should be tailored to meet the needs of particular learners. Recognising that the learning objectives of learners may differ, it is argued that these differences should help shape the design of their learning. It follows that learners may value work-related learning for different purposes and that teachers of work-related learning need to develop ways to vary the focus of work-related learning in the light of what learners want and need.

Teaching work-related learning

The purpose of this book is to inform and develop the teaching of work-related learning – what might be called work-related teaching. Although the book aims to demonstrate that both in terms of concept and in terms of practice there is much variation and openness in the field of work-related learning, it does not offer to remedy this with a tighter definition or universal principles for implementation. The aim rather is to help teachers to master a repertoire of related practices and to find out how they can be adapted for their own students and contexts. Teachers will want to know what purposes work-related learning has been supposed to achieve but should expect to go on to negotiate with their colleagues, their students and their partners to agree and prioritise shared goals. Many teachers have found that they can make use of work-related learning activities to serve other objectives, such as the development of subject learning or personal development. Others have found that work-related learning can be made to serve the distinctive ethos of their schools or colleges, which may be distinguished by religion, cultural aspirations or the communities that they serve.

Work-related learning represents a set of teaching opportunities that are more loosely prescribed and less well supported than a traditional subject or discipline. Work-related learning does not offer as much as a subject; that is to say the content, method and style of teaching are not so well developed and the resources for learning are less clearly defined. On the other hand, the opportunities for teachers of work-related learning are remarkable. Outside of the school and the classroom are offices, shops and factories – all of which can be places for learning. In addition to teachers, there are workers, employers, volunteers, entrepreneurs and trainees – all of whom can, in their own fashion, teach or support learning. Work-related learning offers opportunities to put learning to use in realistic tasks, to gain recognition for learning and to connect education to career and personal goals which conventional subjects are less likely to address.

The aim of this book then is to empower teachers to take advantage of these opportunities. This involves learning from the practice of others. However, it also requires a capacity to work with a diversity of objectives and to take account of local contexts. The question is not so much how to teach work-related learning but how teachers might teach work-related learning in a particular institution, with particular students and in given circumstances.

This book will appear at a time when education policy is under review and the priorities, institutions and language of education are changing. There are some signs that the status of work-related learning in the curriculum will be downgraded by ministers, who have said that they favour a more traditional subject-based schooling. However, the picture is by no means clear: technical and vocational education appear to have a renewed importance, as does employability. The underpinning economic changes that have led to the development of work-related learning appear to be accelerating rather than slackening. The Secretary of State for Education, Michael Gove, has also made it clear that improvements in educational performance will be driven by improvements in teaching and that increased autonomy for schools and for teachers is critical to improvements in teaching (Department for Education 2010). Work-related learning is, as we shall see, a way of teaching as well as being a field that students can study and also a range of capabilities and skills that students can develop. If greater autonomy for schools and teachers leads to greater diversity of educational provision, then school leaders and teachers will have to make decisions about what work-related learning they want to offer and how they want to teach it.

Note

1. Until 2009 this agency was known as the Qualifications and Curriculum Authority (QCA).

References

DCSF (2007) *Building on the Best: Final Report and Implementation Plan of the Review of 14–19 Work-Related Learning*. Nottingham: DCSF. Available HTTP: <http://www.dcsf.gov.uk/14-19/documents/14-19workrelatedlearning_web.pdf> (accessed 16 December 2010).

Department for Education (2010) *The Importance of Education*. London: The Stationery Office. Available HTTP: <http://publications.education.gov.uk/eOrderingDownload/CM-7980.pdf> (accessed 16 December 2010).

QCA (2005) *Work-Related Learning at Key Stage 4: Guidance for School Coordinators*. London: QCA.

QCA (2008) *Career, Work-Related Learning and Enterprise 11–19: A Framework to Support Economic Wellbeing*. London: QCA.

Part I

CHAPTER

1

What is work-related learning?

Julian Stanley

The concept of work-related learning

Work-related learning is a complex educational phenomenon. It is at once a set of educational missions (e.g. careers education), a range of activities (work experience), a collection of topics (understanding credit and work) and a repertoire of teaching and learning styles. There is currently a defined statutory educational requirement at Key Stage 4 for work-related learning and for careers education (QCA 2003) and there are non-statutory programmes of work for Economic Wellbeing and Financial Capability at Key Stages 3 and 4, which include key work-related learning elements such as careers education and enterprise education.[1] In addition, the government has published extensive guidance on the value, relevance and interpretation of work-related learning for learners from Early Years Foundation Stage through to post-16 (DCSF 2009). Work-related learning is also regarded as a way of delivering other programmes, such as Diplomas or mathematics. At times it is used broadly to refer to any educational programme that has any connection to work, at other times as part of a family of activities; for example, the Qualifications and Curriculum Authority (QCA)'s *Career, Work-Related Learning and Enterprise 11–19* framework refers to 'career, work-related and enterprise' education as collectively serving 'economic wellbeing' (QCA 2008, p. 2).

For many years, it has been common to distinguish between the process, the matter and the purpose of work-related learning. When work-related learning became statutory at Key Stage 4 in 2004, all of these dimensions were included:

The statutory requirement is for schools to make provision for all students at Key Stage 4 to:

- learn through work, by providing opportunities for students to learn from direct experiences of work (for example, through work experience or part-time jobs)
- learn about work, by providing opportunities for students to develop knowledge and understanding of work and enterprise (for example, through vocational courses and careers education)

- learn for work by developing skills for enterprise and employability (for example, through problem-solving activities, work simulations and mock interviews).

(QCA 2003, p. 2)

This makes it clear that work-related learning should not be defined just in terms of learning outcomes, that is the knowledge, skills and understanding that learners are to acquire. Work-related learning has come to refer to a range of teaching and learning activities, which involve distinctive teaching and learning processes. Another important characteristic of work-related learning is that it is explicitly concerned with teaching and learning in context. A large part of the conventional school curriculum focuses on knowledge and skills which have a general value and truth; for example, scientific, mathematical and historical knowledge, essay writing and reasoning. This kind of knowledge and skill are supposed to possess a general value far greater than any particular use that one might make of them. Work-related learning also claims to provide some general skills and knowledge (e.g. employability), but it is also concerned with learning in relation to particular situations, particular problems and particular organisational or personal objectives (e.g. individual advice and guidance). Another way in which work-related learning differs from the conventional curriculum is that there is a greater emphasis on emotional and practical as opposed to intellectual learning. Obviously, how people feel and act is of importance in work situations so work-related learning will be concerned with emotions and actions as well as facts and theories.

The challenge is to sustain a multi-dimensional and complex understanding of work-related learning. Work-related learning is not just a matter of process; it does claim to support particular learning outcomes. Work-related learning is not just to do with activities and attitudes; it does also address understanding and judgement. Work-related learning does deal with local problems and local knowledge; but it also makes use of and generates more general knowledge. Some writers argue that these kinds of distinctions are based on the mistaken, though venerable, tradition that the most worthwhile knowledge is intellectual (not practical or emotional) and that the priority of education is to transmit intellectual knowledge (Hager and Halliday 2006). For our purposes, it is enough to recognise that work-related learning should not be conceptualised as something other than academic learning; rather it is something which cross-cuts a number of concepts of education – we need to be tolerant of some ambiguity.

Even if we focus on activities (rather than purposes, topics or teaching and learning styles) it is not easy to agree about the scope of work-related learning since it depends on what criteria are being used. If, for example, the key criterion is *location* then work-related learning might be defined as education that makes use of workplaces as well as classrooms, as for example in work experience or business visits. If, however, a criterion is the involvement of *workers* or *employers* then work-related learning will include such activities as mock interviews or mentoring, even if they take place outside the workplace. Alternatively, a learning event may be related to work because its function is derived from a work situation, for example writing a letter of application for a job or calculating a profit – even though the activity is led by a teacher in a conventional classroom.

One way of getting a grasp on the distinctive character of work-related learning is to make a general comparison between learning as it goes on in a classroom, directed by teachers and making use of educational resources, and learning that goes on in the workplace, where workers learn from carrying out their jobs alongside co-workers. Table 1.1 differentiates work-related learning from traditional classroom-based learning and work-based training. The basic idea is that work-related learning offers

TABLE 1.1 Dimensions and degrees of work-related learning

	'TRADITIONAL CLASSROOM' OR 'FORMAL' LEARNING	'WORK-RELATED LEARNING'	'TRADITIONAL WORK-BASED' OR 'INFORMAL' LEARNING OR TRAINING
Purposes	Educational goals: subject mastery and qualifications	Educational and work purposes	Work goals, e.g. quality outputs, targets, profit
Content (knowledge, understanding and skills)	Academic or school subjects	Sociology, business studies and economics plus generic and vocational skills plus attitudes and dispositions relating to work, consumption, economic activity, etc.	Knowledge of organisational and work processes plus relevant technical or scientific knowledge
Environment	Classroom or workshop in school or college	Workplace *and* school or college (dual system) or hybrid learning/training centre	Workplace
Teachers	School or college teacher	Teachers *and* workers or hybrids, e.g. employer as teacher	Supervisors and co-workers
Resources	Specialist educational resources, e.g. textbooks	Educational *and* work resources or specialist hybrid resources, e.g. training kitchen	Work tools and infrastructure
Conditions	E.g. 50-minute lesson with 26 students controlled by 1 teacher	Lessons *and* work conditions or hybrids, e.g. 'collapsed timetable day'	Normal work conditions
Tasks	Educationally designed, e.g. exercises, note taking	Both educational *and* work tasks or jointly designed tasks, e.g. redesigning a real product outside the work place	Live work tasks
Learning processes	Conventional educational, e.g. listening, writing	Both educational *and* work processes or blended processes, e.g. observation, imitation	Routine work processes, e.g. making, selling, discussing work tasks

a middle ground between work-based and classroom-based learning. However, this idea is elaborated on in two ways. First, it is useful to recognise that work-relatedness is a matter of degree. In other words, learning activities can be judged to be more or less work-related, and many activities, such as simulations and case studies, can be regarded as blended. Second, it is helpful to analyse work-relatedness not as a simple, variable quality but as a complex one in which we can distinguish eight different dimensions. For example, a learning task might be given a *purpose* in relation to a work situation, but it could take *place* in the classroom. The students might be taught or briefed by a business professional (rather than a teacher) and the students could be asked to carry it out under the time conditions normal in the workplace but with educational *resources*, such as textbooks, to help them. The *content* of the learning may be focused narrowly on work processes or work organisations or it may be closely related to subject knowledge such as sociology or business studies. Learning which is strongly work-related in many of the eight dimensions is *more* work-related than learning whose relationship to work is 'one dimensional' or only weakly work-related in a number of dimensions. Many traditional, secondary school maths problems, for example, are about buying and selling, but this is a nominal work-relatedness which is not expected to make any difference to how the calculation is regarded by learners or how they carry it out.

Table 1.1 reveals that work-related learning possesses some of the characteristics of formal or 'school' learning and some of the characteristics of informal or work-based learning. It also shows that work-related learning is characterised by a focus on how the context of learning, in a broad sense, makes a difference to learning. This means that while there may well be knowledge or skills that are acquired through work-related learning, rather as knowledge is acquired within conventional academic learning, work-related learning is also concerned with learning in particular kinds of situation, or with particular people or in relation to certain tasks (Felstead *et al.* 2005). The table also reveals that there are a considerable variety of ways to design and perform work-related learning because there are different ways in which the connection between work and learning can be made.

The development of work-related learning

It would be possible to write separate histories of how policy makers, experts and teachers have sought to develop the different strands of work-related learning: careers education, work experience, personal financial education, enterprise education and so on. Some of these histories are extraordinary success stories: early experimentation by pioneers with relatively small groups of learners gets copied by other teachers and, critically, gains support from local authorities, educational agencies, central government, third-sector organisations, head teachers and teachers more widely. What starts as an experiment gradually becomes an expectation and ultimately an entitlement.

The growth of work experience in the 1970s and 1980s represents a fairytale story of educational innovation and adoption. Before 1970, fewer than 2 per cent of students did work experience; by 1990, 71 per cent did. The apparently unstoppable rise of work experience (see Figure 1.1) has inspired enthusiasts for other kinds of work-related learning and for educational innovation in general. However, as we shall see

Work experience was mentioned in the report of the Newsom Committee (Central Advisory Council for Education 1963) as being of value for some students aged over 15 in their final year of schooling. It was estimated by the Institute of Careers Officers in 1968/69 that fewer than 2 per cent of students reaching the school leaving age had been on work experience placements (Miller *et al.* 1991). The Education (Work Experience) Act 1973 and Department of Education and Science (DES) Circular 7/74 (DES 1974) confirmed that work experience was permissible and stated that it had value for *all* pupils. A DES survey of 1975–78 found that 37 per cent of secondary schools had schemes but very few of these were for all students (DES 1979). The late 1970s and 1980s saw the development of third-sector organisations, most notably Project Trident, that provided advocacy, support and services to make work experience happen. 1982 saw the launch of the Technical and Vocational Education Initiative (TVEI), which included a work experience component, so that by 1986 a survey by Her Majesty's Inspectorate of Education (HMI) found that 66 per cent of schools offered work experience for some students (though only 17 schools out of 371 offered it for all students in their final year) (HMI 1988). However, with the extension of TVEI to all schools and colleges of further education in 1988, work experience became a general requirement, so that a DES survey of 1988/89 found that 91 per cent of schools and 71 per cent of students were involved in work experience (DES 1990). Success breeds success and the late 1980s saw the Department of Trade and Industry (DTI) providing additional support for work experience. In 1988 the DTI launched the Enterprise and Education Initiative, which led to the appointment of 140 DTI Advisors with a brief to increase the supply of work experience places, and from 1990 the DTI provided funding for the development of local education–business partnerships to support initiatives for schools and businesses to work together, including work experience (Miller *et al.* 1991).

FIGURE 1.1 The history of work experience.

in Chapter 4, work experience now faces challenges in relation to its funding, organisation and purpose. Moreover it is unlikely that every kind of work-related learning can achieve market saturation; indeed, it may be that the predominance of work experience has crowded out other forms of work-related learning and that other kinds of work-related learning can grow only at the expense of work experience. Viewed over the last 30 years some work-related activities, such as enterprise education and careers education, have followed volatile cycles of growth and decline, whereas others, such as work shadowing, have remained minority pursuits (see Chapters 4, 8 and 9).

The purposes of work-related learning

A variety of purposes have been associated with work-related learning, and different purposes are given different priorities by different stakeholders. The purpose of work-related learning has shifted over time, with changing economic and political circumstances. Distinctive goals are attributed to different work-related learning activities and these are explored in more depth in the chapters that follow. However, it is possible to summarise the broad purposes which have influenced the development of work-related learning:

1. Work-related learning as an alternative to academic education for all

In England, work-related learning has developed alongside comprehensive schools and it is closely connected with the challenge of creating a curriculum which is relevant for *all* young people. Work-related learning represents an alternative to both a traditional grammar school curriculum (which does not directly relate to work at all) and vocational training (which historically was orientated directly towards craft or technical employment and took place out of school). Work-related learning aims to deliver capabilities, socialisation and understanding to *all* learners, not just the 'unacademic'. Work-related learning claims to relate to all kinds of work – not just to those involving manual skills. Work-related learning is intended to be part of a common rather than a selective curriculum.

Work-related learning is also associated with the issue of transition: how to support successful passage from school into employment. Work experience, careers education and business visits have been rationalised as meeting the needs of older students in their final year or years of school. The raising of the school leaving age to 16 in 1972 and the Technical Vocational and Education Initiative (TVEI) and Diploma initiatives have, in turn, raised the profile of work-related learning. The underpinning argument seems to be that older students need a curriculum that is more work-related than do younger students (because in the past they would have been in work) and that a longer education should incorporate a transitional phase between school and work.

Jim Callaghan's famous Ruskin College speech in 1976 articulated the concern that a traditional liberal curriculum would not do for a comprehensive school system which extended to 16-year-olds. Callaghan urged that education should, in addition to addressing liberal goals, be concerned to prepare all young people for work. Callaghan's speech gave legitimacy and support to a plethora of public and private initiatives that promoted and developed different kinds of work-related learning from the late 1970s onwards.

2. Work-related learning to develop the skills and knowledge required by employers

Another perspective is that of employers. A key driver for the development of work-related learning has been the voice of employers' organisations expressing concerns about the skills of young people or their readiness for work. What employers have asked for has varied. In recent times, these concerns have found their expression in two ways.

First, there is the pursuit of 'employability': the variously defined general skills, capabilities and behaviours supposed to be necessary to gain employment and perform successfully in employment. For example, in March 2007, the Confederation of British Industry (CBI) published a report entitled *Time Well Spent: Embedding Employability in Work Experience*, which endorsed work experience in so far as it serves to develop employability and suggested changes in practice which would strengthen this function (Confederation of British Industry 2007). In 2008–9, the UK Commission for Employment and Skills (UKCES) published research and guidance into employability culminating in *The Employability Challenge*, which called for employability to be given parity of esteem with academic educational outcomes and for action by government, schools, colleges, employers, training providers and universities to make this happen (UKCES 2009).

Second, there is the concern of particular employment sectors to promote awareness, appropriate skills and knowledge, and aspirations for employment in their particular sector. This concern has been addressed through campaigns and programmes originating in particular sectors, such as engineering and financial services, and more systematically through the development of Diplomas (see Chapter 6).

3. Work-related learning concerned with the application or use of knowledge and skills

This approach is supported by accounts of how professionals and workers learn in the workplace: by doing and learning from their actions and those of their peers. Work-related learning is justified as a particularly effective way of learning and contrasted with learning by reading, memorising or listening to lectures. Learning by doing is held to be attractive to young people, and likely to be useful for employers since it ensures that knowledge and skills can be made operational.

Work-related learning has been characterised in terms of teaching and learning styles, for example aiming for learning through first-hand experiences, supplying opportunities for practical action in real or realistic work situations, backed up by review and feedback. This justification of work-related learning has been particularly prominent in the promotion and development of Diplomas. However, work simulation, problem solving, role plays, competitions and mini-enterprises have always been associated with work-related learning and have been variously described as 'experiential' or 'active learning'.

4. Work-related learning to cope with economic and technological change

Advocates of work-related learning have often regarded it as a means by which to respond to changes in the economy and employment. It has been argued that the growth of work experience schemes at the end of the 1970s was closely associated with economic recession and rising youth unemployment (Huddleston and Oh 2004): policy makers saw work experience as a tool to equip young people with the skills and attitudes they were believed to need to compete for employment in an adverse market. Likewise, in 2009 the government announced a graduate internship scheme, *The Graduate Talent Pool*, in a similar economic environment (Department for Business Innovation and Skills 2009).

Work-related learning has also been supposed to help to develop skills or attitudes which are judged to be of growing importance in employment. Information technology (IT) skills were integral to the TVEI in the 1980s and are currently recognised as a functional skill, that is a skill with operational value in employment and life. Skills related to problem solving, teamwork, self-management, communication and creativity, for example, are supposed to be becoming more valuable because of the changing character of work tasks and/ or the changing structure of organisations or industry (see Chapter 7). Another popular notion has been that, in the future, work will increasingly require the development of new knowledge and skills and that workers will increasingly work in a number of different occupations and organisations through their working lives. Accordingly, work-related learning should aim to give young people the capacity and disposition to continue to learn throughout their lives (Edge Foundation 2009).

At times, the introduction and promotion of a particular kind of work-related learning have been justified as a mechanism for achieving particular economic goals. For example, it was argued from evidence that higher levels of economic growth are associated with higher levels of new business formation that enterprise education could contribute to a higher level of economic growth in the UK. Alternatively, and more subtly, it has been claimed that globalisation has resulted in higher levels of economic uncertainty and more opportunities for risk taking and that enterprise education should develop a capability to respond to these circumstances (Gibb and Cotton 1998).

In some cases, the motivation for the development of a strand of work-related learning appears to owe its origin to a fairly narrow concern. Financial capability education is closely associated with the emergence of the Financial Services Authority (FSA) as a body to regulate the financial services industry and to protect and support the consumers of financial services. Education for financial capability can be understood as a concomitant of financial liberalisation and a consequence of a Treasury policy to shift the responsibility for financial planning (in relation to savings and pensions, for example) from the state to the individual.

5. Work-related learning to engage young people in learning

Another argument for work-related learning is that it is a way of making education more worthwhile for at least some young people and thereby increasing their motivation and engagement in learning (Edge Foundation 2009). This kind of thinking is often associated with the provision of vocational or pre-vocational programmes for some students (Steedman and Stoney 2004). These may be targeted at students who are thought to aspire to particular vocations, to be likely to profit from more practical styles of learning or simply to have rejected conventional subjects. In some cases, there may be issues of maturity and social management as well, with schools looking for other environments to help manage the learning of some 'difficult' learners.

This kind of rationalisation has informed the development of the Diplomas which are supposed to be largely delivered through work-related learning. Diplomas are intended to offer an alternative curriculum to conventional academic disciplines. The work-related character of Diplomas is generally accepted, particularly by practitioners, as being the feature most likely to attract and engage students. Similarly, work-related learning is influential in shaping the pedagogy of Foundation Learning programmes, which provide an alternative to GCSEs and vocational qualifications at Level 1 and Entry Level (QCDA 2010).

6. Work-related learning to empower learners

The so-called 'liberal' tradition insists that education is not merely concerned to meet the needs of society as a whole or of different stakeholders, such as employers or the government, but that it also serves the interests of the individual learner. Although the case for work-related learning has often drawn attention to the interests of stakeholders outside education, it is also possible to make out a student-centred case for work-related learning.

Careers education, in particular, is said to enable pupils to:

- understand themselves and the influences on them
- investigate opportunities in learning and work
- make and adjust plans to manage change and transition.

(DCSF 2008, p. 9; see also Chapter 8)

Financial capability education is supposed to help equip young people to make the right decisions in relation to saving, borrowing, pensions and so on, and so to contribute to their economic wellbeing. Enterprise education has been advocated, for example by Enterprise UK, as an opportunity for self-determination and personal freedom:

Make it happen – take control!
In an ever changing world we encourage people to be in control of their own destiny. By following your passions and setting up from home, utilising the skills you've picked from your college course and turning it into an enterprise or taking the plunge after a career break, the future is in your hands, so take control today!

(http://www.enterpriseuk.org/make_it_happen)

Official guidance on work-related learning typically brings together many or all of these six different kinds of purpose discussed (see, for example, Figure 1.2). This can have the effect of seeming overambitious or even confused. On the other hand, it should be remembered that work-related learning covers a variety of activities, often spread across the curriculum, and that different learners can benefit in different ways.

Organisations and agencies for work-related learning

The organisational and institutional landscape for work-related learning is famously complex and mutable. In some quarters, there is a perception that work-related learning organisations are particularly pushy and self-aggrandising. According to Miller and colleagues, for example, the 'so-called schools-industry movement has been variously described as a "galaxy", an "alphabet soup" and a "mafia"' (Miller *et al.* 1991, p. 6). In fact, there are many competing and overlapping agencies because work-related learning is composed of many missions. The mutability of these organisations is due to the instability of work-related learning – subject both to frequent changes in policy, funding and leadership and to market competition. Furthermore, negotiation and brokerage is the normal mode of operation, because there are lots of separate schools and businesses which need to work and communicate with one another.

It is useful, however, to distinguish some different types of player without claiming to provide an exhaustive list.

The underlying aims of work-related learning are to:

- develop the employability skills of young people;
- provide young people with the opportunity to 'learn by doing' and to learn from experts;
- raise standards of achievement of students;
- increase the commitment to learning;
- enhance motivation and self-confidence of students;
- encourage young people to stay in education;
- enable young people to develop career awareness and the ability to benefit from impartial and informed information, advice and guidance;
- support young people's ability to apply knowledge, understanding and skills;
- improve young people's understanding of the economy, enterprise, finance and the structure of business organisations, and how they work; and
- encourage positive attitudes to lifelong learning.

FIGURE 1.2 The aims of work-related learning (the work-related learning guide). Source: DCSF (2009).

Government departments

The Department for Education (DfE), previously the Department for Children, Schools and Families, has a policy and funding responsibility for all aspects of work-related learning and has taken a leadership role in initiating and driving new work-related learning programmes such as enterprise education, Diplomas, Young Apprenticeships and new institutions and agencies such as studio schools and Academies. The Department for Business, Innovation and Skills (BIS) determines policy and funding with regard to work-related learning post-19, but it also takes an interest in some aspects of work-related learning such as enterprise education and business–education partnership.

Parliament

Parliament enacts laws (usually proposed by government departments) which define educational requirements and entitlements and authorise new institutional arrangements and funding. For example, work experience was authorised by statute in 1973 and the entitlement for 14- to 19-year-olds to study work-related learning was enacted in the Education Act 2006.

Curriculum and inspection agencies

The Qualifications, Curriculum and Development Agency (QCDA) has had a responsibility to develop and review the curriculum, including work-related learning. It publishes authoritative statements of requirements and also issues guidance for practitioners and managers. However, in 2010 the new coalition government announced that it intends to abolish this body.

Ofsted (Office for Standards in Schools, Children's Services and Skills) inspects the delivery of work-related learning in schools, further education and publicly funded skills and employment-based training. From time to time, Ofsted publishes thematic reports on aspects of work-related learning, usually based on inspections that sample national practice, which provide an authoritative statement of what is happening in relation to the requirements defined by statute or departmental directive. However, the new government is currently reviewing the scope of Ofsted's work.

Funding agencies

Work-related learning programmes have been supported by additional funding from government or from companies or other foundations. For example, schools received additional funding to carry out enterprise education for 11- to 19-year-olds. Targeted funding of this kind has functioned as an engine to encourage providers, such as schools, to adopt work-related learning programmes.

Different mechanisms have been used to deliver and control funding. Sometimes, the DfE directly funds and controls a programme, for example the Young Apprenticeship programme. Sometimes additional funding is distributed through local authorities attached to the rest of educational funding but separately identified, for example the funding for enterprise education. On occasion, the government has chosen to create a funding agency, which is delegated resources and charged to develop and operate a strand of work-related learning. Until 2010, the Learning and Skills Council exercised such a responsibility with regard to the funding of work experience for secondary schools, though this funding responsibility will be exercised by local authorities and schools in the future.

The DfE has chosen to directly fund a number of national work-related learning providers, often third-sector organisations, such as Young Chamber UK or the Enterprise Education Trust, whereas BIS directly funds, for example, Enterprise UK, a campaigning body aimed at promoting enterprise. Of course, many of these bodies raise funding in a variety of ways, including income from services and through business sponsorship.

Another arm's-length funding body is UKCES, which has been given responsibility for managing and funding the agencies tasked with workforce planning and qualification development for employers (the Sector Skills Councils) and, along with them, Diploma development. UKCES also commissions research and advises the government on skills development and employment issues.

Other educational agencies and charities, such as the National Endowment for Science, Technology and the Arts (NESTA) and The Edge Foundation, are also active in research, promotion and funding of work-related learning – though such agencies are involved in non-work-related learning initiatives as well.

Other significant funding authorities have been the English Regional Development Agencies and European agencies, such as the European Social Fund and the European Regional Development Fund.

Support agencies

A number of support agencies have developed expertise in providing guidance, professional development and resources for work-related learning. Sometimes this support has been commissioned by the DfE and sometimes by specialist commissioning agencies such as the Learning and Skills Improvement Service (LSIS). The Vocational Learning Support Programme (VLSP) is part of the Learning Skills Network (LSN) and it has provided support for Diplomas, vocational qualifications and functional skills.

The Specialist Schools and Academies Trust (SSAT) has been commissioned to provide networks, professional development and resources in support of Diplomas, vocational qualifications and enterprise education.

Brokers

Sometimes known as Education Business Link Organisations (EBLOs) or Education Business Partnerships (EBPs), these are usually local organisations that specialise in matching the need for work-related learning from schools with the provision of work-related services, usually by local businesses. EBLOs can be free-standing companies or they may be part of a local authority or of another larger organisation, such as a local Connexions partnership or a Chamber of Commerce. EBLOs can operate at county, city or district level. EBLOs used to receive a core funding; however, it has been announced that this will not continue in the future. In addition, they charge schools for some of the services that they provide. In practice, many EBLOs act both as a broker and as a provider of work-related learning.

EBLOs are not the only brokers; in 2009 there were 260 Young Chambers, which together formed Young Chamber UK. This organisation, funded by the DfE, aims to engage young people with businesses through the brokerage of local Chambers of Commerce.

Work-related learning providers

The growth of work-related learning in schools, backed up by national curriculum requirements and increased funding, has stimulated the growth of specialised organisations that provide work-related learning services or brokerage on a national or local scale. Many of these organisations started up with a particular focus, perhaps gaining short-term funding from a particular business or from the government. In the past, organisations such as Royal Mail, 3i Investments and Shell have all sponsored distinct organisations that provided work-related learning. Successful organisations have then gone on to develop a distinctive product or service, some of them developing a national network and an extensive range of activities. On the other hand, some work-related learning providers are small, sometimes short-lived organisations.

Many work-related learning providers include a brokerage element. In other words, one of the services that they offer is access to business organisations and business people. This may be a highly developed system. Business in the Community, for example, has developed extensive networks and membership systems and can draw upon its business members in a variety of educational and social projects. The growth of enterprise education in schools has created a demand for contact with young entre-preneurs who can provide at once an insight into their work and a role model for young people. Naturally, a number of entrepreneurial young business people have taken the opportunity to sell their services to education!

The market for the provision of work-related learning services and resources is competitive and recent years have seen the emergence of new providers but also some consolidation, for example a three-way merger to form the Enterprise Education Trust, and the winding up of Project Trident, at one time the largest provider of work experience places in the country.

Careers education and information, advice and guidance (IAG) are delivered partly by careers teachers and tutors employed by schools but partly by local careers com-panies, in most cases part of the Connexions service. The Education and Skills Act 2008 gave local authorities the statutory authority (and the funding) to operate the Connexions service. This includes careers information and IAG for 13- to 19-year-olds but also some targeted social support and assessments relating to learning needs (see Chapter 8).

Businesses

A number of individual businesses run their own their own schemes for work experi-ence or careers education (e.g. the law firm Linklaters, and McDonald's Restaurants) or financial education (e.g. Royal Bank of Scotland), whereas other corporations (e.g. Deutsche Bank) provide funding and other support through other work-related learning providers.

The Sector Skills Councils (SSCs) are publicly funded agencies with a brief for workforce planning, development, and vocational and occupational qualifications. They are expected to work closely with employers and to represent their views. There are 15 SSCs corresponding to 15 different employment sectors. The SSCs have been given a lead role in the development of the 17 new Diplomas, with a particular respon-sibility for engaging employers in the development process. Some of these SSCs have been active in supporting the development of work-related learning, at various levels, both in relation to Diplomas and more widely.

The National Council for Excellence in Education was a working group of senior figures from industry and higher education charged by Gordon Brown, when Prime Minister, to make recommendations for improvements in education, including the way that education connects to work and higher education. This working group led to the formation of a charity, the National Education and Employers Taskforce, charged by the government to develop standards and quality in education–business partnership.

Quality assurance providers and professional associations

The Centre for Education and Industry (CEI) is a research centre at the University of Warwick. In addition to carrying out research into work-related learning, evalu-ating programmes and developing resources, the CEI has developed a number of quality awards which are intended to support evaluation, quality improvement and quality recognition. Currently, the CEI offers awards for Excellence in Work-Related Learning, Excellence in Enterprise Education, a National Standard for Work Experience Organisers and a National Standard for School Work Experience.

In 2009 the Institute for Education Business Excellence (IEBE) gained recognition as the professional body for individuals and organisations involved in education–business partnerships and brokerage. The IEBE aims to share practice, provide status and promote quality. It offers the Award for Business Education Excellence to EBLOs which assesses the quality of core processes and optional areas of activity, such as work experience and professional development.

The Institute for Careers Guidance and the Association for Careers Education and Guidance are membership bodies for those working in careers education, information, advice and guidance.

Local authorities

Many local authorities provide some support for work-related learning across their schools. Some local authorities operate EBLOs themselves or work very closely with EBLOs. Since April 2010, the funding of EBLOs has been a responsibility of local authorities, which is likely to lead to closer collaboration between education–business partnership work and the rest of educational development. Many local authority Children's Services Departments employ some kind of 14–19 Adviser who is likely to take a lead on work-related learning. Local authorities usually take a leadership role in 14–19 Partnerships, which are local authority- or area-wide collaborative groups charged with delivering the reforms in 14–19 education in general and employer engagement in particular.

Schools

Schools have different ways of managing work-related learning. Some have appointed a Work-Related Learning Co-ordinator with a general responsibility for developing, monitoring and delivering all work-related learning. It is not unusual for schools to allocate responsibility for leading careers education and work experience to different teachers, though in some cases one individual may carry several of these responsibilities. Many schools appoint an administrator to undertake much of the work associated with work experience placements, particularly if the school organises its own placements rather than depending on an EBLO. In most schools, a member of the Senior Leadership Team will have strategic responsibility for work-related learning; this role is sometimes combined with a responsibility to develop links with businesses. Schools with a specialism in business and enterprise appoint a Head of Specialism.

Consortia

Some work-related learning is managed by consortia which can include schools, colleges of further education, EBLOs and sometimes training providers. This usually means that the institutions share funding to organise and manage delivery jointly – though often one institution takes a lead role. Consortia have gone about their work in a variety of ways: they may share planning and delivery, or they may just provide shared support and employer engagement or they may commission another service provider. Many consortia have commissioned existing EBLOs to help develop work-related learning for Diplomas (see Chapter 6). Consortia have been used for the delivery of programmes such as work experience, Diplomas, Young Apprenticeships and Foundation Learning.

Teaching and learning work-related learning

The analysis of work-related learning given at the start of this chapter showed that teachers need to make decisions about the purpose of learning tasks, the conditions under which learning takes place, its location, the personnel, resources, task design and learning processes. There is considerable evidence that the appropriate and extensive use of work as a context does engage learners (Steedman and Stoney 2004; O'Donnell *et al.* 2006). Motivation to learn is increased, knowledge and skills appear to be easier to develop, and attitudes and personal development are encouraged (Taskforce on Education and Employment 2010). Some capabilities, such as coping with uncertainty and responding to customers, may be uniquely well supported by work-related learning. However, it does not follow that *any* use of work contexts will improve teaching and learning nor that the more extensively or intensively work contexts are used the more will be learnt.

Just how to go about teaching the different strands of work-related learning will be addressed in each of the chapters that follow. For the moment it must suffice to identify some of the key stages in teaching any kind of work-related learning:

1. Determine objectives: what knowledge, skills and understanding do we want to teach or what experiences, opportunities or support do we wish students to enjoy?

    In order to determine the learning objectives teachers will need to take account of:

    –   nationally prescribed entitlements and requirements for learning

    –   local or school entitlements and requirements for learning

    –   requirements set out in the specifications by an awarding body if work-related learning is to be externally assessed

    –   the plans of other teachers who may also be teaching work-related learning to the same learners in other lessons or at other times during their schooling

    –   the learning experiences of students outside of school

    –   the learning needs, aspirations and preferences of learners.

2. Explore and identify opportunities for work-related learning: which particular contexts, partners and resources are available and how can they support particular learning objectives?

    –   Teachers will need to husband and manage work-related learning opportunities since there are likely to be alternative uses for work-related learning contexts and alternative ways of teaching particular learning objectives.

- Teachers will usually work with colleagues and brokers to share contexts that have already been used successfully or to build on good will and *savoir faire*. Groups of providers are likely to find that, over time, they can improve the quality and reduce the cost of work-related learning by collaborative provision which involves the sharing of specialised resources, facilities and personnel.

3. Select and plan and prepare for work-related learning activities:

- Teachers will want to plan ahead and be flexible about the sequencing of learning and assessment activities in order to take advantage of work-related learning opportunities.
- Teachers will work closely with their managers, colleagues and administrators in order to ensure that the potential of work-related learning is maximised and quality standards, including equal opportunities and health and safety, are met.
- Teachers will work with partners and colleagues to ensure that work-related learning partners and resources are used in a sustainable manner.
- Preparation is likely to involve professional development, communication and formal agreements with partners.

4. Deliver and evaluate:

- Delivery may involve practitioners other than teachers.
- Evaluation can include formative assessment of student learning, formal feedback from participants, monitoring, observation, debriefing, action research, external evaluation, formal assessment of learning.

Although this formal summary must appear dry and lacking in scope for creativity, this is not the case for work-related learning in practice. Organising and teaching work-related learning draws upon the full range of knowledge, skills and personal capabilities that are required for any teaching. In addition, teachers of work-related learning need to be able to explore opportunities for learning outside of their schools and colleges; communicate and negotiate effectively with a range of non-educationalists to organise and deliver work-related learning; teach and manage learning outside classrooms; and co-ordinate their own teaching with the work of colleagues across their institutions.

Evidently teaching work-related learning is no pushover. If it is to work then schools and other providers must put into place the systems and support to help individual teachers carry it out safely and successfully.

Points for discussion

1. 'An 11–18 girls' school with business and enterprise specialist status and a strong commitment to work-related learning runs its timetable over a nine-day period with every tenth day becoming a "focus day"' (QCA 2007, p. 6). Consider how

this kind of timetabling could facilitate the design and delivery of work-related learning in terms of all eight of the dimensions identified in Table 1.1 on page 13.

2. Are the aims set for work-related learning realistic? Is it possible for work-related learning activities to achieve so many different purposes for so many different stakeholders?

3. What might young people learn from work experience that might help them to cope better with economic recession and a tight labour market?

4. Joanne has a background as a business advisor working for a Chamber of Commerce. From 2005 schools were funded to provide enterprise education to 14- to 16-year-olds, which created a demand for providers to come into schools to run enterprise activities. Joanne set up a business to provide these services building on her experiences in providing business advice and the fact that she loves working with young people. She went on to develop a DIY enterprise teaching resource and has built up a successful business selling this resource to schools. Joanne enjoys her business activities but has decided to train as a teacher so that she can spend more time directly teaching young people.

    a. What difference will it make to education if business people work as teachers or become teachers?

    b. What opportunities exist for teachers to become business people?

Note

1. Chapter 3 deals with the relationship between work-related learning and economic wellbeing and financial capability.

Further reading

The *Work-Related Learning Guide* is a clear and accessible official statement on work-related learning (DCSF 2009).

The QCA has published a non-statutory framework to support economic wellbeing and additional guidance and case studies to support work-related learning in different contexts (QCA 2005, 2007, 2008).

What Is to Be Gained is a useful summary of what research shows about the benefits of work-related learning (Taskforce on Education and Employment 2010).

Hager and Halliday (2006) provide a book-length account of what informal learning is, including work-based learning, and they make the case that there should be more of it. The book also contains many examples of the different ways in which different kinds of workers experience learning.

References

Central Advisory Council for Education (1963) *Half Our Future* (Newsom Report). London: HMSO.

Confederation of British Industry (2007) *Time Well Spent: Embedding Employability in Work Experience.* Available HTTP: < http://www.cbi.org.uk/pdf/timewellspent.pdf> (accessed 27 July 2010).

DCSF (2008) *The Work-Related Learning Guide*. London: HMSO.

DCSF (2009) *The Work-Related Learning Guide*. Nottingham: DCSF.

Department for Business Innovation and Skills (2009) *The Graduate Talent Pool*. Available HTTP: <http://graduatetalentpool.direct.gov.uk> (accessed 27 July 2010).

DES (Department of Education and Science) (1974) *Work Experience, Circular 7/74*. London: DES.

DES (1979) *Aspects of Secondary Education in England*. London: HMSO.

DES (1990) *Survey of School Industry Links, Statistical Bulletin 10/90*. London: DES.

Edge Foundation (2009) *Six Steps to Change Manifesto*. Available HTTP: <http://www.edge.co.uk/our-manifesto> (accessed 22 July 2010).

Felstead, A., Fuller, A., Unwin, L., Ashton, A., Butler, P. and Lee, T. (2005) 'Surveying the scene: learning metaphors, survey design and the workplace context', *Journal of Education and Work*, 18 (4): 359–383.

Gibb, A. and Cotton, J. (1998) *Creating the Leading Edge: Work Futures and the Role of Entrepreneurship and Enterprise in Schools and Further Education*. London: Department of Trade and Industry.

Hager, P. and Halliday, J. (2006) *Recovering Informal Learning*. Dordrecht: Springer.

HMI (Her Majesty's Inspectorate) (1988) *Secondary Schools: An Appraisal by HMI*. London: HMSO.

Huddleston, P. and Oh, S. (2004) '"The magic roundabout": work-related learning within the 14–19 curriculum', *Oxford Review of Education*, 30 (1): 83–102.

Miller, A., Watts, A. G. and Jamieson I. (1991) *Rethinking Work Experience*. London: Falmer Press.

O'Donnell, L., Golden, S., Nelson, J. and Rudd, P. (2006) *Evaluation of Increased Flexibility for 14–16 Year Olds Programme: Delivery for Cohorts 3 and 4 and the Future*. DfES Research Report. London: DfES.

QCA (2003) *Work-Related Learning for All at Key Stage 4: Guidance for Implementing the Statutory Guidance from 2004*. London: QCA.

QCA (2007) *Work-Related Learning at Key Stage 4: Providing for More Able Learners*. London: QCA.

QCA (2008) *Career, Work-Related Learning and Enterprise 11–19: A Framework to Support Economic Wellbeing*. London: QCA.

QCDA (2010) *Delivering Foundation Learning: Guidance and Case Studies*. Coventry: QCDA.

Steedman, H. and Stoney, S. (2004) *Disengagement 14–16: Context and Evidence*. London: Centre for Economic Performance, London School of Economics and Political Science.

Taskforce on Education and Employment (2010) *What Is to Be Gained?* Available HTTP: <http://www.educationandemployers.org/> (accessed 15 December 2010).

UKCES (2009) *The Employability Challenge*. Available HTTP: <http://www.ukces.org.uk/tags/employability-challenge-full-report> (accessed 17 October 2010).

Engaging and linking with employers

Prue Huddleston

Why education–business links?

Links between education and business have been a feature of the English compulsory education system for well over 30 years. Even as long ago as 1884 the Samuelson Report (McClure 1964) raised concerns about England's lack of competitiveness vis-à-vis its continental European neighbours and attributed this to its failure to train young people in the technical skills required to compete in an industrial economy. During periods of economic uncertainty the interest in education–business links appears to assume even greater importance and what is now commonly referred to as work-related learning has much broader aims than simply linking education with business.

A major strand of recent government policy for the reform of 14–19 education and training was predicated on increasing exposure of young people to the realities of the workplace, including aligning qualifications more closely to the needs of employers. This emphasis on both work-related and work-based learning puts pressure on a range of stakeholders, not just on employers, although they are expected to assume significant responsibility and on a voluntary basis (Huddleston 2009).

Over the same period employer bodies have been calling for the outputs of the education system to be aligned more closely with the needs of employers (CBI 2007; NCEE 2008; UKCES 2009). Again, this is not new; Huddleston and Keep (1999) highlighted the alleged mismatch between employers' demands of the education system and the supply of recruits available to them, although identifying these needs with any specificity appeared to be a challenge. Why might this be the case?

Employers are not a homogeneous group; any pronouncements allegedly representing the views of employers need to be considered within the context of the sector of employment, the size of the organisation and its product market. Since both the retail and hospitality sectors depend upon a steady supply of student labour to run their businesses, it cannot be assumed that all young people are devoid of the employability skills much lauded by employers. Similarly, whilst undertaking part-time work as students young people may be acquiring some of the employability skills necessary for future employment. Put simply, many young people are already in the labour market. So why work-related learning?

An examination of the purported benefits of work-related learning suggests that it is the 'cure-all' for a range of social, economic, demographic and technological challenges faced by society at large and not just by employers (Huddleston and Oh 2004). Education policy brings together both social (inclusion) and economic (competitiveness/survival) goals. The Nuffield Review of 14–19 Education and Training, which was conducted between 2003 and 2009 (Nuffield 2009), identifies three reasons why 14–19 education and training is in need of reform:

- to raise standards in order to produce a well qualified workforce capable of competing in global markets;
- to promote social inclusion to ensure that young people become contributing members of society, and as such part of a more prosperous economy;
- to ensure economic relevance so that what is taught in schools, colleges and universities provides students with the knowledge and skills they require to gain employment and to contribute to the economy.

(Nuffield Review 2004, p. 12)

Work-related learning has been seen as a significant instrument for addressing these economic and social policy goals. Engaging employers in this process has been central to the mission.

The mission for employer engagement

We look to employers to play their part in helping to shape the flow of young people as they progress through school, college and university, so that they enter the labour market with the skills, knowledge and attributes that employers are looking for. There is a wide range of ways in which employers can get involved with the education service, and so ensure that the realities of the modern labour market are understood at all levels of the learning and skills system. But we recognise that the sheer variety of ways in which employers are able to engage, and the difficulty of understanding what opportunities are available and how to get involved, can itself be off-putting and confusing.

(DfES *et al.* 2005, p. 15)

The expectation on employers to engage with the education system, and to support it in various ways, now extends far beyond the provision of work experience placements, once thought of as synonymous with work-related learning. The Employer Engagement Taskforce has been charged with the responsibility of securing more employer engagement within all schools, including primary schools, and has set out an agenda for employers and schools to progress these targets (Mann *et al.* 2010).

In 2008 the Department for Children, Schools and Families (DCSF) published *Building Stronger Partnerships Employers: How You Can Support Schools, Colleges, Children and Families* (DCSF 2008a) outlining the broad areas in which it was felt employers' contributions could make a difference. These included leadership and governance; enterprise and employability; and the curriculum (once thought of as the preserve of education professionals). A companion document was published for the Education and Children's Services communities: *Building Stronger Partnerships Schools, Colleges and Children's and Families' Services: How Employers Can Support You* (DCSF 2008b). These documents relate not simply to work experience, but to the much wider field of education–business partnership, although it is clear that work experience is seen as potentially contributing to the enterprise and employability agenda, as well as to the curriculum dimension. It is also the largest single work-related learning activity in which employers and schools engage. According to a poll by Ipsos Mori (2009) 83 per cent of school pupils between the ages of 5 and 16 will engage in some form of work-related learning experience; a large proportion will be involved in several activities and by association with employers.

Reading the documents gives a sense of the substantial demand that is being made of employers to support the education community. In 1998 research undertaken by the Centre for Education and Industry (CEI) at the University of Warwick identified at least 40 activities ranging from primary schools to higher education institutions (HEIs) in which employers were asked to engage with education. The demand has not diminished subsequently and it is surprising to see how, or why, employers have continued their involvement.

Employers are encouraged, amongst other things, to provide cash and equipment for schools and colleges; mentor students; contribute to the design of qualifications; serve on governing bodies and councils; provide work experience placements for students (and sometimes teachers); support enterprise activities; and fund, design and manage academies. This list is by no means exhaustive and excludes mention of education- and training-linked activities beyond schools. It is a huge request and it is not surprising that employers sometimes do not understand how they 'might be involved' and why the world of education–business links can be 'off-putting and confusing'.

In addition to individual or company involvement with education there is a veritable cottage industry of broker organisations and intermediaries seeking to match-make between education and business. There is a further layer of private providers peddling their wares to schools in an attempt to inject a 'real life' dimension into the curriculum. It is not surprising that schools too can be confused by the array of offerings, and more importantly about their quality. At a time when budgets are being devolved to schools to make such spending decisions, rather than being given to local authorities, or to intermediary organisations, it is even more important that quality benchmarks be in place and that schools can act as informed consumers.

What's in it for employers?

This level of employer engagement over such a sustained period suggests that employers must derive benefit from relationships with the education community, or at least believe that they do. Many large companies employ dedicated education liaison staff and education partnerships feature within the community investment portfolio of 'blue chip' companies. Clearly, some companies are investing significant amounts of time and money in supporting education. A recent study by the Education and Employers Taskforce (2010) suggests why this might be the case and supports the guidance offered by the DCSF to employers in *The Work-Related Learning Guide*.

Work-related learning benefits *employers* by:

- giving them fresh ideas and perspectives that can help deliver their business objectives;
- helping them to keep abreast of modern qualifications and developments in education;
- providing opportunities to demonstrate the jobs and careers available within their organisation (or employment sector) and to find recruits from a regular supply of school leavers who are more 'job ready', thereby helping to reduce their recruitment and training costs;
- providing opportunities to contribute to local communities and to build links which will enhance the profile and reputation of their own organisation and sector;
- providing opportunities to contribute directly to young people's education, through influencing their attitudes towards work and helping them to develop their capabilities;
- providing motivational and personal development opportunities for those members of their staff who are directly involved with young people and their schools and colleges – through broadening their own perspectives, developing their communication and management skills and increasing their sense of responsibility, self confidence, self esteem and job satisfaction;
- demonstrating the diversity of the school-age population and widening the potential recruitment pool beyond traditional stereotypes of industry and sector workers.

(DCSF 2009, p. 5)

If we compare these alleged benefits with the economic and social policy drivers outlined at the beginning of this chapter how might these be aligned? Clearly, some of these points relate to notions of employability: 'job readiness', 'attitudes towards work', 'develop their capabilities'. Others speak more directly to company objectives: 'enhancing the profile and reputation of their own organisation and sector', 'developing communication and management skills', 'reducing recruitment and training costs'.

What is also being hinted at, but is perhaps less well developed, is the notion of company staff learning through the experience in a way that supports the concept of work-related learning in a more holistic way – the recognition that there is, or could be, joint learning. As Rainbird (2000) suggests: 'The workplace is enormously significant as a site for learning, both for accessing formal learning opportunities and for many informal learning opportunities which result from the nature of work and from social interaction with work groups' (Rainbird 2000, p. 1).

Research evidence (Miller 1998; Huddleston and Muir 2009) suggests that company personnel gain significantly by engaging with young people both within their workplaces, for example when supporting work experience students, and within schools, for example when acting as mentors or supporting reading. Benefits are reported as motivational and confidence building, developing interpersonal skills, and other benefits relate to the opportunities to give something back (Huddleston and Muir 2008, 2009).

For companies more generally there are likely to be reputational benefits, particularly for those companies which receive bad press as a result of environmental concerns. Some petrochemical companies have a long history of support for education, for example. Major retail banks continue to provide education resources, speakers in schools, even school banks. Clearly, they will need to redouble their efforts to try and rehabilitate their tarnished image following the banking tsunami of 2008. The engineering sector has been concerned to raise the profile of the industry and its career opportunities through a variety of initiatives and programmes, including Ambassador Schemes, Challenges, teacher placements, and curriculum support for STEM (science, technology, engineering and mathematics) subjects.

It is clear that education–business partnership is not a one-way street; companies engage with education for commercial as well as for altruistic reasons. A survey undertaken by Edge, the Institute for Education Business Excellence (IEBE) and Business in the Community (BITC) in 2007 of 500 private sector businesses showed that one in four would hesitate to engage in education unless there was a clear business benefit (Institute for Education Business Excellence *et al.* 2007). There is also the opportunity for wider corporate recognition within the awards offered by high-profile organisations, such as Business in the Community's 'Big Tick' award for community engagement. Basically, it is good for the letter head and for reputational benefits, and if competitors are engaged then there are compelling reasons for being involved as well. However, quantifying such benefits is difficult to achieve.

Successive governments have encouraged businesses to get involved; the most recent, and perhaps most extreme case, has been the involvement of employers, via the 14–19 Diploma Development Partnerships (DDPs), in the design of qualifications, namely the new 14–19 Diplomas (see Chapter 6). Whether or not employers should be involved in the design of qualifications, which after all is a highly specialist, technical endeavour, is open for debate. It does however raise issues over the control of the curriculum.

Who controls the curriculum?

The design and delivery of work-related learning depends upon a complex set of relationships between government departments, the Qualifications and Curriculum Development Agency (QCDA), schools/colleges, teachers/lecturers, employers, brokerage organisations, voluntary organisations and possibly others. Arguably, there is no other area of the curriculum in which so many players are engaged and in which there are so many vested interests. Little wonder that it gives rise to confusion – what is it and where is it? Perhaps, most importantly, why do we do it?

We have said that a useful definition, and one that is widely used, is 'learning through', 'learning for' and 'learning about' work. Although this is helpful its generality suggests that it could be everywhere and anywhere. Are dedicated programmes of study, resources and personnel required to deliver it? Is there a danger that by involving outsiders in the 'secret garden' of the curriculum we are giving control to those whose business is not education but business? Can the aims of education and the aims of business be reconciled?

If we look at some of these ideas through a different lens, we can see that workplaces can provide a context for learning, by which we mean opportunities for students to experience rich and varied learning environments. They can also provide opportunities for students to engage in real and authentic work tasks. These can help to enhance learning that takes place in classrooms and workshops. However, this type of learning cannot be taken for granted because it requires shared understanding of the purposes of the experience, clear learning objectives and agreement about intended outcomes. It also requires learners to be able to make sense of their learning and recognise how it might contribute to other aspects of their studies (see Chapter 7). Employers need to be aware of these educational aims as well.

An important question and one that is insufficiently considered within the context of work-related learning is, as one young man put to me during an observation I was undertaking of some classroom activity, 'Just what are we supposed to be doing here?' A good question, since I found it hard to grasp as well. If there is no explicit purpose and intended outcome from the activity then, like any other form of educational practice, it is not worth doing. The workplace visit is a prime example – nice to have, but without any specific curriculum purpose and associated learning aims it is simply a waste of time. Three visits to the same workplace in three years represent an even bigger waste of time.

However, if the visit has some real purpose, for example gathering data for a school-based assessment on business organisation, or interviewing staff about customer service within the organisation, then this gives the visit an educational focus and one which enriches classroom-based subject teaching. Where there are clear curriculum aims, for example providing practical experience of theoretical concepts taught in the classroom, this is clear cut. If we take for example a programme such as a Young Apprenticeship (YA) in engineering, students will learn about the theoretical aspects of workshop procedures – drilling, cutting, polishing – in the classroom, but during their work experience, up to 50 days in the YA programme, they will carry out these procedures in a workplace using industry-standard equipment. In other words it is an authentic task in a real workplace context. This is very much about learning 'how to do something'. The output of the effort can also be judged against recognised industry-standard criteria.

It is hard to argue that this sort of experience could be realistically provided in a school; it may be easier in a college, but a college lacks the urgency of a real workplace. Although colleges do provide realistic learning environments for their students – hairdressing salons and restaurants with paying customers – their purposes are training-focused, emphasising the centrality of the learner, rather than business-focused, in other words making a profit. However, instructional input from 'real' hairdressers and chefs can provide significant value to the learning experience as well as offering role models to aspiring young craftspeople.

Where the intended outcomes are less clear cut, for example 'developing self-confidence', 'improving motivation', 'enhancing employability', then identifying learning gains is extremely challenging. The evidence base is limited and there is a paucity of longitudinal studies tracking young people from education into employment to identify how their work-related learning experiences have impacted upon their employability. It is also impossible to identify control groups. This is very much about learning 'to be or to become', rather than about 'learning to do'. In recent years the employers' demands have shifted much more to the former rather than the latter, with complaints about young people's lack of 'soft skills', 'employability skills', 'customer focused' skills being trumpeted by the Confederation of British Industry (CBI), UK Commission for Employment and Skills (UKCES) and DCSF.

Experiences designed to develop these workplace skills, or workplace readiness, require monitoring and regulation. If significant parts of curriculum time are to be given over to interaction with employers then there needs to be assurance that these experiences add value and have some educational merit and that any potential role models actually possess these skills themselves. Clearly, there are opportunity costs. Of course, there are many ways in which employers engage with education outside 'normal' curriculum time, for example through participation in clubs and activities such as Young Enterprise, Young Engineers and Mentoring, as well as the time spent by employers as school governors or helping with school sports fixtures. Many employers also engage with schools as parents. These are 'naturally occurring' events which often pass unnoticed and which are not necessarily evaluated, and yet the learning could be significant.

The Office for Standards in Schools, Children's Services and Skills (Ofsted) (2009), commenting upon the role of employers within the roll-out of the first phase of the new Diploma qualifications, suggests that young people respond positively to employer involvement with their programme in terms of classroom activities, workplace visits and development of learning materials. The inspectors suggest that employers provided 'a range of inputs and visits, which significantly enhanced their learning and enthusiasm for the subject.' They concluded: 'In almost all the consortia visited, [students] were well motivated by the applied nature of their learning and the opportunity to work in realistic vocational contexts' (Ofsted 2009, p. 36).

In summary, the research so far, albeit limited and patchy, indicates that many students enjoy their work-related learning experiences, they find the applied learning style engaging and they enjoy the practical aspects of learning. Those employers who engage also report benefits. However, of course, many still choose not to. It is to this group that the most recent call to employer engagement is now directed.

If schools and employers are required to devote more time working together to enhance the educational experience of young people and to prepare them to engage with the world of work, whatever the future workplace might look like, then there is a need for clear guidance on what such engagement might entail and how it can be monitored and regulated.

Delegation and regulation

Both the DCSF (now Department for Education, DfE) and the Qualifications and Curriculum Authority (QCA, now Qualifications and Curriculum Development Authority, QCDA) have set out guidance for the delivery of work-related learning in schools. Currently, work-related learning is a statutory requirement for all Key Stage (KS) 4 students, which 'aims to ensure all KS4 students have suitable and high quality work-related learning opportunities as part of a broad and balanced curriculum' (DCSF 2009, p. 22). The QCA (2008) guidance, *Career, Work-Related Learning and Enterprise 11–19: A Framework to Support Economic Wellbeing*, sets out a nine-point framework covering the range of work-related learning opportunities that would deliver the KS4 statutory requirement (see Chapter 3). Decisions about how and where to provide these opportunities for their students are delegated to schools. Schools will also need to decide upon the appropriate range and balance of opportunities and about the personal needs of students; this is an entitlement for all. The framework is used by Ofsted as the basis for carrying out its inspections of work-related learning.

There is a high degree of flexibility for schools in designing work-related learning programmes in that they are encouraged, in the guidance, to take account of their local circumstances and to adopt differing approaches depending upon learner needs. This requires imagination and creativity, and in a 'results driven' climate the justification of work-related learning activity has to be couched in 'outcomes' terms. However, we have shown above that outcomes expressed in behavioural terms are difficult to quantify, particularly when there are no longitudinal data and when there are no control groups. To some extent it is an act of faith.

Given the difficulty associated with providing hard evidence, what might be suitable metrics for assessing the impact of work-related learning? Perhaps there is a case for thinking much more about processes rather than about outcomes? Essentially work-related learning draws upon a pedagogical approach which privileges experiential learning, facilitative teaching styles, expansive work-based learning environments and personalised programmes. How can these be judged?

These questions challenge both the education and business communities. Since using company time and resources to engage with education is not cost-neutral, most companies are looking for some hard numbers and outcomes to set against the activity. The type of 'results' which companies might welcome, for example 'customers through the till', would sit uneasily with many education professionals, who would not endorse interventions in education by employers aimed at increasing 'footfall' or building brand loyalty. Nevertheless, it can be argued that teachers and employers have a shared interest in preparing young people for the world beyond school, including the workplace, and in developing skills for employability, including self-confidence, interpersonal skills and problem solving. Employers should also have an interest in developing such skills in their own employees. In that sense involving company staff in education links could provide cost effective staff development, particularly where such activity is aligned to company training goals, for example in the area of 'soft skills'.

In the absence of robust, longitudinal research data, but with an abundance of anecdotal evidence, it appears that the best way to proceed is to determine, as far as possible, the necessary pre-conditions that need to be in place in order to ensure a successful employer intervention. The DCSF publications (2008a,b) endeavour to set out good practice in terms of planning, delivering and reviewing employer engagement.

What does good practice look like?

As for any business activity, employers should ensure that engaging with education conforms to the quality standards and procedures that they apply to their normal business; schools should expect no less. Similarly, education professionals should have clear procedures in place to ensure quality in their engagement with those organisations and individuals who support learning within and beyond the classroom. You might wish to consider what, within your own school context, you would expect to be in place for effective employer engagement. In planning such activity one would take into account many of the same features that would be included within normal lesson planning:

- What are the main objectives/aims?
- What are my intended outcomes?
- How will I deliver this session?
- What resources will I require?
- How will I know if learning has occurred?

In addition to this basic template one would expect to ensure that the person responsible for the delivery had the necessary professional knowledge and skills to undertake the task and that an appropriate learning environment was assured. One would also want to ensure that appropriate evaluation was in place to allow students to reflect upon the learning and to inform future plans for similar activities. This also provides useful feedback to the company.

In Chapter 3 you will find more detailed information about quality aspects of work-related learning delivery. However, a few key best-practice questions are worth considering in the context of the issues raised in the opening sections of this chapter: 'the sheer variety of ways in which employers are able to engage, and the difficulty of understanding what opportunities are available and how to get involved, can itself be off-putting and confusing' (see Table 2.1).

Best practice within companies engaging in these types of activities reflects a similar set of questions, including those in Table 2.2.

It is important to remember that very often schools and companies will not be making these decisions in isolation; at the very least it is to be hoped that much of this planning, delivery and reflection will be undertaken in partnership. In many cases it will be facilitated by an intermediary, or broker, such as an Education Business Partnership or other Education–Business Link Organisation, or by a sector-representative body. Over the past 30 years the number of these 'middle men' has grown to the extent that there is now a wide array of choice within a mixed market of provision. Education–business link activity is operating within a changing policy environment where budgets and choices are to be delegated much more to the individual school level.

Although it is too early to say how this new agenda will unfold, it is useful to consider how notions of choice could impact upon the delivery of work-related learning in the future.

Mixed market

It has been suggested (CBI 2007; DCSF 2008a,b) that, although much has been achieved in terms of work-related learning and employer engagement over the past decade, quality remains patchy and that the absence of hard data on outcomes limits

TABLE 2.1 Questions and issues for schools

QUESTIONS	ISSUES
Does the company/individual know what they have signed up for, its purpose, and what is expected?	Aims, objectives, outcomes, delivery, resources
Is this a one-off event/activity (for example attending a careers evening), or is it part of a longer-running relationship (weekly mentoring sessions; providing work experience placements)?	Delivery, resources
Is there a clear brief for the employers/employees, which includes a profile of the groups involved, age, gender, ethnicity, prior experience (there is a danger of information from guest speakers, for example, being pitched at an inappropriate level)?	Aims, objectives, delivery, resources
Do the contributors understand how what pupils are doing in/with the company relates to their work in school (is a work experience placement contributing to a pupil's Diploma qualification; is the host company expected to assess the pupil)?	Aims, objectives, outcomes, evaluating learning
Is there a dedicated school contact from whom the business person can seek information and advice?	Resources
Are the necessary health, safety, child protection protocols in place?	Resources
Is this type of engagement going to add value to what I do, will it enhance/enrich learning?	If not, why am I doing it?
Can you think of other 'good practice' pointers?	

TABLE 2.2 Questions and issues for companies

QUESTIONS	ISSUES
Why are we doing this?	Staff development, recruitment, building company profile, raising the profile of the sector, our competitors do it!
What types of education link activity are best suited to a company such as ours?	Subject-specific knowledge, employability skills development
Is this a compulsory or voluntary activity for staff?	Reputation and motivation
Is there a dedicated company contact for the schools/colleges?	Resources
What is the extent of our resource?	Personnel, time, finance
How is the engagement valued within the company?	At board, branch, department, line management level, through appraisal
Is it making a difference, how do we know?	Monitoring, evaluation
Can you think of other 'good practice' pointers?	

a compelling case for investment in this area. Research undertaken by the Education and Employers Taskforce (2010) has attempted to distil the evidence available to build a case for not only more engagement but more research into outcomes for pupils, teachers and employers/employees (public, private and third sector). But what precisely would they be trying to measure?

There is a mixed market in provision of work-related learning experiences. Some are provided by brokerage organisations, which have grown in number over the past decade; others are provided directly to schools by voluntary organisations and charities; some schools organise their own work-related learning programmes and have strong links with local employers and organisations on whom they rely regularly. Some schools offer a wide range of activities and experiences, whilst others may focus activities on KS4, or on a particular dimension, for example careers education. Given such a diversity of demand and supply it is hard to design robust mechanisms for measuring the impact of such activity. It is also hard to predict what future demand and supply might look like. However, where there are compelling reasons for work-related learning, either in curricular terms or in extra-curricular enrichment opportunities, then using the key questions outlined above can help to shape the experience and can act as a monitoring and evaluation mechanism to assess the learning that has taken place. This is just as relevant for employers as it is for schools and colleges.

Figures 2.1 and 2.2 give two examples recently observed (autumn 2010) in 11–18 schools in the West Midlands. They were not deliberately sought out but were naturally occurring in the sense that they were observed during school visits to trainee teachers on placement at the two sites.

These two case studies have indicated how individual teachers have succeeded in integrating a work-related learning dimension into the curriculum. In case study 1 it was dependent upon the enthusiasm of an individual trainee and a willing volunteer. Case study 2 illustrates the practice of an advanced senior manager who has years of experience of organising and delivering work-related learning and who holds a specific brief for enterprise education. He also has strong external networks of companies, both large and very small, on which to draw. He currently has a budget for this type of activity.

These two examples did not involve the use of an intermediary brokerage organisation to arrange visits and speakers, although both schools use such an organisation for arranging and delivering pupil work experience. They also use contacts through former pupils and parents to access particular opportunities. This serves to point up the complexity of the field and the multiplicity of ways in which work-related learning can be delivered. It is also worth reflecting on the extent to which staff in any particular school have an overview of just what is happening. In such a mixed market, to what extent are consumers, that is both schools/colleges and employers, able to exercise an informed choice about what is on offer, how do they assure quality and what are the benefits?

Conclusions

We have demonstrated that work-related learning, and in particular the attempt to engage employers in the processes of education, has grown significantly over the past two decades, although attempts to align the outputs of the education system more closely with the needs of employers are not new. The debate has been characterised

A Year 10 business studies class was covering the topic *Communication in business* as part of its coursework. Having covered the theoretical aspects of the topic in the classroom, the trainee teacher had invited the marketing, communications and public relations manager of a local charity to talk to the group about the ways in which a national charity handled its communications, both internal and external.

The speaker's input consisted of a 15-minute PowerPoint presentation to the whole class, succinctly covering the preferred communications methods used by the charity, their target audiences and why particular modes of communication were selected, for example email, letters, posters, newsletters. This was followed by a question-and-answer session and individual group tasks were set, with the expectation that groups would feed back their responses to the speaker by the end of the session. During the completion of the group tasks the speaker confidently moved between groups offering advice and responding to pupils' questions. At the end of the session each group was able to respond appropriately to the tasks set and to receive comment from the speaker. The pupils also asked supplementary questions about the charity's work.

Good practice points

- The speaker had been very well briefed on the requirements of the talk; there was close alignment of his presentation with what had been covered by the teacher in the theory session.

- The tone, level and content of the presentation were appropriate for the group.

- The speaker engaged positively with the pupils and was a strong role model (a successful young man from a neighbouring community who was engaged in a humanitarian aid charity).

- The focus on a charity as a 'business' provided a useful counterpoint to the more usual large corporation case study.

- The host teacher had ensured that all necessary Criminal Records Bureau checks had been carried out and that the visit had the approval of the head teacher.

- The visiting speaker was comfortable with what he had been asked to do and gained some valuable publicity for his charity to the extent that pupils may well be inclined to support its work in the future.

Reflection

How many of the key planning points referred to previously in this chapter (aims, objectives, delivery, resources, outcomes, evaluating learning) have been addressed? Do you think that the visitor gained something from his visit; if so what?

FIGURE 2.1 Case study 1: visiting speaker.

by concerns that are social as well as economic. The impact of globalisation and the emergence of strong new competitors within international markets have caused governments to turn increasingly to education to provide answers, as well as school/ college leavers and graduates who are 'oven ready' in terms of their employability.

This raises a fundamental question about the purposes of education: to what extent should education be a preparation for employment or a preparation for life (in which employment may, or may not, play a significant part)? Conflating social and economic

---

In the second school a group of sixth form students, studying a variety of subjects, visited the regional outlet of a large multinational furniture and home ware company. The visit was hosted by the company's human resources (HR) manager as part of its community outreach programme (the company employs large numbers of staff from within a five mile radius of the store; the school is within this radius).

The visit was planned by the school's Head of Enterprise and Community Learning in collaboration with the company. The teacher is very experienced in working with external groups and in organising whole school enterprise events. Although the visit was not subject specific it clearly had links to areas such as business studies, geography, maths, English, sociology, art and design, technology, IT, as well as to more generic 'employability skills'.

The visit included a talk by company staff covering, amongst other things, company history, organisation, customer profile, product range, logistics, recruitment and selection policies, a tour of the site and a question-and-answer session. Prior to the visit students had been asked to seek information on particular topics, to complete a worksheet, and to reflect upon what they had seen and heard about the company from the perspective of their own subject area. For example, who designs the products? Where does the company source its products? How does the company deal with communications across its different sites across the world? What is the company's policy on environmental issues?

On return to school the students had to prepare a collage presentation of photographs taken during their visit to illustrate different topics identified. These included: logistics, stock control, customer service, merchandising, stock rotation, recruitment and selection, waste disposal, communication, display, working environment. In addition to the displays, students presented their findings to the group, relating their experiences to theoretical concepts learned in class.

Good practice points

- The Enterprise Coordinator had visited the site prior to the visit to discuss the brief with the HR manager and to identify learning opportunities.
- Students had been briefed on the visit and the associated tasks, and they had a clear focus for the activity with intended learning outcomes, some of which were generic, for example customer service, and others of which were subject specific, for example business location.
- A bespoke worksheet had been designed for use on the visit.
- Students were encouraged to develop their own research skills.
- The visit was part of a wider whole school programme of enterprise education.
- The company benefitted from enhanced profile within the local community and had an opportunity to promote itself as a potential employer.

FIGURE 2.2 Case study 2: the visit.

> ### Reflection
>
> How many of the key planning points were achieved (aims, objectives, delivery, resources, outcomes, evaluating learning)? Why do you think that this company wishes to provide dedicated staff time for community links?

FIGURE 2.2 Case study 2: the visit (*continued*).

goals within the context of education has on occasions polarised the debate between those who embrace a more instrumental perspective and those who see wider purposes for education in terms of educating the whole individual. This chapter has attempted to suggest that adopting a work-related learning dimension can enhance the curriculum in terms of providing both context and content for learning and by espousing an active learning approach. In this way work-related learning provides a holistic approach to the curriculum for all learners rather than a default offering for those who are marginalised or who fail to be engaged by more traditional approaches. As such it goes beyond merely a preparation for work.

However, this is also to argue that work-related learning is not of itself a 'good thing', but that it needs careful planning, integration, delivery and evaluation, like any other educational endeavour, to ensure that it meets the needs of learners and serves curricular purposes. In the future it is likely that schools and colleges will be providing for their work-related learning needs in house or buying services directly from providers; they may be less reliant on intermediaries and brokers who charge for their services, but who have often provided some degree of quality assurance.

If this proves to be the case then having sound market intelligence about the services on offer and robust systems of quality assurance will be important. Continuing professional development for staff will also be essential. This will be equally important for the large number of companies and employers who engage with education, and who are currently being encouraged to do so even more. Unless there are clear benefits for all parties, particularly in terms of enhancing the learning experiences of students, teachers, employees, trainees and employers, then the opportunity cost of work-related learning may be too great.

References

CBI (Confederation of British Industry) (2007) *Time Well Spent: Embedding Employability in Work Experience.* Available HTTP: <http://www.cbi.org.uk/pdf/timewellspent.pdf> (accessed 16 May 2011).

DCSF (2008a) *Building Stronger Partnerships Employers: How You Can Support Schools Colleges, Children and Families.* London: DCSF.

DCSF (2008b) *Building Stronger Partnerships Schools, Colleges and Children's and Families' Services: How Employers Can Support You.* London: DCSF.

DCSF (2009) *The Work-Related Learning Guide*, 2nd edn. London: HMSO.

DfES, DTI, HMT and DWP (2005) *14–19 Education and Skills.* London: HMSO.

Education and Employers Taskforce (2010) *What Is to Be Gained through Partnership? Exploring the Value of Education–Employer Relationships.* London: Education and Employers Taskforce.

Huddleston, P. (2009) 'Preparing students for the world of work', *Curriculum Management*, 98: 3–10.

Huddleston, P. and Keep, E. (1999) 'What do employers want from education? Questions more easily asked than answered', in Cramphorn, J. (ed.) *The Role of Education in Economic Development: International Perspectives*. Coventry: University of Warwick.

Huddleston, P. and Muir, F. (2008) *Evaluation of the Brokerage Citylink Schools' Programme*. Coventry: CEI.

Huddleston, P. and Muir, F. (2009) *Evaluation of the Hackney Schools' Programme: 'Linking Work with Learning'*. Unpublished report for Linklaters LLP. Centre for Education and Industry.

Huddleston, P. and Oh, S.-A. (2004) '"The magic roundabout": work-related learning in the 14–19 curriculum', *Oxford Review of Education*, 30 (1): 81–100.

Institute for Education Business Excellence, Edge and Business in the Community (2007) *Raising the Bar and Removing the Barriers: What Employers Can Offer Education*. Available HTTP: <http://www.educationandemployers.org/research/research-reports/schoolcollege-performance/raising-the-bar/> (accessed 16 May 2011).

Ipsos Mori (2009) *Young People Omnibus 2009 Wave 15: A Research Study on Work-Related Learning among 11–16 Year Olds on Behalf of the Qualifications and Curriculum Authority (QCA)*. Available HTTP: <http://www.qcda.gov.uk/resources/assets/Young_peoples_omnibus_survey.pdf> (accessed 16 May 2011).

McClure, S. (1964) *Educational Documents England and Wales 1816–1967*. London: Chapman and Hall.

Mann, A., Lopez, D, and Stanley, J. (2010) *What Is to Be Gained through Partnership? Exploring the Value of Education–Employer Relations*, 2nd edn. London: Education and Employers Taskforce.

Miller, A. (1998) *Business and Community Mentoring in Schools*. DfEE Research Report No 43. London: DfEE.

NCEE (2008) *The National Council for Educational Excellence: Recommendations*. London: Department for Innovation, Business and Skills.

Nuffield Review (2004) *Nuffield Review of 14–19 Education and Training Annual Report 2003–2004*. Oxford: Oxford Department of Educational Studies.

Nuffield Review (2009) *Education for All: The Future of Education and Training for 14–19 Year Olds: Summary, Implications and Recommendations*. Oxford: Department of Education.

Ofsted (2009) *Implementation of the 14–19 Reforms, Including the Introduction of Diplomas*. London: Ofsted.

QCA (2008) *Career, Work-Related Learning and Enterprise 11–19: A Framework to Support Economic Wellbeing*. London: QCA.

Rainbird, H. (ed.) (2000) *Training in the Workplace*. London: Macmillan.

UKCES (2009) *The Employability Challenge: Full Report*. Wath-upon-Dearne: UKCES.

Part II

A co-ordinated approach to work-related learning

Faith Muir

As discussed in the introduction to this book, work-related learning is a complex subject and one that appears unconventional when compared with other aspects of the curriculum. It can encompass teaching and learning related to all kinds of work and workplaces and has relevance in all curriculum subjects, at all Key Stages and for all young people. However, it is recognised that different students acquire it in various ways and schools are at liberty to choose to deliver work-related learning through 'the most appropriate work-related activities according to students' individual needs and local capacity' (QCA 2004). Consequently, there can be no single 'right' way of organising and delivering work-related learning, as evidenced by the multiplicity of forms it takes in different schools, and the diverse range of interpretations of its content and purpose.

Although in some respects such a flexible approach to work-related learning may be seen as a positive benefit for curriculum planners, teachers and learners alike, it also raises several important questions. For example, a school may be able to prove that it is fulfilling its legal responsibility to provide opportunities for careers education at Key Stage 3 and for career and work-related learning at Key Stage 4 – but what about the quality and consistency of this provision? Do all young people enjoy equality of access at a level appropriate to their individual needs, interests and abilities? Does the school community have a shared vision and understanding of the purposes of work-related learning and how are these communicated to partners and stakeholders? Who holds overall management responsibility for work-related learning and are they fully aware of the range and quality of work-related activities taking place across the curriculum?

In effect, without careful planning and co-ordination, an individual young person's experience of work-related learning may turn out to be patchy, repetitious and with little meaning or relevance for them. It will lack a sense of coherence and progression, with little connection being made between the different activities and no opportunity to apply the learning and skills gained from one work-related experience to another. Often, scant recognition is paid to learners' prior knowledge and understanding of the world of work despite the fact that many primary schools enhance their curriculum with 'visits and visitors', enterprise learning, careers education and work-related simulations, and that many older learners have part-time jobs.

So, what needs to be done? The purpose of this chapter is, first, to consider the extent to which recent developments in the secondary national curriculum may help to promote a more coherent approach to work-related learning provision at Key Stages 3 and 4. Second, it explores some of the key factors for achieving successful co-ordination of provision.

Economic wellbeing and financial capability

Building on the Best (DCSF 2007), the Review of 14–19 work-related learning,[1] refers to work-related learning as an 'umbrella' term encompassing a broad range of activities, including 'awareness of the local and broader economy; the connections between the national curriculum and other subjects and learning with the world of work; and which encompass careers education' (p. 8). Nevertheless, one of the key findings of this Review was that there was no shared understanding of work-related learning, the activities it could involve or the learning outcomes it could support. In some ways, this is hardly surprising given that work-related learning and its stated components – particularly careers education and enterprise education – have regularly been treated at national, regional and school levels as separate subjects or aspects of the curriculum.

Discrete guidelines and frameworks have been prepared for each aspect, thereby reinforcing their distinctness and potentially undermining the possibility of developing a holistic, co-ordinated approach to work-related learning provision. At national level, policy and strategy were inconsistent, with statutory status as well as funding being conferred on some but not all of these aspects – and at some but not all Key Stages. This has led, for example, to a lack of recognition in schools of the value of work-related learning below Key Stage 4 and confusion regarding the relationship between enterprise and work-related learning. Regionally, different agencies and individuals have often been tasked with responsibility for careers, enterprise and work-related learning activities, resulting in the development of uneasy alliances in some places and outright competition in others. In schools and colleges, organisation and delivery of the three aspects may have been the responsibility of different individuals who do not always share a common vision or plan, despite the demonstrable overlap in terms of content and learning objectives.

No wonder, therefore, that the 2007 Review recommended that there was urgent need to develop and begin to communicate a new vision for work-related learning. As part of the strategy for achieving this goal, it was recommended that the existing framework for work-related learning (introduced in 2003) should be revised to take into account the proposed 14–19 curriculum reforms, including Diplomas (see Chapter 6). However, the greatest opportunity to bring about real and lasting change came with the introduction of a new subject area – personal, social, health and economic education (PSHE education) – as part of the revised secondary curriculum (September 2008). Under the previous government, this was due to be made statutory from 2011.

The notion of bringing together personal, social and health education with work-related learning, including economic and business understanding, enterprise, careers education and financial capability, is not new. Indeed, when personal social education

(PSE) was first identified as a cross-curricular 'dimension' in the 1990 national curriculum, it was underpinned by five cross-curricular 'themes': economic and industrial understanding, careers education and guidance, health education, education for citizenship and environmental education. A major difference in 2008, however, was the underpinning of PSHE education with two new non-statutory, interrelated programmes of study at Key Stages 3 and 4: *Personal Wellbeing* (PW) and *Economic Wellbeing and Financial Capability* (EWFC). Both programmes of study were based on the five outcomes for Every Child Matters (ECM)[2] and took account of the existing guidelines and frameworks for their respective areas.

It is true that the various aspects of work-related learning have continued to evolve in their own separate ways, as evidenced for example by the publication of statutory guidance for Impartial Careers Education (October 2009) and the development of national quality standards for enterprise education. Nevertheless, whether statutory or not, the introduction of EWFC and PSHE education had – and still has – the potential to act as a catalyst for schools and colleges (reinforced by Ofsted inspection requirements) to review their existing practice and the needs of young people in order to create a more co-ordinated, coherent and progressive approach to work-related learning on a whole-school basis.

Framework for economic wellbeing 11–19

The revised non-statutory framework recommended in the 2007 Review of 14–19 work-related learning is intended to reinforce the content of the new EWFC programme of study. Entitled 'Career, work-related learning and enterprise 11–19: A Framework to Support Economic Wellbeing', it sets out to 'improve provision by drawing together three important and distinct aspects of the curriculum in one simple tool' (QCA 2008, p. 2). It aims to complement rather than to replace existing guidance on the three aspects and to offer scope for conflating the range of learning opportunities incorporated within them to nine basic 'elements of provision for all learners' (see Figure 3.1).

In addition, the new framework seeks to establish a common baseline in terms of minimum provision for each Key Stage – namely, the minimum range of work-related activities and opportunities to be provided for learners per element of provision – and to clarify the possible learning outcomes. In this way, it attempts to foster a more coherent approach to planning and co-ordination of provision in schools and colleges. It encourages schools to look at work-related learning as an experiential learning cycle[3] across the entire 11–19 age range, thereby offering scope for better progression and continuity at post-16. This move makes sense, given the national focus on 14–19 curriculum reform, although some teachers of Key Stage 3 learners may find it difficult to interpret the learning outcomes from their perspective given that the framework also covers possible work-related achievements for Key Stage 4 and post-16.

The advantages of using the new framework as a co-ordinating resource would seem to be that it offers managers, practitioners, external partners and learners a common language, vision and checklist of aims and objectives. It can be used with teachers from different subjects to plan aspects of work-related learning provision across the curriculum, helping them to set learning goals relating to a range of different elements of provision. It can support a whole school policy linked to strategic

---

Economic Wellbeing 11–19 Framework

Elements of Provision for All Learners:

1. Recognise, develop and apply their skills for enterprise and employability
2. Relate their own abilities, attributes and achievements to career intentions, and make informed choices based on an understanding of available options
3. Develop an awareness of the extent and diversity of opportunities in learning and work
4. Use their experiences of work to extend their understanding of careers and work
5. Learn from contact with people who work
6. Learn about how and why businesses operate
7. Learn about working practices and environments
8. Undertake tasks and activities set in work contexts
9. Engage with ideas, challenges and applications from the business world.

(QCA 2008, pp. 20–21)

FIGURE 3.1 Career, work-related learning and enterprise 11–19: a framework to support economic wellbeing.

development founded on a balanced approach to all three work-related learning aspects. It also offers a means of developing tools for mapping and monitoring existing provision and assessing the impact on young people. In effect, it has the capacity to be a non-prescriptive starting-point from which schools can develop and personalise their approach.

On the other hand, at first glance the framework may suggest that as long as the minimum provision is in place at each Key Stage no more effort is required – and that the quality of individual activities, or coherence of the overall programme, is of minimum importance. By separating out the nine elements of provision, their inter-relationship may be overlooked; for example, a task focused on learning from contact with people who work (element 5) can also be used to provide opportunities for exploring changing patterns of employment (element 3) and for applying enterprise skills (element 1). Above all, as with any tool of this nature, it needs to be shared, understood and fully integrated across the school if it is to make a real impression on school practice. This is particularly important where post-16 providers and senior staff are concerned; awareness of the framework appears weaker in these two areas than in other parts of the school/college community (QCA 2009a).

The purposes and functions of the EWFC programme of study

The programme of study for Economic Wellbeing and Financial Capability also draws together the three 'distinct but interrelated' curriculum aspects of careers education, work-related learning (including economic/business understanding) and enterprise education. However, unlike the 11–19 Framework, this time financial capability – whose value and status in the eyes of the then government[4] are made clear by its inclusion in the programme title – is singled out as a fourth distinct aspect (see DCSF 2008). The programme complements the revised national curriculum by supporting the fifth ECM outcome in particular: 'achieve economic wellbeing'.

The overall purpose and scope of education for EWFC is articulated in an 'importance statement'. It is intended to:

- equip young people with knowledge, skills and attributes necessary for making the most of changing opportunities in learning and work;
- help them understand the nature of work, the diversity and function of business and its contribution to national prosperity;
- enable them to develop skills and strategies for fulfilling their future roles as questioning and informed consumers, producers and citizens.

Through participation in a planned programme of EWFC learning opportunities and experiences, young people can develop their enterprise capabilities, self-esteem and self-efficacy. Such skills, qualities and attributes can help them make informed career, learning and financial choices, leading to a positive and successful future of benefit to themselves and to those around them. These objectives are further unpacked under four 'Key Concepts', identical for both key stages:

- *career* – focus on lifelong progression through learning and work; personal identity and what having a 'career' means; what makes someone employable;
- *capability* – what it means to be enterprising and a critical consumer; money management; ability in transition planning;
- *risk* – positive and negative in different contexts; taking risk, being able to manage the consequences and learn from mistakes;
- *economic understanding* – the economic environment and a range of business types; money uses and functions.

Also, there are four sets of 'Key Processes' or essential skills that students need to learn to make progress in EWFC. These vary slightly at Key Stage 4 in order to encourage more opportunities for independent learning to take place in 'real' work-related contexts such as work experience:

- *self-development* – developing self-esteem; managing major life roles; understanding of personal preferences, abilities, attitudes and achievements in relation to future plans and choices;
- *exploration* – of different information sources relating to personal career options and financial contexts, and the main trends in employment; ability to research, clarify and review, recognise bias and inaccuracies;
- *enterprise* – developing and applying enterprise qualities and capability, such as risk management, understanding of economic and business ideas, creativity,

self-reliance, open-mindedness, ability to improvise, having a 'can-do' approach and the drive to make things happen;

- *financial capability* – money management; financial risk and reward; understanding of financial terms and products; the importance of finance in one's future life and achieving aspirations.

The breadth of the subject on which practitioners should draw when teaching the key concepts and processes is outlined in a section on 'Range and Content'. The list supplied is intentionally non-prescriptive, fairly flexible and open-ended, with an emphasis on personalisation and the embedding of basic economic and business ideas. It covers a diversity of topics such as different types of work and work roles; the organisation, structure and financial operations of businesses; opportunities in learning and work at local, national and international levels; the personal review and planning process (careers education); personal budgeting and financial risk and reward. Some topics clearly reflect the relationship between EWFC and Personal Wellbeing/Citizenship; for example the investigation of social and moral dilemmas regarding the use of money and, at Key Stage 4, rights and responsibilities at work and values in relation to work and enterprise.

Again, much of the suggested range and content for EWFC is identical for Key Stage 3 and 4 learners with opportunities for progression built primarily through the inclusion of a number of more complex economic and business concepts for the older age range. The final section of the programme of study, closely linked to 'Range and Content', aims to clarify the range of 'Curriculum Opportunities' that young people should be offered. These are 'integral to their learning and enhance their engagement with the concepts, processes and content of the subject' (QCA, 2007a, p. 240). Importantly, the suggested curriculum opportunities directly relate to and enrich the nine elements of provision described in the 11–19 Framework discussed earlier; so the two main tools for supporting a co-ordinated approach to EWFC delivery can be seen to be integral to each other.

Overall, the EWFC programme of study appears to have achieved what it set out to do; namely, to combine the salient features of all four curriculum aspects into a single structure for teaching and learning which is balanced and yet preserves the integrity of each individual aspect. It strongly supports the argument for all students to have a basic understanding of economics and business[5] although this may prove challenging at Key Stage 3. It is non-prescriptive because of its non-statutory status, thereby allowing for flexibility, personalised learning and local interpretation of content and process, built on existing practice and values. Moreover, it promotes links and learning on a cross-curricular basis and yet there is an implicit expectation that some specialist teaching should take place to cover specific career- and work-related concepts, knowledge and skills. Particularly welcome is the expansion of EWFC into Key Stage 3, given that careers education is currently statutory at Key Stages 2 and 3 and work-related learning/enterprise activities regularly feature in the curriculum at both these levels. The programme of study can certainly help teachers to plan such activities in a less ad hoc manner and to identify clear learning objectives and curriculum relevance.

Nevertheless, education for EWFC does raise some issues and concerns. To begin with, why use the title 'economic wellbeing' rather than work-related learning, if the latter already has the reputation as the 'umbrella term' for such activities? Clearly, the title may promote the importance of economic understanding as a major factor in our future wellbeing and happiness but it could be confusing for teachers who are more familiar with economic wellbeing in the context of Every Child Matters. Although it may go some way to explaining the purpose behind the programme of study, to what extent can economic wellbeing be said to truly describe the content in a way that is instantly meaningful to the majority of stakeholders? Perhaps what it does is to create a level playing field for careers, work-related learning and enterprise in which none of the three strands is privileged. Who should own this curriculum hybrid? Should it be treated as an add-on, new subject, a means of enriching an existing curriculum programme or an opportunity for closer collaboration between discrete partners with similar goals?

In this respect, it is important to recall that the 2008 secondary curriculum places EWFC alongside Personal Wellbeing within the broader context of PSHE education, the purpose being to 'provide opportunities to address real life and topical issues and show pupils they can make a difference to their own and others' lives' (from working definitions agreed by PSHE education strategic partners, February 2008). Both programmes of study can make a significant contribution to each other[6] and to young people's personal development, particularly in relation to skills identified in the framework for Social and Emotional Aspects of Learning (SEAL) under five key aspects: self-awareness; managing feelings; motivation; empathy; and social skills. They also have much in common with Citizenship. However, there are implications for timetabling combined delivery of both or even all three subjects, as some schools may assume to be the required approach. EWFC could suffer in terms of quality of delivery and impact because of lack of time and availability of teacher expertise for delivering its specialist elements in such a packed programme.

Finally, some points about structure and content. The opening lists of key concepts and processes provide a comprehensive, straightforward overview of what is to be achieved. Some goals do tend to be overly ambitious or ambiguous, such as key concept 1.4, 'Understanding the economic and business environment' – a huge undertaking, if treated literally, which would prove particularly daunting for teachers with limited personal economic knowledge on which to draw – and key process 2.4c: being able to 'explain' financial terms and products' is unlikely to make a young person financially capable unless they also understand how to apply such knowledge appropriately. The need to draw so much together under one programme of study has resulted in a far more complex web of information in the final sections. For instance, the considerable breadth of the subject as outlined under 'Range and Content' may be a useful checklist for more experienced staff working as a team but could well deter less experienced teachers working alone. The same may be said for the suggested range of 'Curriculum Opportunities', particularly when time and other resources are constrained. Clearly, the methods chosen for managing and maintaining EWFC in a school or college will be crucial to the quality of provision.

'Done well, everybody wins': success factors for effective co-ordination

Evidence from Ofsted, QCDA and other sources (for example, Harris *et al.* 1996/7) shows that where effective practice takes place in careers, work-related learning, enterprise and financial capability, as well as in PSHE education and citizenship, this is commonly underpinned by a number of key enabling factors. In order to make the best of current opportunities for firmly establishing work-related learning (in the context of EWFC) in the curriculum for all 11- to 16-year-olds, logic suggests that these key factors should be carefully considered and implemented. Therefore, this section sets out to present some of the evidence, illustrated by examples of good practice, using a structure based on the framework for developing organisational excellence produced by the European Foundation for Quality Management (EQFM).[7]

The EFQM model is a useful resource for helping organisations reflect on their existing practice and identify what needs to be done to improve. The framework consists of nine elements which are grouped into:

- *'enablers'* – five elements or aspects of an organisation which help it to carry out its functions and meet its aims: 1. Leadership; 2. Policy and strategy; 3. People; 4. Partnerships and resources; 5. Processes, products and services;

- *'results'* – four elements which cover the measured outcomes of all the organisational effort placed in the 'enabler' aspects: 1. People results; 2. Customer results; 3. Society results; 4. Key results.

Effective co-ordination of work-related learning provision depends on constantly working to develop and improve the quality of the enabling aspects: *Leadership*, which drives *Policy and strategy*, which in turn is delivered through the *People*, *Partnerships and resources*, and *Processes, products and services* associated with work-related learning. The positive impact of this effort is shown by the levels of satisfaction demonstrated by staff, students and other internal/external partners (the 'customers'); also, by the impact the school has on its local community – including other schools – in relation to work-related learning provision, and particularly by the quality of teaching and learning achieved in this area. For the EFQM, 'innovation and learning' both help to improve the 'enablers' which in turn can lead to improved 'results' in a continuous cycle of development.

Leadership, management and co-ordination

Gaining the active support and commitment of the senior leadership team is vital to the achievement of excellent whole school work-related learning/EWFC provision. In schools where senior leaders, especially the headteacher, also have a good, up-to-date understanding of its purpose and potential benefits, work-related learning is more likely to be reflected in the school's priorities, on a par with other subjects, and to figure in whole school curriculum planning. In particular, staff deployment to work-related learning/EWFC is more likely to be treated seriously where the most appropriate members of staff are selected. Committed Senior Leadership Team (SLT) members can support staff responsible for provision by helping to communicate the school's vision for work-related learning/EWFC, both internally and externally. For example, deputies and senior staff from mainstream and special schools in one county are members of a multi-agency working group for careers information, advice and guidance (IAGS). Several are also trained as IAGS Champions and do much to promote careers within their own schools, bringing in new ideas from the IAGS network. In some schools, the head actively supports employer engagement by seeking out new partners and initiatives to enrich existing provision. A headteacher of a London girls' school takes on a specific responsibility for raising sixth formers' career aspirations through linking them with women business leaders.

The way in which senior leaders actually run their school can serve to illustrate work-related learning in action. In one school, an Ofsted report commented on the 'can do' culture demonstrated by the SLT and the headteacher – a prime example of enterprise capability. This generated a strongly motivational effect on staff and students alike, inspiring them to seek success and bring about further improvements.

A second factor for success relates to management of provision. As mentioned in Chapter 1, schools can choose whatever management system suits them and this has led to a wide variety of practice, including individual managers being appointed for each discrete aspect; a general work-related learning manager/co-ordinator responsible for several aspects; or, noted recently by Ofsted (2010) as a growing trend, a specialist PSHE education team or faculty responsible for delivery of all aspects, including work-related learning/EWFC. Whichever approach is selected, the person who has overall responsibility for planning, monitoring and delivering EWFC should be a senior member of staff with sufficient time and resources to carry out their management responsibilities, particularly in light of the range of topics and activities to be covered and the potential number of external partners involved.

A good example is the approach taken by a school in the North West[8] which has created a new faculty of personal development and vocational education. Previously, there were separate co-ordinators for PSHE and citizenship, for careers, and for business education, including vocational education, work-related learning and enterprise. The PSHE education/citizenship co-ordinator is now head of the new faculty. His team comprises careers co-ordinator; head of business/vocational education; head of PE; three personal development teachers from other faculties; and an administrator. An assistant head of faculty, who leads on economic wellbeing, including careers education and guidance/IAG, has recently joined the team.

Policy and strategy

Although schools tend to have policies in place for careers, work-related learning and enterprise, in order to achieve a co-ordinated approach it is important to establish an integrated policy for work-related learning/EWFC identifying the intended learning outcomes at each Key Stage. This should set out the aims and rationale for the programme and its relationship to PSHE education, including value added to the wider curriculum, and outlining key roles and responsibilities. It should indicate the students' entitlement at each Key Stage and criteria against which to assess outcomes. Aims should reflect the school's strategies for raising standards, school improvement, equality and diversity, and staff development. Harris and colleagues (1996/7) in their investigation of effective teaching and learning in work-related contexts found that schools demonstrating best practice in work-related learning had a whole school culture which valued work-related activities: they had a vision, values and goals which supported work-related learning. This was reinforced by the translation of policy into accessible entitlement statements for students which helped to make them aware of work-related learning.

Programme design

How a school chooses to deliver work-related learning/EWFC may inevitably be influenced by a range of circumstances including school priorities, resources, staff availability and timetable space. However, it is worth considering the curriculum models that research has shown to have a positive impact on the quality of provision. In Ofsted's experience (Ofsted 2010) , schools where the most effective teaching occurs combine dedicated lessons, often as a module within the PSHE education programme, and 'suspended timetable' days such as enterprise days, to work through a range of topics. They note that, where schools rely solely on 'suspended timetable' days, the students develop only a partial understanding of the whole programme even though they enjoy the days. Earlier findings on PSHE provision (Ofsted 2005) also confirmed that themed days lack continuity, may not be rooted in young people's wider experience of the curriculum and tend not to connect with prior experiences: 'they have the potential to enrich programmes, but not to replace them' (p. 16).

Other possible models need careful consideration. For example, if work-related learning/EWFC is entirely taught through other subjects across the curriculum, it can be difficult to co-ordinate and monitor quality, often leading to repetition, fragmented learning and failure to understand underpinning concepts. Nevertheless, a well-planned use of cross-curricular opportunities can add depth to provision, help build curriculum relevance and increase staff awareness and participation. Some aspects may be best taught by subject specialists, such as financial capability in maths or citizenship or elements of economic understanding by business studies staff. In some schools, a particular focus for cross-curricular development may be subject specialism or a whole school strategic priority such as science, technology, engineering and mathematics (STEM). One school in the North East with such a priority has recently appointed a 'STEM Enrichment and Enterprise Manager' whose responsibilities include developing STEM-related business partners and also co-ordinating work experience.

Another common but less effective means of work-related learning/EWFC programme delivery is through tutor time. In this case, problems may arise from lack of allocated time combined with insufficient preparation or lack of appropriate knowledge as seen in many schools (Ofsted 2010). These schools had attempted to combine careers and citizenship for delivery by tutors but had not allowed sufficient lesson time for high-quality teaching and learning to develop, nor for extended activities or meaningful discussion to take place. Even so, when combined with other methods, involving tutors can prove an excellent strategy as evidenced in the model used by the North West school mentioned earlier. Here, the amount of time allocated for teaching increases from Year 9 onwards, as illustrated in Table 3.1.

TABLE 3.1 Example of allocated timetabled time for personal development

PERSONAL DEVELOPMENT	Y7–8	Y9	KS4
Lesson – week 1	1 × 70mins	1 × 70 mins	1 × 70 mins
Lesson – week 2	n/a	1 × 70 mins	1 × 70 mins
Weekly tutorial time	2 × 20 mins	2 × 20 mins	2 × 20 mins

Students in both key stages follow an integrated programme of personal development delivered by a faculty staff member, which covers the full range of PSHE education together with citizenship. The scheme of work, organised around themed modules, is mapped against relevant national frameworks and programmes of study and each lesson is colour-coded to enable students and teachers to see where the component curriculum areas occur (also a useful means of identifying and addressing gaps in provision). Further work, planned by the head of personal development to ensure coherence and continuity within the overall programme, is covered by tutors during additional weekly tutorial sessions. The school also enhances personal development work through a range of enrichment activities and links with the community.

Programme development

Regularly reviewing and developing work-related learning/EWFC provision is important to ensure that programme content and delivery are relevant and fit for purpose. As described above, mapping existing curriculum provision against the EWFC programme of study and the 11–19 Framework is an essential part of this process. It should focus on identifying where the intended learning outcomes are being achieved at different Key Stages rather than solely acting as an audit of activities or topics. Equally important is to link programme development planning to whole school improvement planning. For example, embedding EWFC in STEM learning (DfE 2010) could be used strategically to emphasise the transferability of STEM skills for employment and raise awareness of STEM-related careers. At one school, raising aspirations to higher education (HE) was a major priority identified by the SLT. This prompted development of a themed module for delivery from Year 7 to Year 11 which incorporated careers education (routes to HE and graduate employment opportunities), financial capability (managing your finances at university) and work-related learning (workshops and discussions with professionals and university representatives).

Developing strategies for monitoring student, staff and other stakeholders' satisfaction, including parents, is important in informing future curriculum planning and target setting. Some schools use student forums and focus groups for evaluating activities and capturing the 'learner voice'. Others have developed surveys for Year 11 students to gauge how well their whole work-related learning experience has prepared them for transition, plus online surveys for parents/carers of all year groups to feed back on their observations of work-related learning/EWFC provision. Outcomes are fed into an annual report which is presented to governors, and provision is adapted to take account of responses. A local Connexions service trained a team of young people aged 11–16 to become student Connexions Champions in their schools. As well as helping to raise awareness of Connexions, they were involved in planning and evaluating materials and activities. As one school co-ordinator observed, young people are both interested and willing to engage with professionals to help shape a service such as Connexions in their school.

Finally, developing strategies for monitoring learners' prior experiences of work-related learning/EWFC is essential and can be linked to school policy and practice on primary–secondary transition. The recent Ofsted survey (2010) found very little evidence of curriculum liaison with primary schools or that secondary schools were building on students' primary school experiences of enterprise and personal finance. Consequently, this led to repetition, work often not matched to maturity and ability, and early disenchantment.

People management and development

Ensuring consistency in the quality of teaching across all aspects of work-related learning/EWFC provision is a challenge for schools, particularly in light of the range of content to be covered and the amount of specialist knowledge required. Whether delivery involves specialists or non-specialists, tutors or other subject teachers, a planned programme of continuing professional development (CPD) is valuable in ensuring that the vision for work-related learning/EWFC is shared and understood, that there is commitment to its rationale and that staff are aware of the intended learning outcomes and how to assess progress. In addition, training may be needed on specific topics relating to aspects of careers, financial capability or economic understanding as well as appropriate pedagogy.

Some CPD may be delivered in-house, possibly linked to the school's appraisal system. For example, at a school in Lancashire the personal development faculty runs a system of regular 'faculty reviews', which are seen by staff as supportive and constructive in that they identify and address teachers' needs. The model of CPD adopted by the school focuses on enabling staff to lead initiatives, for example through action research groups, which also promotes strong teamwork and a shared sense of purpose. Other opportunities may be offered externally by agencies such as an Education Business Partnership (EBP) or Local Authority 14–19 Partnership. A good example is a training programme run by a 14–19 Partnership and Connexions aimed at staff with no previous responsibility for teaching impartial careers information, advice and guidance (IAG). The programme is intended to help them understand careers IAG and their role within it. It is based on the premise that all staff need to understand the complexity of decisions facing young people, how to inform and advise them and where to refer them for in-depth guidance. Participating teachers complete an accredited 'reflective practice' workbook after the course. The initiative is making a positive contribution to IAG capacity building and workforce development.

Professional development for other stakeholders such as governors, business and community partners is helpful in preparing them for their roles in work-related learning/EWFC activities. In addition, there is potential for using work-related learning/EWFC to strengthen and update the whole school curriculum. The 2007 Review of 14–19 work-related learning observes that work-related learning: 'is as important to the education workforce as it is to the learners they help to achieve. It can help [teachers] update knowledge, gather case study and stimulus material and develop resources to support enterprise activities' (DCSF 2007, p. 17). In the case of the Review, this statement refers to the benefits of teacher placements into business. It also suggests that effective work-related learning/EWFC provision can make a contribution to professional development for the whole school community by opening up regular opportunities for interaction with work environments, people and practices.

Resources

Effective and sustained co-ordination of this complex area of the curriculum requires adequate resourcing. This should include appropriate accommodation and, if possible, administrative support for dealing with external partners and work experience placements; a budget for work-related learning/EWFC enrichment events, activities, materials and CPD; and sufficient non-contact time to enable the subject leader to carry out their management responsibilities such as meeting the teaching team to develop materials and review teaching and learning.

At delivery level, effective teaching which engages and interests students regularly draws on the wide range of resources available for work-related learning/EWFC, including the expertise of external agencies (Ofsted 2008). Where funding is limited, working collaboratively with other schools and external partners can often help to supplement provision. For example, in an area of the East Midlands, whenever students or teachers visit an employer they make a video of their visit for use by other schools, as a 'virtual visit' or as a case study. This enables access to a much wider range of small employers who can host one visit, but not several.

Involving external agencies can help in many ways. In one London borough, an EBP has assisted its schools to improve relationships with employers. Working with employers, they have defined three common 'tools for schools': a code of practice for effective employer engagement, an agreement on the key ingredients of successful work experience and a definition of employment skills. Another example is a school which has integrated Connexions support into its provision. Connexions advisers visit students on work experience and are also involved in the Year 9 options programme and in Year 11 progression events; they also regularly teach modules on the use of IAG computer software.

Effective teaching also makes use of the expertise of employers and community representatives but ensures that their contribution is well planned, relevant to classroom learning and fully integrated within it. This is demonstrated in the way a Birmingham school uses engagement with others to help its students break down barriers and remove any potential stereotyped views of Muslim girls. The school draws on former students and members of the local community as role models to inspire students to raise their aspirations and make informed choices about their future.

Teaching and learning: aspects of content and delivery

The programme of study for EWFC and the 11–19 Framework together provide guidance for schools on programme aims and appropriate content linked to clearly defined learning outcomes for each Key Stage. However, individual schools will decide exactly what to deliver and how it should be taught, taking into account institutional and local circumstances and priorities, and the specific learner needs. Particularly effective examples of work-related learning/EWFC provision share a number of key characteristics, including those deemed essential for the development of employability skills (adapted from UKCES 2009, p. 4):

- *Experiential action-learning*: using skills rather than simply acquiring knowledge, placing emphasis on trial and error (risk), and with a clear focus on the pay-offs for the learner in terms of employment and progression;

- *Experience of work*: a work placement in an actual business, or an authentic classroom simulation based on a real workplace;

- *Opportunities for reflection and integration*: learners do not recognise their enterprise and employability skills when these are delivered without time for reflection and recording (see QCA 2009b).

In line with findings on the characteristics of a 'good' PSHE programme, effective provision should also offer young people frequent opportunities to take responsibility for their own actions and make informed choices, and provide all students with the chance to achieve success and be recognised and rewarded for achievement (Ofsted 2005). The latter point is particularly significant; Harris and colleagues (1996/7) found that, where student learning and achievement in work-related activities was directly linked to some mechanism for recording and rewarding achievement, students were more likely to recognise and value the learning. In an increasing number of schools, formal accreditation is the preferred method for recognising achievement in both personal and economic wellbeing. For example, as part of Key Stage 4 personal development in a school recently noted by Ofsted (2010, p. 32), all students take two GCSE-equivalent courses: a Certificate in Enterprise and Employability in Year 10 and Preparation for Working Life in Year 11. Preparation for Working Life prepares and develops transferable skills for life beyond school and covers topics such as personal awareness, relationships, enterprise, healthy lifestyles, 'world of work' and employment opportunities, hazard identification, and economic and financial aspects of life.

Recent research by Ofsted (2010) indicates that provision for financial capability is often weaker than for enterprise or careers education, implying that students do not understand basic concepts such as credit or debt. Whatever the underlying reasons, lack of specialist staff or curriculum time, this finding highlights the importance of ensuring that no work-related learning/EWFC aspect is allowed to dominate provision to the detriment of another. Whether treated as a stand-alone subject area or integrated into a larger programme of PSHE education, such as life skills or personal development, a coherent scheme of work for work-related learning/EWFC should endeavour to provide a balanced approach to teaching and learning of the various aspects. Effective teachers help students to recognise and understand the nature of the learning taking place and provide different contexts and types of activity in which to apply the knowledge and skills gained. Even where specialist staff are unavailable, compelling work-related experiences can be developed using real-life situations and contexts, such as fundraising, enterprise projects, the management of school events such as music and drama performances, and citizenship projects based in the community.

Two further points arise with regard to programme content: first, a co-ordinated approach to work-related learning/EWFC requires that provision be built around key 'milestone' events such as Year 10 work experience, Year 7 induction and Year 11 transition to post-16. Second, if work-related learning/EWFC is to be an entitlement for all, provision must be inclusive, offering breadth and depth, stretch and challenge to suit every individual. This may require eliciting whole school support as in the case of a London school where work experience is held in high esteem for both Years 10 and 12. For those students needing more support the school raises funds to run a bespoke training programme, ensuring that every student is able to benefit from work-related learning at a level that meets their needs.

Using the interface between EWFC and Personal Wellbeing

When comparing EWFC with Personal Wellbeing, it is clear that they are not only interrelated programmes of study (see QCA 2007a,b) but also potentially complementary and, in some respects, interdependent. Many of the key concepts and processes set out in one resonate with those in the other, as demonstrated in Table 3.2. In many cases, work-related contexts can be used for in-depth exploration of Personal Wellbeing concepts. For instance, Year 10 work experience would offer an excellent opportunity for 'exploring relationships and understanding that people have multiple roles and responsibilities in society' (PW: 1.4) whereas, in order to manage the processes involved in self-development (EWFC: 2.1), it would be valuable for young people to understand how to apply the skills for critical reflection (PW: 2.1).

With regard to range and content, further overlaps arise. For example, students would have ample opportunity for considering the 'effect of diverse values' and 'clarification of personal values' (PW) when exploring 'attitudes and values in relation to work and enterprise' and 'social and moral dilemmas about the use of money' (EWFC). At Key Stage 3, they can apply 'the knowledge and skills needed for 'setting realistic targets and personal goals' (PW) when undertaking the 'personal review and planning process' or developing understanding for 'personal budgeting' (EWFC). Similarly, when both the curriculum opportunities sections are analysed they show a number of common components. With respect to both programmes of study, the curriculum should provide opportunities for students to:

- use case studies, simulations, scenarios, role play and drama for exploring important issues;
- develop research skills in order to make real choices and decisions;
- meet and work with people from the wider community (such as business partners);
- take part in discussions on issues relating to different contexts (such as work);
- develop teamwork skills;
- evaluate their personal development and learning and set realistic targets and goals for future life choices (PW), which is inextricably linked with writing/reviewing a personal statement and developing an individual learning and career plan for transition (EWFC);
- make links between PW and EWFC learning with other subjects and curriculum areas.

TABLE 3.2 Interface between Personal Wellbeing and Economic Wellbeing/Financial Capability

	PERSONAL WELLBEING	INTERFACE WITH EWFC
Key concepts	1.1 Personal identities – identity is affected by a range of factors, including a positive sense of self	1.1 Career – developing a sense of personal identity for career progression
	1.2 Healthy lifestyles – healthy lifestyles, and the wellbeing of self and others depend on information and making responsible choices	1.2 Capability – becoming critical consumers of goods and services
	1.3 Risk – understanding both positive and negative risk and that individuals need to manage risk to themselves and others . . . ; developing the confidence to try new ideas and face challenges safely, individually and in groups	1.3 Risk – understanding both positive and negative risk; understanding the need to manage risk in financial and career choices; taking risks and learning from mistakes
	1.4 Relationships – relationships affect all we do in our lives and relationship skills have to be learnt and practised; understanding that people have multiple roles and responsibilities in society	1.2 Capability – exploring what it means to be enterprising (applying skills, attitudes and qualities) 1.4 Economic understanding – understanding the economic and business environment
	1.5 Diversity – linked with both personal identities and relationships; similarities and differences in society, attitudes and behaviours, the need to challenge prejudice and discrimination	Scope for exploring diversity in work-related settings and as part of preparation for work experience or in reflecting on students' own experience of part-time employment

Key processes	2.1 Critical reflection – reflect on personal strengths, achievements and areas for development	2.1 Self-development – assess needs, interests, values, skills, abilities and attitudes in relation to options in learning, work and enterprise
	2.2 Decision making and managing risk – processes for 'finding and using accurate information, weighing up the options and identifying the risks and consequences . . . to make an informed choice' can all be applied in EWFC contexts	2.2 Exploration (KS4) – identify, select and use information sources to research, clarify and review options and choices in careers and financial contexts relevant to needs
		2.3 Enterprise – assess, undertake and manage risk
		2.4 Financial capability – understand financial risk and reward
		Economic and business understanding – 'make informed choices between alternative uses of scarce resources'
	2.3 Developing relationships and working with others – use social skills to build and maintain positive relationships; use communication, negotiation, assertiveness and collaboration; demonstrate empathy	2.3 Enterprise – approaches to working with others, problem-solving, action planning; key attitudes for enterprise . . . open-mindedness, respect for evidence
		Application of skills in work experience situations, working with adults

Sources: QCDA 2007a and b; Programmes of Study for KS3 and 4.

Monitoring and assessment

Overall, Ofsted's most recent findings on the state of EWFC (2010) show that schools are delivering a great deal of useful activity to develop students' basic economic understanding and enterprise skills. However, little of this work is underpinned by clearly identified learning objectives, monitoring or assessment systems. Although it is true that the non-statutory nature of EWFC means that formal assessment methods are not mandatory, if schools do not consistently identify and track what the students have learnt, it will be almost impossible to judge whether provision is effective. It is essential to 'check that learning is taking place, to identify what learners can do well, and where and how they can do better' (Macdonald 2009, p. 33) in order to sustain the momentum, value and purpose of the course, the motivation of learners and the commitment of teachers and parents/carers to the programme. Given that work-related learning/EWFC is still at a relatively early stage in terms of being accepted and integrated, this would seem of paramount importance for its long-term survival.

In conclusion, it is worth reflecting on the findings of the PSHE Strategic Partners Group as quoted in the Macdonald Review (2009, p. 33) into the potential impact of effective assessment on PSHE education, which is also relevant to developing co-ordinated and coherent work-related learning/EWFC provision. It can:

- enable staff to tailor provision and practice to the learners' needs;
- track the progress learners make;
- motivate learners and boost their self-esteem;
- encourage and help them to take increasing responsibility for their learning; and
- help to prepare them for a working life in which they will shoulder most of the responsibility for assessing their own performance and identifying and meeting their training and development needs.

Discussion questions

1. What are the benefits and challenges of having a single Programme of Study for EWFC at Key Stage 3 and Key Stage 4?

2. What should be taught in terms of 'economic and business terms' at Key Stage 3 and why?

3. Is the suggested range and content for EWFC at Key Stage 4 (see QCA 2007a, p. 239) achievable? If not, how could it be improved?

4. How would you work with other teachers to help them manage delivery of work-related learning in tutor time and/or within their subjects?

5. What would be your priorities for CPD sessions on effective work-related learning delivery?

Tasks

1. When planning your work-related learning provision for Key Stage 3 it is essential to consider the range of knowledge, skills and attitudes to work young people are bringing with them from primary school and their personal life. For example:

   – What does 'being enterprising' mean to them – is it different from your interpretation?

   – What kinds of work and work environments have they already investigated, perhaps through meeting employers, visiting a workplace or via a family member – where are the gaps?

   – What other work-related activities have they been involved in and what did they gain from them – might the activities you are planning be repetitious for some young people?

   – How have these work-related learning experiences influenced their personal development – what do they see themselves doing in the future as a result?

   Devise a practical means of gathering some of this information from learners – and from teachers at your main feeder primary schools – either just before they move from Year 6 or early on in Year 7. How can their achievements be celebrated and shown to be of value?

2. Choose a particular work-related experience such as an enterprise activity, work experience or work simulation, and identify the ways in which it could be used to help young people at Key Stage 4 develop a range of skills and knowledge for managing risk in the context of personal finance.

Notes

1. The Review was carried out as part of the process of implementing the reforms to qualifications and curriculum set out in the 14–19 Education and Skills White Paper and the Implementation Plan.
2. Every Child Matters (DfES 2003) identifies five wellbeing outcomes for children and young people: be healthy; stay safe; enjoy and achieve; make a positive contribution; achieve economic wellbeing.
3. For information on the experiential learning cycle, see QCA (2005).
4. As Jim Knight MP said when Minister of State for Schools: 'Education has to prepare children and young people for the real world beyond the school gates, and financial literacy is a skill that every citizen needs to function effectively in society' (parliamentary debate, April 2007).
5. 'The economy is a key part of all our daily lives, young and old. It can have a marked impact on the opportunities we have, the uncertainties and risks we face, and our standard of living in general . . . I believe that teaching young people about the economy as part of citizenship education will help them to understand a key aspect of the way our society works, how we each contribute, and how it affects our everyday lives' (Dr Andrew Wardlow in Ofsted 2006, p.14).
6. Ways of building on the interface between EWFC and PW are considered later in this chapter.
7. See EFQM Introducing Excellence at http://www.efqm.org. The EFQM Excellence Model is widely used by private and public sector organisations across Europe, including schools and colleges, as a means of benchmarking good-quality practice and building sustainable excellence.

It is equally appropriate for small and large organisations and has been used by schools alongside Investors in People to improve their overall performance and effectiveness. The Centre for Education and Industry's schools award for Excellence in Work-Related Learning reflects the EFQM Model in its self-review framework.

8.   With acknowledgements to the Specialist Schools and Academies Trust website.

References

DCSF (Department for Children, Schools and Families) (2007) *Building on the Best: Final Report and Implementation Plan of the Review of 14–19 Work-Related Learning*. Nottingham: DCSF.

DCSF (2008) *Guidance on Financial Capability in the Secondary Curriculum: Key Stages 3 and 4*. Nottingham: DCSF.

DfE (Department for Education) (2010) *STEM and Economic Wellbeing [EWB], Planning Tools and Resources for Key Stage 3*. Crown Copyright. Available HTTP: <http://www.nationalstemcentre.org.uk/elibrary/resource/2544/stem-and-economic-wellbeing-ewb-planning-tools-and-resources-for-key-stage-three> (accessed 18 May 2011).

DfES (Department for Education and Skills) (2003) *Every Child Matters*. London: DfES. Available HTTP: <https://www.education.gov.uk/publications/eOrderingDownload/CM5860.pdf> (accessed 18 May 2011).

Harris, A., Jamieson, I. Pearce, D. and Russ, J. (1996/7) *Effective Teaching and Learning in Work-Related Contexts: Report of a Research Project Funded by the Department for Education and Employment*. Rotherham: DfEE.

Macdonald, A. (2009) *Independent Review of the Proposal to Make Personal, Social, Health and Economic Education Statutory*. London: Department for Children, Schools and Families.

Ofsted (Office for Standards in Education) (2005) *Personal, Social and Health Education in Secondary Schools*. HMI 2311. London: Ofsted.

Ofsted (2006) *Towards Consensus? Citizenship in Secondary Schools*. HMI 2666. London: Ofsted.

Ofsted (2008) *Developing Financially Capable Young People: A Survey of Good Practice in Personal Finance Education for 11–18-Year-Olds in Schools and Colleges*. 070029. London: Ofsted.

Ofsted (2010) *Personal, Social, Health and Economic Education in Schools*. 090222. London: Ofsted.

QCA (Qualifications and Curriculum Authority) (2004) *Changes to the Key Stage 4 Curriculum: Guidance for Implementation from September 2004*. London: QCA.

QCA (2005) *Work-Related Learning at Key Stage 4: Maximising Learning from Work-Related Experiences*. London: QCA.

QCA (2007a) *PSHE: Economic Wellbeing and Financial Capability – Programme of Study (Non-statutory) for Key Stages 3 and 4*. London: QCA.

QCA (2007b) *PSHE: Personal Wellbeing – Programme of Study (Non-statutory) for Key Stages 3 and 4*. London: QCA.

QCA (2008) *Career, Work-Related Learning and Enterprise 11–19: A Framework to Support Economic Wellbeing*. London: QCA.

QCA (2009a) *Career, Work-Related Learning and Enterprise 11–19: QCA Survey of Practice*. Unpublished report.

QCA (2009b) *Maximising Learning from Work-Related Experiences*. London: QCA.

UKCES (UK Commission for Employment and Skills) (2009) *The Employability Challenge: Executive Summary*. London: UKCES. Available HTTP: <http://www.ukces.org.uk> (accessed 18 May 2011).

4

Pupil work experience

Prue Huddleston

Background

Work experience has a long history dating back at least as far as the last raising of the school leaving age (ROSLA) in 1972, although there were some manifestations as early as the 1960s. However, its purposes have been redefined over the past 30 years to adapt to changing circumstances and policy imperatives; rather than being viewed as an option for the few it has become a universal entitlement for all pupils during their last year of compulsory schooling and beyond. It is the most ubiquitous form of work-related learning (95 per cent of pupils undertake work experience during Key Stage 4) and yet its purposes, outcomes and value for money have been questioned throughout its history. More than 10 years ago, the Davies Report (DfEE 1999), *A New Agenda for School Business Links*, recommended that government departments [Department for Education and Employment (DfEE) and Department for Trade and Industry (DTI)] should review the provision of work experience bearing in mind the significant investment by both government and business in its provision and the lack of clarity around learning outcomes and quality issues.

The Confederation of British Industry's (CBI) *Time Well Spent* revisits similar themes when urging employers, schools and pupils to consider carefully the aims, content and intended outcomes of work experience so that pupils can benefit from the 'key role [work experience has] to play in preparing young people for the adult world [and the] opportunity to bring home to them the attributes, skills and knowledge they need to succeed throughout their working lives' (CBI 2007, p. 6). Providing young people with learning experiences that extend beyond the school gate has been encouraged by successive curriculum initiatives, but there has been concern about the quality of such experiences and, most importantly, what can be learned from them. Despite these criticisms the CBI recognises the value of work experience for both employers and students and urges its members to engage with the process.

In 1995, the DfEE described work experience as 'a placement on employer's premises in which the pupil carries out a particular task, or duty, or a range of duties, more or less as would an employee, but with the emphasis on the learning aspects of the experience' (DfEE 1995, p. 5). Similarly, the Qualifications and Curriculum Authority (QCA 1998) placed emphasis upon the need for the young person to engage in tasks and activities that are authentic and relate to the role of a young worker rather than that of an observer, as in work shadowing. The significance of work experience is that, at best, it involves real work tasks, in real work settings, where the young person is encouraged to develop the workplace skills, often described today as skills for employability. It also provides opportunities for the young person to engage with 'communities of practice' to observe and learn from people at work.

This chapter will review the current position of work experience within the curriculum, its rationale, organisation and delivery and provide opportunities for you to reflect upon approaches to practice in order to maximise the potential of this particular type of work-related learning experience.

Purposes and functions of work experience

Defining the purposes and functions of work experience is rather like the salesman of snake oil describing the virtues of his product: it has been seen as a 'cure-all' for many conditions. It has been described variously as helping to develop workplace skills, both generic and specific, to increase self-confidence and motivation, to allow career sampling, to enable young people to understand the *savoir être* as well as the *savoir faire* of the workplace. Delivering all this would be a tall order, especially from an average two-week work experience placement. That is why it is essential, if a placement is to have some success, for its aims to be clear from the outset and for those to be shared with all stakeholders: young people, teachers, employers and those intermediary bodies that source and provide work experience placements.

For different young people the purposes of their work experience have differed over time, and may still differ. For example, work experience was once thought of as an option or pathway for some, often those described as 'benefitting from a more practical learning experience' as in the case of the Increased Flexibility Programme at Key Stage 4 (Golden *et al.* 2005, p. vii). Here pupils spent one or two days each week within a workplace setting, often working towards occupational or vocational qualifications whilst at the same time following their core curriculum in school on the other days. The Key Stage 4 Engagement Programme had similar features, allowing students to combine practical and theoretical learning though a combination of workplace experience in a chosen sector of interest with classroom-based core curriculum activity. Work experience has also been advocated for those disengaged from mainstream education, and a variety of programmes and charitable projects have provided work experience opportunities alongside basic skills training for those excluded from school, for example the YMCA and the Prince's Trust.

For students following particular types of vocational qualification, for example BTECs, work experience may be embedded within, and closely aligned to, the main learning programme. Those 14- to 16-year-olds following a Young Apprenticeship pathway are expected to complete 50 days' work experience over the course of two years and this is specifically aligned to the employment sector in which the apprenticeship is based. Within Diplomas (see Chapter 6), it is suggested, though not mandatory, that the compulsory 10-day work experience should be closely aligned to Principal Learning.

Nowadays work experience is a universal entitlement and the assumed benefits deriving from it are couched in more general rather than vocationally, or occupationally, specific terms. It is suggested that all young people can benefit from the opportunities provided by work experience to develop the 'attributes, skills and knowledge' necessary for employability (CBI 2007, p. 6). However, such claims are problematic, and difficult to prove, since employability is something of a 'chimera' concept, connoting different meanings for different people. This applies both to those undertaking the experience and to those hosting placements. If young people are unclear as to the purposes of work experience and employers are similarly vague, then it is unsurprising that outcomes are mixed.

An engineering employer, recently interviewed, stated that he could not understand why he had been sent a particular pupil for work experience, 'since the lad had no interest in machinery'. Similarly, a pupil placed in a law firm reported that she was 'not interested in law but in IT'. The young woman had not realised how extensively IT (information technology) was used in the company and how she might have benefitted from opportunities whilst on placement to enhance her IT skills and learn about careers in IT, albethey in law firms. Those in the company with responsibility for arranging this placement had not taken this student's interests into account either. Jack, who spent his work experience at a local branch of a national hotel chain, said that 'he had learnt nothing, because all he did was collect dirty linen from bedrooms and serve coffee at breakfast'. Upon closer questioning it was clear that Jack had learnt a great deal about the terms and conditions of employment within the hotel industry (CEI 1999a). Following the experience he decided to follow a different career route.

It has been suggested elsewhere (Huddleston 2000) that work experience has sometimes been viewed as 'compensatory' education – to be offered to those not capable of pursuing the academic route – whereas by others it is viewed as 'complementary' to mainstream education in that it provides experiences which enhance and extend learning and are unavailable in schools. The foregoing section demonstrated some of these different perspectives. Current thinking is that work experience should be available to all students, irrespective of their career intentions or pathway of study, specifically because of the broader educational aims that it can serve.

As long ago as 1991, Miller, Watts and Jamieson (1991) outlined the range of purposes for which work experience might be used and commented upon the narrow approach adopted by some schools, teachers and pupils. In summary, Miller and colleagues argue, and this has been further supported by work undertaken by the QCA, Ofsted and DCSF (QCA 1998, 2007; Ofsted 1998, 1999; DCSF 2007), that work experience can support different areas of the curriculum: personal, social, health and economic education (PSHEE); careers education and guidance; linkages to core curriculum subjects; opportunities to develop generic personal, learning and thinking skills; and explicit linkages to vocational programmes. In this way the rationale for work experience links with the wider rationale for work-related learning: learning 'for', 'through' and 'about' work.

What has been demonstrated above is that reactions to work experience are often located within a particular view of the purposes of work experience, for example career tasting. The challenge is reconciling these particular views of work experience in order to provide a holistic learning opportunity for young people that can potentially serve a multiplicity of learning goals, including contextualising learning, workplace socialisation and engagement with a community of practice. The even greater challenge is helping learners to make connections between these experiences.

Work experience delivery

The organisation and delivery of work experience for all Key Stage 4 students in a large comprehensive school is a significant undertaking and involves a set of complex relationships between students, parents/carers, teachers, employers (public, private and third sector), training providers, intermediary bodies, the local authority and governors. Essentially, it is a shared enterprise across a range of stakeholders.

The delivery of work experience may vary from area to area, or even from school to school. Some schools organise their own work experience programmes, either by finding their own placements or by asking students to find their own. However, a common means of delivery is through a central organiser, often an education–business link organisation (EBLO) such as an education–business partnership (EBP). The advantages of using a central organiser are promoted as 'reducing the burden on employers', 'reducing the administrative burden on schools', 'ensuring that quality features are in place, for example health, safety and insurance'.

Where the services of a central organiser are contracted there is likely to be a service-level agreement between the school and the provider setting out the number of placements needed, with details about types of placements, including any special requirements. In addition the school as 'buyer' should insist on appropriate quality assurance for all aspects of delivery, including risk assessment of placements and any special health and safety issues.

Recent work by the Institute for Education Business Excellence (IEBE), in partnership with the DCSF (DCSF 2008a), has resulted in the development of a set of quality standards for education–business link activities. Essentially, any organisation offering such a brokerage service to schools should meet the quality criteria set out in the IEBE's standards. In future a pre-condition of Department for Education funding will be an organisation's possession of the standard.

Since 1989 core funding from central government has been available to support the delivery of work-related learning activity in general, a large proportion of which has gone to the organisation and supply of pre-16 work experience. Core funding has been paid to central work experience organisers and has been subject to variations over time in terms of the level of funding, the targets imposed (reflecting the composition and size of the area served) and the quality standards expected of those organising work experience placements. Schools were also provided with an element of funding to support work-related learning, including work experience, and could make decisions about how they would spend this allocation in terms of work experience provision.

As these arrangements are subject to change it is important to consult with a local work experience organisation to receive up-to-date information and advice. Central organisers of work experience will charge schools for the service. In addition to organising placements, many of these bodies provide networking opportunities for schools to share good practice and to engage in continuing professional development (CPD). From 1 April 2010 the Learning and Skills Council (LSC) ceased to have responsibility for the funding stream which provided work-related learning support to schools often through EBPs. Instead this funding has been routed in full through local authorities, which also have full responsibility for the health and safety of learners whilst engaged in any work-related learning, including work experience.

Some schools successfully organise their own placements and do not rely on the services of central organisers. Where this is the case, schools will usually have strong, existing links and will be able to call upon a core of supportive local employers, sometimes involving parents, governors or former pupils. In some schools pupils are encouraged to find their own placements. Clearly, this can prove quite a challenge in areas of significant unemployment or where there is narrow sector representation. Whereas it may be relatively easy for the son or daughter of a professional to call upon established parental social networks, it is extremely difficult for those whose parents are unemployed, or where there is little experience of continuing education.

Whatever model is adopted, schools have to ensure that there is adequate co-ordination of the process with designated responsibility given to a member or, in the case of a large school, several members of staff. Issues to consider include: the quality and quantity of placements required in any year; defining roles and responsibilities for school staff, including support staff; identifying potential curriculum linkages; securing the capacity to support delivery, including the infrastructure in school; funding requirements; health, safety and insurance; and investment in the CPD necessary to support those involved in managing work experience in school. This planning and support extends to administrative as well as teaching staff; in some schools, for example, the administration of work experience will be undertaken by a non-teaching member of staff. In other schools work experience co-ordinators may be recruited from business backgrounds.

The co-ordinator is the main point of contact for all activities involved in the smooth running of work experience, including liaison with students, staff, parents, outside bodies, employers (in the case of schools finding their own placements), controlling, monitoring and evaluating the programme. The commitment of the head teacher, and other senior managers, is essential to ensure that work experience is given appropriate priority and resource within the school's development plan.

Schools have the ultimate responsibility in ensuring that work experience placements offered to their pupils conform to health and safety requirements, that employers have the necessary insurance in place and that they are clear about their legal responsibilities towards those undertaking placements in their companies. Where the school has devolved responsibility for its work experience programme to an outside agency, for example an EBP, these checks will have been made by that agency. However, ultimately the school must be assured that all placements meet all the current health and safety requirements and that risk assessments have been carried out on the suitability of placements. Where students are encouraged to find their own placements, the school will have to arrange for such placements to be visited to ensure that all the necessary conditions described above pertain. In addition there are the necessary child protection issues to be addressed.

Health and safety in pupil work experience is a specialist area and it is important that anyone involved in organising and managing work experience be clear about the current legislation and the roles and responsibilities of all parties, and that they be satisfied that they are not putting students at risk by placing them in particular locations for their work experience. More detailed information can be found in DCSF 2008b.

Supply and demand

From what has been said so far it will be clear that the annual demand for pre-16 work experience placements puts a significant strain on the resources of employers, many of which are small enterprises, or even micro businesses. Education–business partnerships usually have good knowledge about local employers and the opportunities available within their area. These vary across different parts of the country, for example rural to urban (in rural areas problems can be particularly acute because of the limited range of placements and also because of travel issues). In other areas a particular sector may dominate, for example distribution or electronics; in coastal areas business is seasonal and places can be restricted to certain months. The public sector provides significant numbers of placements, for example in schools, hospitals and local government offices. In one large metropolitan borough in the West Midlands the Council House is the largest provider of work experience. Third-sector bodies can also provide useful experiences as well as training providers.

Although in general terms matching demand and supply within a given area may not be insurmountable, it is more difficult to find enough close fits to meet specific demands. Some placements are highly prized and may be open to competition between schools, or for pupils within a given school. For some placements companies may impose application and selection procedures – this can be the case with big City corporates. A young woman interviewed recently during her work experience placement in a large City firm reported: 'One of my mates is dead jealous, he said, how did you get that, I'm in a bloomin' garage.' She went on to say that she felt that the reason she had been successful with her first choice was because, in her words, 'she kept pestering the teacher to make sure her name was on the list.' She was aware that the number of places was limited and word travels fast from year to year about which places are 'cool' and which are not (Huddleston and Muir 2009, pp. 32, 33).

The role of employers

We know that partnerships with employers support leadership and governance. They also help to support a broad, rich and relevant curriculum, and make learning more engaging. They can help in ensuring young people enter adult life prepared for the world of work. And they can help raise aspirations and broaden horizons.

(DCSF 2008c, p. 3)

This is the case made for employer engagement within the education community, but what specifically should employers contribute to work experience and what advantages are to be gained by them for doing so?

What employers can offer will depend upon the size and nature of their business; for example a large metropolitan borough council in the West Midlands can accommodate about 30 placements a year across its many departments, and also has a designated member of staff dealing with this area, whereas an estate agent in a southern coastal town can take a maximum of four. A small art gallery and gift shop in a seaside resort takes one student a year on work experience, but relies on part-time student labour to staff the shop during weekends and in the holiday season. It may be that the part-time student employee could simply ask to extend the weekend seasonal job into a two-week work experience, as in the case of a young man interviewed in the Centre for Education and Industry (CEI) research (CEI 1999a) who used his weekend part-time retail job as a work experience placement.

This is not generally encouraged, as it is suggested that experience as a part-time worker differs from that of the work experience student (Percy 2010). There are clearly some areas of commonality, for example doing real work tasks, understanding the routines and procedures of the workplace, operating in real working environments; however, the degree of responsibility is likely to be different, and also the motivation. The majority of Year 10 students will not be in part-time employment anyway.

The nature of some companies' business will preclude their offering work experience; for example there may be confidentiality issues, or the jobs and tasks available are unsuitable for young people to undertake. The company may not have a member of staff available to provide the necessary supervision and support for the young person. This can occur in large companies where Head Office has signed up to the concept in general terms, often with significant recognition at government department level and in the board room, but where local delivery is hindered by unco-operative branch managers, or simply a lack of capacity.

In the best arrangements employers will have identified the departments, posts and tasks most suitable for a student; any health, safety and welfare implications (including equal opportunities); the time, cost and resource required to run the placement (this can be significant if professional time is factored in); any likely disruption to normal working practice; any inherent risks; and the benefits of company involvement.

Clearly, within some types of organisation it will be possible for students to do actual jobs; in others students may have to undertake tasks by helping others to do their jobs. In some situations there may be specially designed tasks for work experience students; in others students will be given 'odd jobs' to complete. In some companies the experience may also involve some observation of others, this is more akin to work shadowing than real work experience, but if it is limited to a small percentage of time then it can provide useful insights into different types of job available within one company, or sector. In many cases a placement will involve all the activities above.

Let us take, for example, a placement within a hairdressing salon:

■ doing actual jobs – receiving clients, checking booking and dealing with cloakroom and 'gowning', preparing hot drinks for clients, maintaining salon tidiness;

■ helping others to do their jobs – collecting products from stock room, passing equipment to stylists during procedures;

■ observing others doing their jobs – watching stylists cut and colour hair.

Employers need to ensure that the foregoing is possible and in place; it is not the responsibility of the employer to set the educational agenda, although best practice suggests that there should be some dialogue between all parties in terms of shared goals and expectations for learning. These will be considered later, but it is to be hoped that the employer will wish to ensure that the activity has educational aims and that it is not simply two weeks off school, or another pair of 'cheap' hands to help out at a busy time. The average length of time spent on a two-week work experience is equivalent to about half the time spent on a GCSE programme; clearly there are opportunity costs.

It is important for the employer to ensure that there is a programme of work available for the young person, that there is a designated supervisor appointed and that appropriate induction, briefing, debriefing and evaluation processes are in place. The employer should also make clear the hours of work, break times, health and safety issues and confidentiality requirements. Employers may also welcome a pre-placement meeting with prospective work experience students and a visit from a teacher during the placement. These are optimal arrangements; unfortunately not all placements follow this model.

The large number of employers continuing to offer work experience placements suggests that they must feel that there is something to be gained from participating. Clearly, benefits are difficult to quantify, but on the whole research suggests that benefits fall into the following broad areas:

- Accessing current and future customer base
- Raising the company profile within the local area
- Influencing young people's career choices
- Identifying potential future recruits
- Influencing the quality of future employees
- Providing development opportunities for company staff.

(Education and Employers Taskforce 2010, p. 55)

These could be said to apply to a range of education–business links, not just to work experience. However, during work experience the student has contact with employers and their businesses over a sustained period; he or she has significant exposure to actual workplaces and to work processes. This is not the case in other types of work-related learning activity. Similarly, the employer has an opportunity to see young people at first hand in real working conditions. In an unpublished survey conducted by the CEI for the Learning and Skills Council (CEI 2004), employers reported that work experience was the most common work-related learning activity in which they engaged. They did so because they knew exactly what was required of them, the objectives were clear and it was relatively easy for them to do once capacity issues had been resolved. It is also an activity that can be repeated year on year.

Recent research by KPMG for the Employer Engagement Taskforce (KPMG 2010) supports these findings and suggests that work experience is the one work-related learning activity in which employers most frequently engage. It is often seen as synonymous with work-related learning itself, suggesting perhaps that their knowledge of other types of possible engagement may be less well developed.

Thinking about learning

It has been suggested above that, although there may be multiple aims for work experience, essentially it should be an educational experience. If this is the case then some fundamental questions need to be addressed:

- What is the intended learning outcome of the activity?
- What types of learning opportunities are available within the contexts being offered?
- How can learners make sense of these experiences, internalise them and act upon them?
- How can linkages be made between what young people are learning in their work experience and what they are learning in the classroom and within the wider world?

If we start from the position that workplaces can provide rich contexts for learning, then the identification of potential learning opportunities within placements should be a first step. These may be generic, for example focusing upon 'employability skills', or specific, for example subject linked. We have said above that there are several curriculum areas to which work experience might contribute:

- personal, social, health and economic education;
- careers education and guidance;
- core curriculum and other subjects;
- functional skills (maths, English and IT);
- personal learning and thinking skills;
- vocational programmes (for example, BTECs).

Between 1997 and 1999, the CEI undertook research across a range of employment sectors to identify the potential learning outcomes that might be achieved within different workplace settings for students during their work experience placements (CEI 1999a). The purpose of the study was seen as an attempt to address earlier criticisms of work experience, namely:

> Specific learning outcomes, as opposed to general outcomes such as 'learning about the world of work' were rarely seen as the main objectives of work experience placements.
>
> (Hillage *et al.* 1996, p. 8)

The researchers visited 24 employers, of varying sizes, in each of nine different work experience sectors to identify the work tasks which students regularly undertook whilst on placements in their companies. Further questions attempted to elicit the extent to which placements provided opportunities for students to develop key skills, for example problem solving, working with others, communication. The study was later extended to include other work experience areas: 17 areas were finally covered.

The findings from the research informed the production of a set of Learning Frameworks, one for each sector studied, which helped students, employers and teachers to identify learning outcomes and enhance links with the school curriculum (CEI 1999a). Potential learning opportunities were identified, based on real workplace examples, for each of the 17 sectors in terms of work tasks, work skills and key skills. For example within the child care sector, the following illustrative opportunities were identified (they are not exhaustive; adapted from CEI 1999b):

- work tasks
    - playing with children individually and in groups
    - participating in talking and listening activities with children
    - reading stories to children
    - cleaning and maintaining nursery clothing and equipment
- work skills
    - how to provide opportunities for children's physical play
    - how to play creatively with children
    - how to promote positive aspects of children's behaviour
    - how to maintain a healthy environment for children
- employability skills
    - understanding the importance of good appearance
    - displaying enthusiasm in work with children
    - presenting yourself well to other staff
    - displaying a 'can do' attitude when working with children.

One of the problems when attempting to identify the possible learning outcomes of a placement stems from the fact that the responsibility for the process is shared across a range of stakeholders. Employers may express willingness to offer a placement but may have no knowledge of the intended curriculum focus. They may also be locked into an outdated view of schools and of the way in which the curriculum is shaped, based on their own educational experience. Subject teachers may know little about the placements on offer, even less about their possibilities for curriculum linkage. A careers teacher, with responsibility for work experience, is unlikely to have detailed knowledge across all curriculum areas and is not best placed to match the offers of placement to subject-specific learning objectives. Central organisers of work experience may come from business rather than from education backgrounds. Where students are finding their own placements then all parties are likely to be working in the dark, unless the student is proactive in having clear learning aims at the outset; for example he or she has an interest in making a career within the sector.

Identifying learning opportunities within work placements first depends upon having clear ideas about the proposed learning outcomes for students: what do we hope students will gain from these placements? Are they intended to provide an insight into careers in a particular sector, or are they intended to have wider 'skills' outcomes? Much will depend upon the pool of places available. It will not be possible to meet all learning needs from an existing pool of placements, nor would a placement always provide the best environment for learning. A teacher might start from the position: how can I help students learn about the uses of IT in business? An obvious answer is to find work experience placements that will enable students to observe and use IT within real business settings with real IT professionals. The fall-back position is to invite a speaker from the sector to talk to students in school or to source a DVD, or similar teaching resource. All have a place but the actual work experience provides a 'close' experience through both observation and participation. The other two are 'remote' and mediated through others' perspectives and experiences.

Following the identification of learning aims and appropriate approaches the next step is to scan what placements are on offer and then to attempt an audit of what learning opportunities they might present, in the way in which the CEI study was conducted. This is a significant undertaking, but worth the effort. Although every teacher cannot know in detail what individual placements might offer, it is possible to build up a picture of generic activities which occur within different sectors. For example, within the retail sector (a significant provider of work experience placements) it is clear that customer service, merchandising and display, food handling and hygiene are all areas that will be covered. It is also likely that there will be opportunities to develop generic skills such as working with other people and working to deadlines. Similarly, within office environments there are opportunities to observe and practice subject-specific activities as well as generic skills. These might include preparing papers for a meeting (subject specific, for example information and communication technologies, business, English) as well as answering telephone calls (functional skills).

For learners with particular needs, programmes of work experience need to be closely prescribed to learning goals. These may focus, for example, upon developing self-confidence and independence. A work experience programme for learners with special needs set within the catering department of a further education college enables students to serve customers in the college's bistro. They can take orders, present food to real customers and handle payments under the supervision of the bistro staff. Following this experience, some students have been able to gain part-time employment in external catering outlets. For these students the placements had met their learning objectives: developing self-confidence and independence (author's discussion with tutor during visit to college).

Where there are well-developed systems for work experience in place with a good supply of reliable and well-established placements, job descriptions of possible placements are often available outlining the type of work involved. This enables students to review and select a placement which meets their objectives, for example career tasting or improving their knowledge of particular software packages.

A pre-placement visit can help to identify potential learning opportunities and to match contexts to learner needs, whether these are aligned to a course specification or to developing self-confidence. Some companies insist on a pre-placement interview, even involving selection, where potential students are asked about their learning objectives. This also provides opportunities for functional skills development, for example oral communication skills. This is best practice; unfortunately not all placements are as well planned.

During and after the placement there should be ample opportunities for learners, teachers and employers to review what has been learned in order to ensure that there is clear alignment between work experience aims and practice. Because this particular way of learning may be unfamiliar to some students they may be unaware of what they are learning, or have learned, from their work experience (remember Jack's comment?). They need to be encouraged to reflect on their learning through discussion with workplace supervisors, teachers and others; often students may do this through the completion of a work experience diary or log. Although there is a danger that completing the log can be a mechanistic box-ticking exercise, if the log is thoughtfully constructed it can prompt learners to think more deeply about what they have learned. In some cases students may complete a piece of coursework aligned to their work experience, for example how different types of communication are used in workplaces.

Schools should ensure that there is adequate curriculum time for work experience preparation, debriefing and follow-up, including any suggested amendments to the experience for successive years. Similarly, host companies should be encouraged to contribute to the process and should be provided with feedback on what worked well and what was less satisfactory. The CBI (2007) placed emphasis on the importance of employer debriefing; in the best cases, in addition to debriefing, students make presentations to their hosts at the end of their placements. This provides feedback for host departments but also allows students to practise presentation skills within a realistic setting; thus contributing to skills development within work contexts.

Keeping learning at the heart of the experience involves thinking about:

- what is to be learned (setting learning objectives with associated learning outcomes)

- how this learning might be achieved (where are the opportunities within the placement?)

- what sort of evidence will be used to confirm learning (diaries, logs, examples of completed work tasks, videos of presentations, witness statements by workplace supervisors)

- how this evidence will be assessed (reports from workplace supervisors, teacher review of pupils' learning through feedback and debrief, teacher visits to students on placement).

The Learning Frameworks, described above, provide an example of a tool to support this process.

What do employers expect young people to learn from their work experience?

A lot has been said about the importance of learning within work experience from an educational perspective. It is also important to consider what employers hope that young people will learn from the experience (CBI 2007; DCSF 2007). Sometimes these views are not well aligned; for example employers make much of the shortcomings of those leaving full-time education, both from schools and even from higher education (CBI 2007), and yet they are happy to staff their businesses with part-time students, particularly within the retail and hospitality and catering sectors. By engaging with work experience employers have indicated that they wish to put something into the education system, so what is it that they hope young people will learn?

When examined a little more fully, in the context of work experience, it can be seen that the criticisms of young people are mainly couched in terms of 'employability' rather than subject-specific knowledge. This is seen by employers as one of the main learning aims of pupil work experience. There is nothing wrong in this; in fact a recent survey undertaken by the United Kingdom Commission for Employment and Skills (UKCES 2010) identifies significant shortages in 'employability skills', including 'customer handling, problem solving, team working, oral and written communication but also extend to cover a basic platform of literacy and numeracy too' (p. 39) within the existing work force. From the employers' perspective, if such skills can be developed during a two-week work experience programme, so much the better. Certainly the CBI Report (CBI 2007) sees this as the main learning outcome of work experience.

Clearly, there needs to be some consensus on what these skills are and how they might be developed. The Institute for Education Business Excellence (IEBE) in its recent report on *Students' Perceptions of Work Experience* (IEBE 2008) defines 'employability' as 'the skills, personal qualities and knowledge needed by all young people so that they can be effective in the workplace, which benefits the young people, employers and the wider community' (p. 18). Developing these within a two-week work experience is a tall order indeed; we are back to the snake oil salesman. However, some case can be made for providing opportunities for young people to practise such skills, if they know what they are and if they have given some thought to how they might do this within the context of their placement.

This supports the earlier argument for having clear, but realistic, learning objectives for the placement and for a shared understanding between the host company, students and teachers about the purpose of the activity. Otherwise there is little merit in doing it, especially if it becomes an annual numbers game of getting everybody out, no matter what. It is an area that requires support at every level.

Employers should be encouraged to identify possible learning opportunities within the context of their business, but it is unlikely that they could be expected to do this without help. In large companies dedicated education liaison staff, or community investment personnel, can work with education professionals to identify potential rich contexts for learning. A recent example from a large city legal practice illustrates such a possibility.

Local teachers were hosted at a day workshop held at corporate headquarters. Following a tour of the company, observation of staff at work and reviewing company literature, teachers were asked to identify the use of functional skills within the company. They were then encouraged to incorporate this into their schemes of work and lesson plans for teaching functional skills in school.

Clearly, the use of functional skills within the workplace is so ubiquitous and routine that staff may be unaware of the potential for a work experience student to practise them. The teachers were able to signpost such opportunities.

Some companies support seconded teachers to work with them on such developments. This was the case in the example cited above. This secondee organises a wide range of education–business link activities for the company, including a work experience programme. In a large food manufacturing company a seconded history teacher was used to research the company archive with a view to identifying resource material for teaching about working conditions in the nineteenth century.

A small employer does not have the luxury of dedicated education liaison staff; here the local EBP may be able to help in identifying opportunities for learning. Once a bank of placements has been built up these can be matched to learners' needs in the same way as the Learning Frameworks. Similarly, a teacher when visiting a student on placement might identify further opportunities within the workplace and discuss these with the employer.

In order for all parties to benefit from participating in work experience the learning aims should be communicated to workplace supervisors. Even when there is clear understanding higher up in an organisation it is all too common for a young person's arrival in a department to be greeted with surprise.

The increasing requirement for student placements, not just for the traditional Key Stage 4 work experience, but for post-16 placements, 14–19 Diplomas and practical experience within vocational programmes, not to mention the wider 14–19 employer engagement agenda, places heavy demands on employers' resources. It is bound to raise questions concerning quality, purpose and relevance. These questions are as important for employers as for the students undertaking the placements.

The Institute for Education Business Excellence's survey (IEBE 2008) of student responses to work experience, which reports the views of 15,025 students undertaking work experience during the academic year 2007–2008, reveals that 80 per cent had found the experience 'very enjoyable' or 'mostly enjoyable', and that 90 per cent were either 'very satisfied' or 'satisfied' with the experience. The majority also reports developing skills useful in the workplace and understanding more about workplaces, but a smaller proportion stated that the experience had influenced their decisions about post-16 destinations.

On a less positive note, research undertaken by Percy (2010) examining data from 2003–2007 comparing young people's experiences of work experience and part-time paid work suggests that 'insight from young people in the 14–19 Learner Panel informs us that work experience poorly *managed* has a negative impact, even where it is well intended' (p. 4, author's emphasis).

The foregoing sections have emphasised the importance of managing not just the processes of work experience but the potential for learning that it can offer. This is an area requiring further development.

Part-time employment

A large number of young people who are in full-time education engage in some form of paid part-time employment; this obviously includes those who reach their sixteenth birthday during Key Stage 4 – the stage at which school work experience is undertaken. Clearly, those involved in work experience in Year 10 would not fall into this category, but there are likely to be substantial numbers of young people who have already found themselves a job. Perhaps we should also consider voluntary work and 'pocket money' jobs such as babysitting or helping in the family business. When we move to post-16 the numbers are even greater. These young people are already experiencing what it is like to be employed, to receive a wage, to mix with others in the workplace, to develop social networks, to enhance their CVs, to fit in, or to move on, if necessary.

Although it can be argued that the two activities, formal work experience and part-time work, are different in some ways – the former has an educational focus, the latter is a means of financial support – it should not be assumed that learning occurs only in the former. If we accept the case argued above concerning the workplace as a rich context for learning, as providing access to communities of practice, allowing opportunities for maturation and socialisation, then we should encourage those young people to reflect upon their learning in part-time employment. Teachers should encourage lessons learned from part-time employment to inform learning in the classroom, and should recognise students also as young workers. The experiences of young people as workers might also inform the selection of work experience placements, their planning and their delivery.

Conclusions

This chapter has outlined the current significance of student work experience in terms of its scope, range, numbers involved: employers and students, purposes and outcomes. It has suggested that much, perhaps too much, is expected from it in the context of the current policy agenda, where it is promoted as the flagship of the EBP. Nevertheless, more remains to be done in terms of the quality of the experience and in identifying and capitalising on the learning opportunities inherent in work placements. Work experience placements are not in themselves 'a good thing'; they require close alignment to purposes and these are not always clearly understood or shared.

Since it is an activity which many young people appear to enjoy and value, and one in which significant numbers of employers are prepared to engage, enhancing its quality and the learning opportunities it can offer appears a worthwhile undertaking.

Some issues to consider

1. How can the amount of time and resource devoted to work experience be justified within a climate of targets driven by examination success?

2. Is work experience really necessary post-16, given that most students now engage in some form of part-time employment?

3. Is work experience appropriate only for those studying on vocational programmes?

4. Percy (2010) reports: 'although interviews and case studies indicate that effective work experience can have a motivational and positive effect on young people, enough work experience placements were not effective in 2005/06 that the aggregate effect of this activity over the country was negligible.' Why do you think this was the case?

Tasks

1. Design a student log book/diary which encourages them to reflect upon skills development – either functional skills or personal, learning and thinking skills – within the following work experience placements: hotel reception; estate agent's office; veterinary practice; museum; garage; pharmacy. Can you think of others?

2. Consider a recent range of workplaces that you have used for student work experience and list the factors that contributed to their success or lack of success.

Further reading

CEI (1997–1999) *Work Experience: The Learning Frameworks*. Coventry: University of Warwick.

Frameworks are available for the following areas: animals; art and design; child care; construction and the built environment; environmental conservation; factories and workshops; farming and agriculture; financial services; floristry; game conservation; garages and vehicle maintenance; hairdressing and beauty; health care; horticulture; hotels; laboratories; leisure centres; media; office; oral health care; performing arts; restaurants and catering; retail; schools.

DCSF (2009) *The Work-related Learning Guide (Second Edition): A Guidance Document for Employers, Schools, Colleges, Students and Their Parents and Carers*. London: DCSF.

Johns, A. and Miller, A. (2003) *Work Experience and the Law: The Essential Guide for Central Organisers, Employers, Schools*. Coventry: Centre for Education and Industry, University of Warwick.

References

CBI (2007) *Time Well Spent: Embedding Employability in Work Experience*. Report sponsored by Department for Education and Skills. London: CBI.

CEI (Centre for Education and Industry) (1999a) *Work Experience: The Learning Frameworks*. Coventry: University of Warwick.

CEI (1999b) *Work Experience Learning Frameworks Tutor Manual*. Coventry: Centre for Education and Industry, University of Warwick.

CEI (2004) *Education–Business Link (EBL) Activity: Research on Structure and Funding Outline Report for Internal Use by LSC National Office*. Unpublished.

DCSF (2007) *Building on the Best: Final Report and Implementation Plan of the Review of 14–19 Work-Related Learning*. London: DCSF.

DCSF (2008a) *Quality Standard for Work Experience*. London: DCSF.

DCSF (2008b) *The Work-Related Learning Guide: A Guidance Document for Schools, Colleges, Students and Their Parents and Carers*. Available HTTP: <http://www.teachernet.gov.uk/publications> (accessed 16 May 2011).

DCSF (2008c) *Building Stronger Partnerships – Employers: How You Can Support Schools, Colleges, Children and Families*. London: DCSF.

DfEE (1995) *Work Experience: A Guide for Employers*. London: DfEE.

DfEE (1999) *A New Agenda for School Business Links* (The Davies Report). London: DfEE.

Education and Employers Taskforce (2010) *What Is to Be Gained through Partnership? Exploring the Value of Education Employer Relationships*. London: Education and Employers Taskforce.

Golden, S., O'Donnell, L., Benton, T. and Rudd, P. (NFER) (2005) *Evaluation of Increased Flexibility for 14–16 Year Olds Programme: Outcomes for the First Cohort*. London: DCSF.

Hillage, J., Honey, S., Kodtz, J. and Pike, G. (1996) *Pre-16 Work Experience in England and Wales*. Brighton: Institute of Employment Studies.

Huddleston, P. (2000) 'Work placements for young people', in Rainbird, H. (ed.) *Training in the Workplace*. London: Macmillan.

Huddleston, P. and Muir, F. (2009) *Evaluation of the Hackney Schools' Programme: Linking Work with Learning*. Unpublished report for Linklaters LLP. Centre for Education and Industry, University of Warwick.

IEBE (2008) *Students' Perceptions of Work Experience*. Available HTTP: <http://www.educationandemployers. org/research/research-reports/young-people/students-work-experience/> (accessed 16 May 2011).

KPMG (2010) *Evaluation of Education and Employer Partnerships Final Report*. London: Education and Employers Taskforce.

Miller, A.D., Watts, A.G. and Jamieson, I. (1991) *Rethinking Work Experience*. London: Falmer Press.

Ofsted (1998) *Work Related Aspects of the Curriculum in Secondary Schools*. London: Ofsted.

Ofsted (1999) *Inspecting Subjects and Aspects 11–18: Work-Related Education and Careers Education and Guidance*. London: Ofsted.

Percy, C. (2010) *Exploring the Impact of Formal Work Experience and Term-Time Paid Employment Using Longitudinal Data from England (2003–2007)*. Available HTTP: <http://www.educationandemployers. org/media/4680/work_experience_vs_part-time_employment_-_lsype.pdf> (accessed 6 September 2010).

QCA (1998) *Learning from Work Experience*. London: QCA.

QCA (2007) *Work-Related Learning at Key Stage 4*. London: QCA.

UKCES (2010) *Skills for Jobs: Today and Tomorrow: The National Strategic Skills Audit for England. Volume 1: Key Findings*. Wath-upon-Dearne: UKCES.

5

Enterprise education

Malcolm Hoare

Enterprise education in England

English enterprise education has experienced a varied response from school and college practitioners over the past three decades. The 'Enterprise and Education' initiative of the 1980s suffered from a perception that there had been ideological capture, with some teachers rejecting the programme as having little educational relevance (MacDonald and Coffield 1991; Smyth 1999). Such views still exist in some quarters and attempts to introduce enterprise education during the last decade have had to overcome this mistrust. Focused around a 'twenty-first-century skills' agenda, there has been an attempt to argue that enterprise education is an entitlement for all young people and therefore deserving of a central place in the curriculum. The Davies Report (Davies 2002) provided a strong argument for the introduction of enterprise education, and the evaluation of the Enterprise Pathfinder pilot projects (2003–2005) led to Enterprise Standards Funding being made available for all secondary schools from 2005. Evidence, in particular from two major Ofsted inspection reports (Ofsted 2004, 2005), suggests that the argument has not been entirely won but that a considerable development of practice has occurred.

The Schools Enterprise Education Network (SEEN) was launched in 2006 to support secondary schools in England and re-launched with a 5–19 remit as the Enterprise Network in 2008. The Enterprise Network is a centrally funded, regional support structure for enterprise education 5–19. The Network brings together employers, providers and education practitioners to develop strategies for the delivery of high-quality provision through local Enterprise Learning Partnerships. There is a nationwide continuing professional development (CPD) offer and a well-stocked resources clearing house (www.enterprisevillage.org.uk). Regional co-ordinators support Enterprise Learning Partnerships in every English local authority to deliver programmes appropriate to the needs identified by local schools and colleges.

Most recently a National Standard for Enterprise Education has been developed and made available to schools in England from April 2011. This standard functions in a similar way to the Sportsmark and the Healthy Schools Award as a way of recording and celebrating the achievements of a school in this cross-curricular area.

Purposes and functions of enterprise education: competing interpretations

The European dimension

The European Union recognised the importance of enterprise education with the Lisbon Strategy for Growth and Jobs (Lisbon European Council 2000) requiring member states to support entrepreneurship education in schools and colleges. Enterprise education has been identified as a priority for many countries within the European Union, as exemplified by a study undertaken as part of the Entredu review. This research (Hytti 2002) identified three main approaches including:

> Programmes which aim at creating and improving the information necessary for business start-up, programmes which strive to create a better understanding of entrepreneurship and programmes which try to help young people to become more enterprising.
>
> (p. 43)

A progress report from the European Commission in 2007 (European Council, Directorate General Enterprise and Industry 2007) showed patchy progress, with only a minority of member states making any real progress towards embedding enterprise education in their core curriculum. The survey prompted a recommendation from the European Parliament and the Council of Ministers that entrepreneurship should be a key competence for all.

The Commission set itself several objectives including showcasing good practice, identifying key issues to be addressed, suggesting measures for a more systematic strategy and triggering action in the member states. An assessment of progress towards these aims was undertaken in 2009 and again the results were disappointing.

> Much entrepreneurship education practice tends to be ad hoc, varies vastly in quantity and quality, is not treated systematically in the curriculum, and has relied heavily on the enthusiasm and commitment of individual teachers and schools. Some activity is structured and ambitious; much is not; some schools have no entrepreneurship education at all. There are some pockets of excellence, and a number of advanced countries.
>
> (European Commission 2010, p. ii)

The United Kingdom was listed amongst the small number of 'advanced' countries and the report provides several best-practice exemplars from English schools.

The English experience of enterprise education

This dichotomy between enterprise and entrepreneurship, whether real or imagined, has become a central theme in the debate about the validity and relevance of enterprise education. In the UK there has been an attempt to integrate the two perspectives, with policy statements to the effect that 'we all need to be more enterprising'. The Entredu research suggests that in Europe a narrower focus on entrepreneurial behaviours and preparation for business start-up has prevailed.

Enterprise education in England, like other aspects of work-related learning, has often been presented as both 'compensatory' and 'complementary' education (Huddleston and Oh 2004). In many instances, it has been offered as an alternative to an academic curriculum for those pupils too disaffected to cope with mainstream schooling. Alternatively, enterprise education has sometimes been presented to high-achieving pupils as an additional 'real life' experience, usually to assist with their university entrance. Only more recently has it been seen as part of the core curriculum entitlement for all young people, linked to employability and the so-called twenty-first-century skills. This, in turn, has major implications for teaching and learning, with an expectation that enterprising experiences will be delivered across the curriculum and in all schools.

The Centre for Education and Industry undertook an independent review (CEI, 2002) into *Learning for Enterprise and Entrepreneurship* for the then Department for Trade and Industry. The findings from this review suggested a very contradictory scene. On the one hand, there was perceived to be a lack of clarity in the vocabulary of 'enterprise' and 'entrepreneurship', whereas there was also found to be an extremely diverse offering of enterprise activity in schools. The majority of provision appeared to be at Key Stage 4 (14–16 years), with Key Stage 3 (11–13 years) provision often missing the opportunity to link into the national curriculum.

Enterprise learning was frequently delivered as a 'one off' lesson or through extra-curricular activities. Interesting developments were taking place linking enterprise education into the Key Skills initiative but this was patchy and often lacked co-ordination. Practitioners needed to be persuaded of the institutional benefits of enterprise learning, and ongoing continuing professional development was identified as a priority. Initial teacher training (ITT) was highlighted as a concern, with many newly qualified teachers having little exposure to enterprise education during their training. Business and community partners were seen as having much to offer the enterprise education agenda but there was also perceived to be a need to support their engagement, directing them to ensure they made best use of their skills and resources. Quality assurance of delivery remained a cause for concern, as did the assessment of impact on teaching and learning and of learning outcomes.

In England, the Labour government (1997–2010) was keen to promote an enterprise culture within education and commissioned Sir Howard Davies to undertake a review of enterprise and the economy in education. Davies defined enterprise capability as:

> the ability to handle uncertainty and respond positively to change, to create and implement new ideas and new ways of doing things, to make reasonable risk/reward assessments and act upon them in a variety of contexts, both personal and work.
>
> (Davies 2002, p. 17)

The government accepted the main thrust of the report, including the funding of the equivalent of five days of enterprise learning for all pupils at Key Stage 4 from 2005.

In preparation for this, the Department for Education and Skills (DfES) established 151 Pathfinder projects, embracing nearly 400 schools from September 2003. The DfES prospectus for Pathfinder bids adopted a more specific definition of enterprise learning to include both economic and business understanding and financial literacy as vital underpinning dimensions to the enterprise capabilities identified by Davies (Figure 5.1).

The DfES Pathfinders prospectus also required project schools to develop enterprise learning within a clearly defined work-related or business/community context. The department subsequently made £180 million available over three years to embed enterprise education in schools. This funding was devolved to schools through the Standards Fund and almost immediately generated controversy through a lack of 'ring fencing'. The issue of how tightly spending on enterprise education should be prescribed was to become an ongoing issue.

Ofsted was tasked to review the success of these Pathfinders and its report (Ofsted 2004) effectively set the agenda for the future development of enterprise education in England. It says much for the state of enterprise education at that time that Ofsted began its study with an account of the attempts to define what is meant by enterprise learning:

> There is no universally accepted definition of enterprise learning. It is often mistakenly regarded as being synonymous with the development of entrepreneurial skills, but an important distinction needs to be made between the two. Entrepreneurship is about starting up businesses, particularly involving risk. Entrepreneurs need to be enterprising to succeed and survive. However, only a relatively small proportion of the working population will become entrepreneurs, while all adults need to be enterprising both in their work and in their personal lives.
>
> (Ofsted 2004, p. 6)

The report goes on to assert that all employees need enterprise skills and capabilities such as problem solving, decision making and coping with uncertainty to work effectively in teams. The development of these skills in young people is therefore an essential part of the preparation for adult life. Enterprise education, from an Ofsted perspective, is clearly aligned with Life Skills.

Enterprise capability – innovation, creativity, risk management, risk taking and a 'can-do' attitude and the drive to make ideas happen

supported by

financial capability – the ability to manage one's own finances and to become questioning and informed consumers of financial services

and

business and economic understanding – the ability to understand the business context and make informed choices between alternative uses of scarce resources.

FIGURE 5.1 Enterprise Pathfinders project: definition of enterprise education.

Ofsted found that the sample of schools visited interpreted enterprise learning in a variety of ways (Figure 5.2). Whereas some adopted the Davies definition and used this to review their whole approach to work-related learning delivery, the majority had a narrower view, largely based around introducing entrepreneurial skills and extending links with local businesses.

Relatively few schools saw enterprise learning as part of a coherent curriculum for vocational and work-related learning which linked with other aspects of the curriculum such as citizenship education, careers education and guidance and personal and social education. Worryingly, in only half the schools was there an explicit and commonly understood definition of enterprise learning. Not surprisingly, many of

---

Although many schools were at a relatively early stage of development, examples of good practice were observed in the majority of schools. In the most effective schools, there was evidence of pupils being motivated by enterprise learning and developing a good range of relevant skills.

Schools making the most effective provision had a strong commitment from senior managers and a clear management structure to support enterprise learning. An enterprise ethos permeated teaching and learning across the curriculum. Schools made good use of local businesses and the wider community to engage pupils in real issues and to support enterprise learning more generally.

In the most effective schools, teaching and learning were characterised by clearly defined aims and objectives, pupils taking responsibility for their own actions and being given significant autonomy to tackle relevant problems. Enterprise learning also involved pupils evaluating the outcomes of their decisions and reflecting on what they had learned. The least effective schools failed to recognise that enterprise education had important implications for teaching and learning styles.

There was no 'blueprint' for the development of enterprise learning. Schools adopted a variety of different curriculum models, each of which had merits as well as shortcomings.

Only half of the schools had an explicit and commonly understood definition of enterprise learning. This was impeding progress.

Only a minority of schools identified desired learning outcomes in terms of pupils' enterprise knowledge, understanding, skills and attributes. Very few schools had effective procedures in place to assess and evaluate pupils' enterprise learning, although the use of logbooks for self-assessment and some pilot frameworks for assessment are emerging. Links to existing vocational qualifications were rare and few pupils were able to make direct use of their enterprise experiences in assessed coursework.

Monitoring and evaluating progress in the implementation of plans for enterprise learning were weaknesses in a substantial proportion of schools.

Although schools often provided a good range of enterprise experiences of high quality, these were rarely planned as part of a coherent curriculum for work-related learning.

The cost-effectiveness of different possible uses of additional resources for developing enterprise learning is not yet established.

(Ofsted 2004)

FIGURE 5.2 Learning to Be Enterprising: main findings.

these schools were unable to clearly identify the learning outcomes they expected from their enterprise education programmes.

It should be acknowledged that the Ofsted evidence of good practice, patchy though it was, was gathered from a selective cohort of schools known to be supportive of enterprise education.

A model for delivery

One researcher (Hoare 2005) has identified a series of 'myths and legends' about enterprise and entrepreneurship that are widely held and need to be challenged if teachers are to fully engage with enterprise education.

Grewcock, Hoare and Stagg (2010) argue that the successful implementation of a coherent enterprise education policy across the majority of English schools will succeed only if:

- Whilst being a national imperative, it allows local and regional solutions to be adopted to suit the particular context.

- Programmes are fully inclusive, involving all students, subjects, teachers, schools and communities.

- The enterprise education provision is seen as an integral dimension of the school development and improvement plan.

- Enterprise knowledge and understanding are delivered through a skills-led approach, with a strong emphasis on moral and ethical dimensions.

- Schools consider the 'hidden curriculum' generated from their culture and ethos. Many schools operate as social enterprises and as such provide an excellent role model for the workplace of the future.

- Social and community enterprise programmes receive as much regard as 'for profit' activities.

- Full compliance with health and safety, public liability and child protection requirements is ensured.

- Staff CPD is of the highest standard and monitored and evaluated to ensure staff engagement.

Best-practice enterprise education recognises that enterprise is not limited to any particular age group, and that there are various kinds of enterprise activity. Enterprise education should encourage originality and creativity. At any one time, the focus may be business related, emphasise community/social enterprise or link to personal finance education and economic wellbeing. The best enterprise education will be both student centred and activity based, encouraging student enjoyment and ownership of activities, allowing decision making and problem solving to be undertaken by the young people themselves.

There are close links to the personalisation agenda and the increasing focus on personal, learning and thinking skills (PLTS; see also Chapter 7). Ofsted (2005) wrote of the need for enterprise education to be delivered as a student-centred experience, with learners taking responsibility for their own learning and accepting the risk of failure. The implications of creating an authentic learning context have been explored by Herrington and Oliver (2000). The real-life context has to allow for students to experience the full enterprise process, involving ideas generation, planning, delivery and review. These four stages will now be considered in turn to identify what is required of practitioners if they really want to move towards excellence.

Research from the evaluation of the Enterprise Pathfinders project (CEI 2006) underlined the need for a shared vision of what is being aimed for. Effective schools thrive on team work, underpinned by a shared understanding of purpose and total commitment to success that allows all participants to benefit from the experience. Any school wishing to be seen as an outstanding provider of enterprise education would show the following characteristics.

Stage 1: Developing the vision

First, there needs to be a commitment to enterprise education provision for all pupils/ students. There will also be a vision for the enterprise curriculum that incorporates activity-based learning and uses student-centred methods. This in turn will ensure that there is a clear view of where enterprise education fits into the school curriculum and annual development plan. The leadership team will show a strong commitment to embedding enterprise education and there will be a shared understanding and support from a majority of school staff.

Schools should be able to demonstrate that enterprise education does not occur only as a 'bolt-on' activity, for example during 'collapsed' curriculum days or through special events using external providers. There is certainly a place for these activities, but the ideal provision would be based on a more integrated approach with enterprise education embedded in the curriculum across a range of subject areas.

There should also be evidence of clear communication processes within the school. Staff should have a shared understanding of the importance of enterprise education, and demonstrate commitment and enthusiasm. There should be evidence that senior leadership has consulted with staff, providing opportunities for them to discuss issues and to make their own contributions. The communication process should make explicit the likely benefits and learning outcomes which enterprise education will provide for pupils/students.

Stage 2: Planning for enterprise education

Effective day-to-day management and planning of enterprise education activities and events is central to the success of the initiative. Planning of enterprise education should be connected with other aspects of school planning, for example featuring in annual plans and self-evaluation frameworks and linked to other key requirements (e.g. national curriculum).

The planning process should be driven by the need to establish an 'enterprise education entitlement' accessible to all students. In addition there will be evidence of a range of other opportunities open to some students extending beyond this minimum entitlement. Involvement of the learners is central to the process. The school should ensure that students understand the importance of enterprise and enterprise skills. They should know when they have opportunities to take part in enterprise activities, and what they should learn as a result of involvement in them.

The school leadership team should ensure that governors are fully consulted about enterprise education and that their support has been secured. Also, parents should be informed of the school commitment to enterprise education, and what it is intended to achieve. There should be also evidence that the school works with a range of external partners to enrich the enterprise education provided for students.

Key features in the planning and management of enterprise education include the following:

- There should be an identified member of staff with specific responsibility for co-ordinating enterprise education on a day-to-day basis. This may be linked to the management of work-related learning in the school or college.

- Adequate resourcing in terms of both time allocations and funding to support the co-ordinator. The costs of enterprise education should be monitored, and there should be evidence of efforts to analyse the benefits.

- Resources and opportunities are made available for appropriate staff development as part of annual plans for CPD.

- Curriculum plans and timetabling should create appropriate opportunities for enterprise education activities. This should allow some enterprise activity at every Key Stage and year group and may be integrated into subject areas, reflected through the introduction of an enterprise week or part of 'collapsed' curriculum days.

- Curriculum planning should seek support for enterprise education through contacts with external businesses, charities or public sector organisations, as appropriate.

- Schools must also show that enterprise education complies with current legal obligations in terms of child protection, health and safety, and equal opportunities.

Conducting an enterprise education audit

Schools are often encouraged to undertake an audit of the full range of enterprise education activities which take place. In order to ensure a complete audit, there needs to be strong support from senior management, establishing clear roles and responsibilities and providing appropriate resources (including time). Staff from all departments should be included and encouraged to feel able to contribute their examples of enterprise activity. Schools should adopt an approach to auditing which best suits themselves. Teachers should be encouraged to take account of not just the amount of activity occurring in the school but how it is managed, supported, planned, organised and delivered. The audit should include assessment and evaluation. This includes assessing and recording the enterprise skills development of individual students. Also, schools should be able to identify strengths and weaknesses in their overall enterprise education delivery and have a clear view about future development and change. Some examples from schools colleges are shown in Figure 5.3.

If the audit exercise is carried out regularly – for example, once every two years – it should demonstrate both continuity and development. It is also recommended that schools complete an action plan at the end of the audit. Exactly what and how much information is entered is best left to the school's own judgement; but the key is that plans should be realistic and achievable. An enterprise education audit framework and a quality framework are available to download at the Enterprise Village website (www.enterprisevillage.co.uk).

Stage 3: Delivering the enterprise education curriculum

Effective programmes ensure that students have opportunities to develop their enterprise skills and capabilities, for example leadership, decision making, problem solving, risk management, teamwork, creativity and financial capability. Effective enterprise learning is student centred and activity based and students have opportunities to consider moral and ethical issues within a context of enterprise education. Students have opportunities to learn about business operations as part of their enterprise education (e.g. designing a product, production, costs, pricing, marketing and advertising) but they also have opportunities to undertake community and social enterprises. There is differentiation in teaching and learning in enterprise activities to cater for different abilities and preferred learning styles amongst students in the school and full involvement of external partners and contacts in the local community.

Stage 4: Assessing and evaluating enterprise education

It is widely acknowledged that assessment and evaluation of enterprise education present a significant challenge. Many of the skills and capabilities that enterprise education seeks to develop are not easily measured. However, high-quality enterprise education must aim to adopt rigorous approaches to assessing the learning outcomes of enterprise education and evaluating its effectiveness.

- A completion deadline was agreed with staff and document sheets were pinned up on a staff room notice-board to allow departmental/faculty staff to add their own contributions.

- The audit was issued directly to various departments where a nominee was given responsibility for their completion.

- A small team, consisting of the teacher with oversight for enterprise and a curriculum manager, was given the task of collecting information, interviewing key personnel and building up their audit report.

- A part-time, non-teaching enterprise co-ordinator was able to dedicate her time to completing the audit, liaising with tutors and giving staff support.

FIGURE 5.3 Some examples of different audit methods.

Assessing enterprise education

Assessment of enterprise education, which can be broken down into formative assessment (assessment for learning, AFL) and summative assessment (assessment of learning, AOL), has been identified as an area of weakness in some programmes (Ofsted 2005; CEI 2006).

Schools need to demonstrate real commitment towards rigorous assessment, and this includes consideration of student progression in enterprise learning. This is acknowledged by a National Foundation for Educational Research study (Spielhofer and Lynch 2008) which reviews a range of approaches being trialled in schools. The study suggests that schools should have identified the specific learning outcomes intended through enterprise activities and planned how their assessment will be undertaken (by staff and by students). The 'tools' to be used in assessment should have been decided upon and decisions should have been made about what enterprise learning will be recorded and how this evidence will be used, for instance as feedback into the school improvement process. Ideally the approach adopted will be consistent with whole school strategy for assessing learning. Schools should not create overly complex tracking systems, which are time-consuming to implement and often misunderstood by staff and students alike. Some of the most effective enterprise education assessment schemes used in schools are based on a simple three-stage model: Working Towards, Working At and Working Beyond and linked to the range of capabilities identified by the Davies report.

Some projects such as Rotherham Ready (more details below) have used a more detailed criteria-based approach which links enterprise capabilities to level descriptors. The Rotherham team has produced six stages of achievement, each stage describing a level of mastery of their 'Big 13' enterprise skills. These learner outcomes are in turn linked to the appropriate age group from Foundation Stage through to Key Stage 5. More details are available at www.rotherhamready.org.uk/13skills.html

Evaluation of enterprise education

Schools and colleges should have systems in place to evaluate the effectiveness of their enterprise education and to disseminate and celebrate successful outcomes. The evidence may come, at least partly, from sampling the results of pupil assessments. Some schools carry out pre- and post-testing of students who are involved in particular activities; others have adopted externally provided accreditation specifically aimed at enterprise education. In the best-practice schools there will be regular and systematic evaluation of enterprise education provision and assessment of the impact on individual student development of enterprise capabilities. There will be regular evaluation of student experience, showing how students have enjoyed and benefitted from their enterprise education activity. Stakeholders such as parents, governors and employers will also be consulted. There will also be an attempt to identify the broader contribution of enterprise education to the school's achievement agenda and the school's overall development plans. Schools need to be able to identify strengths and weaknesses in their overall enterprise education delivery if they are to have a clear view about their priorities for future development and change.

Continuing professional development

The Ofsted review of enterprise education identified CPD for current practitioners as a major priority and most schools now regard such support as vital to their eventual success. Best-practice enterprise education CPD adopts a 'learner centred' approach, with participants encouraged to take on responsibility for their own learning. These events are often run on a 'by practitioners, for practitioners' basis and this seems to add much to their credibility. Practitioners are generally encouraged to experiment with active learning strategies, although providers also need to recognise that this is not always easy for those practitioners more used to a more didactic style of delivery. The implied loss of control may be a fearful prospect for those not used to experimenting with a range of teaching and learning styles. During these events, concerns about health and safety, public liability and child protection issues often come to the fore, adding to the sense of risk. Having experienced and successful practitioners in attendance can add reassurance, allowing trainees to gain a 'warts and all' account of the realities of enterprise teaching and learning.

Enterprise education in action: regional and institutional initiatives

Following the lead from European and national policy makers, some regional and local organisations have accessed additional funding to develop bespoke responses to the specific needs of their communities.

Rotherham Ready

Although externally funded, the Rotherham Ready initiative has developed organically at grass roots level and is now regarded as a model of best practice. South Yorkshire has a long history as a manufacturing region and there is a tradition of having to adapt to changing economic circumstances. Rotherham Ready is an ambitious 4–19 education project which aims to engage all the schools and colleges in the borough in the development of enterprise education. The project, which is currently part funded by the European Regional Development Fund and Working Neighbourhoods Fund, sits within the School Effectiveness Service of Rotherham Council's Children and Young People's Services Department.

Hundreds of teachers have been trained to champion enterprise in schools and colleges, a framework to develop enterprise through the curriculum has been developed and scores of local businesses and entrepreneurs are involved in the programme, working in partnership with schools to promote enterprise and entrepreneurship.

Vision

Rotherham Ready aims 'to equip the borough's young people with the enterprise skills they need to make a success of their future and help create a thriving economy in

Rotherham' (Rotherham Ready 2010, p. 6). The project began in 2006 with funding for a four-year period. Rotherham Ready aimed to create a culture of enterprise in Rotherham schools and colleges which would impact on all pupils and students at all Key Stages and provide a pathway into entrepreneurial opportunities. Over the course of the project a diverse partnership has developed, bringing businesses, schools, children and teachers together in a spirit of collaboration and innovation. Enterprise is perceived as a vehicle of transformation in Rotherham.

Planning

The specific programme objectives identified by the management team focused on the desire to establish a ladder of learning opportunities for all children and young people aged 4–19, in collaboration with local employers. The project has provided funding to establish and train an Enterprise Champion in every school and college in the authority to embed enterprise skills in the core curriculum offer. These champions seek to maximise opportunities to encourage employer engagement and to establish effective education/business partnerships.

Rotherham Ready has developed an extensive training programme, ranging from Enterprise in Early Years and Primary Enterprise Champion training and Secondary and Cluster Inset days, an accredited postgraduate research module and an 'Inspire ITT' enterprise enhancement for trainee teachers studying at Sheffield Hallam University. Notably, the project works closely with local teachers and support staff to design all their training programmes and resources.

Delivery

The project engages businesses and employers in enterprise education through projects such as 'Make £5 Blossom' and the 'Young Entrepreneurs Clubs'. Throughout all these activities children are encouraged to learn about the 'Big 13' – a set of enterprise skills agreed by Rotherham schools and businesses as what young people need to survive and thrive in the twenty-first century.

Another core offering relates to the involvement of local young people who have started out in business supported by Rotherham Youth Enterprise (www.rotherham. gov.uk/info/349/business_advice/1035/rotherham_youth_enterprise).

The project believes that working with young entrepreneurs can empower other young people to reach their full potential. Rotherham Ready Young Entrepreneurs contribute their time and business expertise to work with and support schools in the delivery of enterprise activities. They help to shape training programmes and project delivery, and provide role models for young people. In return, they receive a bursary and an opportunity to develop their people skills.

Assessment and evaluation

Rotherham Ready has achieved particular success with its work in primary schools. The intention of enterprise education at this stage is really no different from the work done with older children, namely to develop the skills and attributes young people need to ensure they thrive in an increasingly fast-paced and competitive world. Working with Key Stage 1 and 2 teachers, it became apparent that primary school pupils are engaged in a wide range of 'enterprise' activities, the quality and impact of which varies enormously and is often dependent on the extent to which pupils have an opportunity to reflect upon and assess their own learning. A pilot study to test scrapbooks as a method for children to record and assess their learning clearly demonstrated that they had a significant impact on children's learning. Students developed a greater understanding and awareness of enterprise skills and concepts and reported that they were empowered by the realisation that they had unique and valuable attributes.

An evaluation (Coldwell *et al.* 2007) described Rotherham Ready as more of a 'movement' than a project, yet the 'replicability' of its achievements has been proved with the successful roll-out of 'Hull Ready' in November 2008. The Inspire CPD training model has also been successfully rolled out in Sheffield, Barnsley, Doncaster, Bradford, Warrington and, further afield, Valencia. A group of teachers from Valencia are developing a 'Valencia Ready' project and have been trained for a week in Rotherham to be able to deliver the Inspire training model to Spanish teachers. The project received recognition in 2010 as the national winner of the Enterprising Britain award.

Toot Hill School: enterprise education and the school improvement agenda

Toot Hill is a medium-sized, mixed non-selective 11–18 school in a market town in Nottinghamshire. The school intake is truly comprehensive and the leadership team prides itself on providing high-quality education for the local community. Toot Hill has been a specialist school in Business and Enterprise and Visual Arts since 2003 and as such has developed a reputation for excellence in this area.

Vision

Enterprise pervades all areas of school life and is taught explicitly through each Key Stage of the curriculum. The head teacher contributed to the *Enterprising Heads, Enterprising Schools* publication (Department for Education and Skills 2007), describing his vision for the school 'to be recognised as an enterprising school by all in our local community'.

Planning

At Key Stage 3, all students are offered an introductory course in enterprise. Enterprise not only forms a major element of traditional GCSE and AS/A2 courses offered by the Business Studies department but is integral to many other formal external accreditations such as information and communication technologies (ICT). The work experience programme has been reviewed to provide a clearer focus on enterprise and entrepreneurship and additional opportunities have been created for developing awareness of enterprising behaviours through careers and interviews days.

Funding has been provided to employ a dedicated Business and Enterprise co-ordinator and this, in turn, has led to the introduction of numerous enrichment opportunities. Improved business links with the local community have enriched the curriculum and raised the profile of enterprise with students, parents and teachers. All staff receive training on enterprise through the internal CPD programme and this has led to several non-specialists teaching the Key Stage 3 course highly effectively. The school has led training in enterprise in the region through the Specialist Schools and Academies Trust (SSAT) Enterprise Hub and Enterprise Learning Partnership (ELP) programmes. It has also delivered two successful enterprise conferences for teachers that received outstanding evaluations and all training materials have been shared with other schools.

Delivery

One important feature of the school's enterprise education programme is a week in the summer term dedicated to enterprise. In 2010 all Key Stage 3 students worked to manufacture a product or provide a service which was sold in the local market. The money generated was given to a charity chosen by the group and each subject area decided which product to manufacture. The school raised a total of £4000 and the evaluations from students and the local community involved in the market day event were extremely positive, as was the feedback from all staff. This has also led to sustainable enterprise initiatives: the community garden and allotment that was created in enterprise week will be expanded as a result of a successful Lottery bid. A current focus has been to facilitate the delivery of young enterprise programmes in local primary schools.

Assessment and evaluation

All subject areas use 12 animated enterprise characters (banker, risk taker, problem solver, decision maker, team player, goal setter, communicator, organiser, evaluator, entrepreneur, negotiator and flexible friend) to assess and reward enterprise. This is monitored through the internal lesson observation process, which includes an evaluation of the enterprise element of the lesson. The school would suggest that this has been a major factor in raising the number of good and outstanding lesson judgements and that the skills and experiences generated through the enterprise education programme have had a major impact on whole school attainment through raised aspirations and enjoyment of learning. A new whole school initiative is being introduced which aims to ensure that students record and evaluate all of their enter-prise experiences across the curriculum through a so-called 'torch of experience'. The school shares its expertise through head teachers' conferences and hosts regular good-practice learning visits.

See www.toothill.notts.sch.uk for more information.

Discussion questions

1. How can teachers of subjects other than business studies be encouraged to engage with the enterprise education agenda?

2. Local entrepreneurs – role models for the twentieth or the twenty-first century?

3. Many practitioners use outside providers to deliver enterprise education in their schools and colleges. Are there any advantages to bringing more of this provision 'in house'?

Tasks

1. Small and medium enterprises (SMEs) already contribute greatly to the UK economy and look set to extend their position. How could a school/ or college undertake an audit of local SMEs willing to support to their enterprise education programme?

2. Outline a strategy for introducing enterprise activities in five different subjects at Key Stage 3.

Selected resources

www.rotherhamready.org.uk
www.enterprisevillage.co.uk
A Guide to Enterprise Education, Department for Children, Schools and Families. (2010)

References

CEI (Centre for Education and Industry) (2002) *Independent Research into Learning for Enterprise and Entrepreneurship*. London: Department of Trade and Industry.

CEI (2006) *National Evaluation of the Enterprise Pathfinder Projects: March 2004–December 2005*. Warwick: DfES.

Coldwell, M., Trickey, S., Gornall, L., Holland, M., Drew, S., Willis, B. and Wolstenholme, C. (2007) *Innovative Methodologies Project Rotherham Ready Final Evaluation Report*. Leeds: Yorkshire Futures.

Davies, H. (2002) *Review of Enterprise and the Economy in Education*. London: DTI.

Department for Education and Skills (2007) *Enterprising Heads, Enterprising Schools*. London: DfES.

European Council, Directorate General Enterprise and Industry (2007) *Assessment of Compliance with the Entrepreneurship Education Objective in the Context of the 2006 Spring Council Conclusions*. Brussels: European Council, Directorate General Enterprise and Industry.

Grewcock, C., Hoare, M. and Stagg, P. (2010) *National Standard for Enterprise Education: Improving the Quality of Enterprise Education in Schools*. Warwick: Centre for Education and Industry.

Herrington, J. and Oliver, R. (2000) 'An instructional design for authentic learning', *Educational Technology Research and Development*, 48 (3): 23–48.

Hoare, M. (2005) 'Creating an enterprise checklist', *Curriculum Briefing*, 4 (1): 12.

Huddleston, P. and Oh, S-A. (2004) ' "The magic roundabout": work-related learning in the 14–19 curriculum', *Oxford Review of Education*, 30 (1): 81–100.

Hytti, U. (2002) *State of Art of Enterprise Education in Europe*. Turku, Finland: Small Business Institute.

Lisbon European Council (2000) *Presidency Conclusions*. 23 and 24 March. Brussels: European Commission.

MacDonald, R. and Coffield, F. (1991) *Risky Business? Youth and the Enterprise Culture*. Lewes: Falmer Press.

Ofsted (2004) *Learning to Be Enterprising*. London: Ofsted.

Ofsted (2005) *Developing Enterprising Young People*. London: Ofsted.

Rotherham Ready (2010) *The Future Is Yours*. Rotherham: Rotherham Ready.

Smyth, J. (1999) 'Schooling and enterprise culture: pause for a critical policy analysis', *Journal of Education Policy*, 14 (4): 435.

Spielhofer, T. and Lynch, S. (2008) *Assessing Enterprise Capability: Guidance for Schools*. Slough: NFER.

6

14–19 Diplomas as work-related learning

Julian Stanley

Much of the work-related learning considered elsewhere in this book has been developed as a supplement to the existing curriculum and has been designed to fit in, as far as possible, with the mainstream curriculum. The Diploma represents a different approach: it was conceived as a tool to reform 14–19 education. The Diploma is intended to create a new educational pathway which is constructed around the concept of work-related learning. All stages of Diploma development – design, roll-out and support – have been marked by the intention that Diploma content and learning processes should be strongly connected to particular employment sectors. As a result, the Diplomas represent a case of 'strong work-related learning' in the sense that they aim to be strongly work-related across a range of dimensions (see Chapter 1). It is no surprise that this ambition has made Diplomas challenging, costly and politically contentious. Indeed, at this point in time the future of the Diplomas is uncertain. However, even if they do not survive, the Diplomas will represent an extremely important educational experiment from which there is much still to learn – particularly for the organisation, design and practice of work-related learning.

Background

In order to get clear what is distinctive about both the content and the pedagogy of the Diplomas it is useful to understand the background of vocational qualifications, such as GNVQs (General National Vocational Qualifications), BTECs (a family of qualifications supplied by the awarding body Edexcel) and AVCEs (Advanced Vocational Certificates of Education) against which they have been developed. These vocational programmes have some common features. They are offered as alternatives to general qualifications such as GCSEs and GCE A Levels, and post-16 they often take the form of a distinctive pathway rather than being one qualification that is taken along with others. They are scoped in terms of broad areas of employment, such as 'business', 'leisure and tourism' and 'IT' rather than in terms of particular occupations as, for example, are National Vocational Qualifications (NVQs). They are taught in schools, colleges of further education and sixth-form colleges rather than in the workplace. Assessment methods have tended to give preference to extended coursework that incorporates 'authentic tasks' rather than written exams.

Student demand for these vocational qualifications has varied as new awards have been developed and marketed. Qualifications serving some employment sectors, such as business and IT, have proved far more successful than those serving other sectors, such as agriculture and manufacturing. However, in general there has been a long-term increase in take-up of these qualifications as post-16 staying on has increased and work-based training has declined or stagnated. Furthermore, these vocational qualifications have found a place in the larger system of qualifications, so that it has been possible for increasing numbers of learners to progress from level to level, for example from a Level 2 GNVQ to a BTEC Diploma (Level 3) and thence to a vocational degree such as Business Studies.

Despite the growth in take-up of vocational qualifications in England there have been many concerns and criticisms which have led to repeated efforts to reform vocational qualifications, and most recently to the Diplomas. Some of the most common and sustained criticisms have been that vocational qualifications:

- are not sufficiently valued by employers so students who achieve them may not get the pay or jobs that they are aspiring to
- are not sufficiently valued by students and their parents so many students, particularly more able students, opt to do A Levels and GCSEs even if these programmes do not match their aspirations or learning style
- only support a narrow or specialised progression in terms of both work and education – they do not permit the breadth of progress that general qualifications appear to support
- are not sufficiently promoted and not always well taught in schools (as opposed to colleges) (see, for example, Hyland and Winch 2007).

Reforming vocational education

Diplomas are intended to build upon what works in vocational education and to remedy what does not. In the first place, the Diploma is a relatively large educational programme composed of different elements which when put together support progression along a variety of different routes: into immediate employment, further vocational education, higher education or work-based training. Diplomas are expected to include theoretical or 'subject' knowledge, for example scientific and social science theories, as well as the skills and knowledge associated with particular jobs and tasks. Diplomas are supposed to develop intellectual and social skills which contribute to the capability for learning either at work or in further and higher education.

The credibility of Diplomas has been addressed through their development process. Development bodies (Diploma Development Partnerships) were set up for each Diploma line and tasked to design qualifications that would recognise the skills, knowledge and understanding that stakeholders really wanted.

The term 'applied learning' has been used to try to communicate the ambition to incorporate both general and practical learning. Applied learning has been defined as:

Acquiring and applying knowledge, skills and understanding through tasks set in sector contexts that have many of the characteristics of real work, or are set within the workplace. Most importantly, the purpose of the task in which learners apply their knowledge, skills and understanding must be relevant to the real work in the sector.

(QCA 2008a, p. 26)

This concept of applied learning has been used to differentiate Diplomas from other qualifications and also to establish a common standard across all Diplomas: 'at each level a minimum of 50 per cent must be concerned with the application of knowledge and skills through tasks, problems and situations that are related to work in that sector' (QCA 2008a, p. 5).

In this way, work-related learning has come to define the Diplomas and, as we will see below, the pedagogy of work-related learning provides much of the good practice for Diploma teaching.

Diploma structure

Diplomas are currently available at three different levels: Foundation, Higher and Advanced. However, at all levels, the standard Diploma has three components: principal learning, generic learning and additional and specialist learning (Figure 6.1). Principal learning focuses on the employment sector which gives each Diploma its vocational identity; for example, the Creative and Media Diploma addresses employment in the areas of performance, art, design, broadcasting and so on. Principal

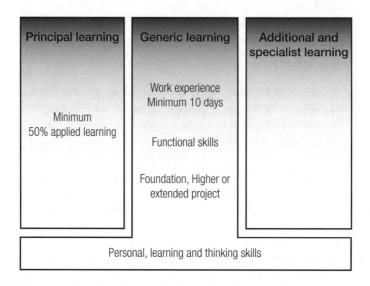

FIGURE 6.1 Adapted from *Practitioner Guide to the Diploma* (LSIS 2009).

learning is predominantly composed of work-related learning, which implies that it is largely concerned with the application of knowledge in work contexts. The 50 per cent rule allows that principal learning may also contain knowledge and pedagogic processes which are not directly addressing application, such as theoretical and factual knowledge. Principal learning is composed of units, some of which must be assessed through an externally set and marked task (at least 16 per cent at Level 3).

Generic learning incorporates a variety of skills and dispositions which are supposed to be necessary for any learner to progress in any kind of education or employment at each level. Generic learning aims to develop capabilities to apply mathematics, English and information technology in learning and work (the 'functional skills') and the ability to apply a range of learning and work skills including teamwork, independent enquiry, self-management, creative thinking, reflective learning and effective participation (for the 'personal, learning and thinking skills' see Chapter 7). Generic learning also includes a student-designed project, related to the employment sector, and a minimum of 10 days of work experience. Both the project and the work experience are supposed to supply opportunities for the development of the generic skills.

The Diploma framework attributes great significance to generic skills: the integration of generic skills does make Diplomas different from other vocational qualifications – generic skills are optional and additional in BTECs for example. Generic skills include 'employability skills', in other words general personal and social capabilities that most employers expect; however, they also include capabilities that are associated with ongoing learning, with individual autonomy and with capabilities for evaluation and judgement. In consequence, it is the generic learning component of the Diploma that preserves, to some degree, the liberal purposes of education that are absent from those training or vocational programmes which are concerned only to bring about competence in relation to pre-defined work tasks. The integration of generic skills into Diploma programmes and Diploma teaching adds to the challenge of the Diploma, both because of the multiplication of learning outcomes and because of the challenge of the outcomes themselves. However, this integration makes it possible for learners to use their Diploma to pursue their own ends rather than just preparing them to meet the requirements of others.

Lastly, the additional and specialist learning component offers a wide range of optional units. Students can either select units that deepen their vocational specialism or they can broaden their curriculum by choosing units from other Diplomas or general qualifications such as GCSEs or A Levels. The assessment rules for the Diploma require students to pass every unit in order to gain an overall pass although they will be accredited for those units that they achieve. These rules mean that a Diploma qualification, particularly at Advanced Level, represents a broad range of capabilities, of which some are closely tied to an employment sector, others are generic and others vary between particular students depending on their options.

Diploma consortia

The consortia reporting the best outcomes have been holding 1 hour progress review meetings amongst practitioners every 2 weeks since teaching began. The most successful consortia also hold regular (but less frequent) meetings of Head Teachers and College Principals.

(Harrison and Ota 2009, p. 7)

In order to try to make Diplomas available to all learners by 2013 and because there were concerns about the capacity of schools to teach the full range of Diplomas, it was decided that schools and colleges should group together into consortia for the purposes of delivering Diplomas. Schools and colleges were invited to form themselves into consortia and then go through a tendering process, known as the Gateway process, in order to gain funding and approval to teach Diplomas. The providers in a consortium, typically at least one college of further education and a cluster of schools, make joint plans about which Diplomas will be offered and how and where they will be taught. Different consortia have developed different delivery models: in some consortia different elements of a single Diploma are taught by different providers on a variety of sites, in some different Diplomas are shared between providers and in others dedicated Diplomas teaching centres have been set up.

In order to gain government approval to deliver Diplomas, consortia had to submit plans that showed not only how they would teach Diplomas but also that they could engage employers to help deliver Diplomas. In many consortia, well-established local education–business link organisations were given a major role in setting up appropriate work experience and building links between Diploma teachers and employers. In some cases, specialist brokers have been appointed, at school, consortium or local authority level, with a responsibility for engaging and co-ordinating employer involvement. Consortia are also required to provide appropriate independent information, advice and guidance (IAG) for students to support their choices in relation to Diplomas. The Gateway process has required that consortia collaborate, plan in advance and commit to provision. Viewed as a way of doing work-related learning, this approach has resulted in a relatively joined-up and comprehensive provision rather than the more flexible and variable provision that has characterised much of work-related learning in the past (Ofsted 2009).

Rather than particular centres focusing on what they are able to do for their own students, managers and teachers working in different institutions have had the chance to set up joint systems and shared resources and to develop their courses and activities together. On the positive side this has opened up channels through which teachers can support one another in developing their practice. It has made it possible for learners to access teachers from outside of their institutions and to benefit from a variety of learning experiences and environments. However, it also implies that centres and individual teachers have come to depend on partnership and collaborative working – which, for some, requires new skills and creates new challenges. Concerns have also been raised in some quarters about the cost and efficiency of collaborative working.

Models for delivery

Choosing the right model of delivery is always a challenge with work-related learning, because work-related learning cuts across the subject-based model by which learning is organised in schools. Diplomas, unlike most of work-related learning, constitute 'subjects' so they can be delivered alongside other subjects, though there are some overlaps, for example between functional mathematics and GCSE mathematics. However, the biggest challenge for Diploma implementation is to develop a comprehensive Diploma entitlement for all learners in an area. It should be remembered that in 2008, when Diplomas were first introduced, it was extremely unusual for any 14-year-old to be offered an extensive range of vocational options. Those responsible for Diplomas at local level have been concerned to put into place the infrastructure for Diploma delivery: getting the right distribution of delivery across centres, setting up managerial systems, co-ordinating support and business engagement and planning for the expansion of provision to meet the entitlement that was supposed to be in place by 2013.

This 'front-end' work, although it is not teaching in the sense of 'interaction' with students, is crucial for the sustainable delivery of Diplomas and for work-related learning in general. The delivery of work-related learning involves partners other than teachers and spaces other than classrooms. Teaching work-related learning involves partnership and organisation as well as communicating with learners. Schools working in isolation from employers and specialist vocational education providers will only be able to offer work-related learning to some learners and in relation to some employment sectors. The Diploma reform, by contrast, represents an attempt to develop the structures and ways of working that would be capable of sustaining an appropriate and extensive work-related learning for all.

Delivery options for the Diploma include:

- moving learners between sites for whole or part of the course
- moving staff to where facilities and learners are; some staff can also work across a consortium
- establishing specialist skills or training facilities
- moving equipment or resources used for specific units
- creating mobile facilities, such as workshops, that travel between sites
- developing a learning platform and creating e-learning resources
- bringing learners together for shared events, for example, induction, employer inputs and higher education events.

(QCA 2008b, p. 4)

In Newham in East London, for example, each Diploma line is developed and planned collaboratively by a team of teachers who come together on a regular basis. Depending on student numbers and level, Diplomas are offered in one or more centres and the learners travel to those centres from across the borough. In Liverpool some Diplomas (for example construction and the built environment, and engineering) are offered city-wide at Liverpool Community College, while other Diplomas are distributed between particular centres within what are known as travel-to-learn partnerships.

In some consortia, Diploma funding has been used to provide specialist skills centres. The Kendray Diploma Skills Centre, for example, in the South East Barnsley Learning Alliance, has two areas:

- the society, health and development area, which includes a 'ward' with hospital beds and mock patients, nursing station and a range of medical equipment; 'care home' setting with bedroom; fully-equipped kitchen; and bathroom
- the construction and the built environment facility, which has two workshops, one for services (plumbing and electrical) and a multipurpose one with a focus on joinery.

(QCA 2008b, p. 8)

In Sheffield, premises have been taken in the City's Cultural Industries Quarter to create a Diploma learning space that is well positioned to enable partnership work between students and creative and digital businesses.

Consortia have also worked to create timetables that facilitate co-operation. Many consortia have managed to develop some form of common timetabling between centres. In North Liverpool a common timetable permits all Advanced information technology Diploma students to spend two days at the Inspire Diploma Centre set up on a new business park and a further half day at Campion City Learning Centre, where they learn about networking and gain vendor qualifications as part of their additional and specialist learning (ASL). Plymouth consortium has timetabled afternoon sessions which can be extended to accommodate ASL. In the Kingswood Partnership in Bristol the Creative and Media Diploma is delivered separately in each centre, though common timetabling means that learners from different centres can be brought together for periodic joint events.

Management

Different consortia have developed different management systems which align with their chosen model for delivery. In Derbyshire, for example, Diploma activity is managed by eight strategic groups corresponding to eight areas or 'learning communities'. Each strategic group comprises headteachers and representatives from the local authority, local higher education institutions, the education–business link organisation and training providers. These groups have sub-groups that focus on curriculum, IAG and pastoral/inclusion issues, and beneath these sub-groups are development groups that co-ordinate the delivery of each line. At county level there is a 14–19 strategic partnership group, chaired by the local authority, with representatives from each learning community, and lead practitioners for each Diploma line. Other consortia have more centralised management structures or structures that reflect the particular Diplomas being offered, as for example with the line of learning partnerships in Plymouth.

Diploma management has led to the creation of new posts and responsibilities, sometimes full time but more often filled through secondment or in the case of further education staff through remission from other duties. The Kingswood Partnership, for example, employs a full-time 14–19 partnership co-ordinator, a business links development manager, an offsite student support manager and several e-learning managers and designers. Barnsley provides identified time (one hour per week) for Key Stage 4 Diploma co-ordinators for each line at each level. Their role is to co-ordinate meetings, act as domain assessor[1] and oversee curriculum development. In addition there are 14–19 area co-ordinators who are seconded for two days a week plus remission time for line leaders from Barnsley College. The consortium in Sheffield has employed consultants who already have strong relationships with particular employment sectors, for example IT and creative and media, and tasked them to broker partnership opportunities for Diploma students.

The scale of Diploma development has made it possible for teachers and managers to take on responsibilities for leadership and support and develop expertise in the collaborative delivery of work-related learning – rather as the Technical Vocational and Education Initiative (TVEI) did in the 1980s. It is possible that this expertise and engagement will, in the future, continue to support work-related learning, even if not all of the Diplomas survive. However, the future of Diplomas is now in question and the posts, structures and partnerships that have been created may not survive.

Pedagogy

The scale and delivery model of Diplomas distinguish them from other kinds of work-related learning. In terms of how they are actually taught and learnt, they have much in common with the other kinds of work-related learning discussed elsewhere in this book. It has always been an objective of the Diploma reform to engage learners by offering an innovative learning experience. This has been characterised in a variety of ways: 'applied', 'active', 'practical', 'experiential', 'personalised' and 'hands-on'. These terms are frequently used in the documentation that supports Diplomas but it is not always clear just how they connect together. There is a broad consensus that Diploma pedagogy is supposed to emphasise:

- learning from experiences and activities (learning by doing)
- learners taking responsibility for learning, for example through planning, reviewing, setting goals
- applying knowledge and skills in work-related contexts
- the enhanced relevance of learning activities because they are work tasks or relate to work problems or involve representatives from the world of work.

However, these ideas draw upon several styles of pedagogy and upon different theories of learning. In 2008, the Qualifications and Curriculum Authority (QCA) commissioned a review of recent research into teaching and learning in order to explore what light this sheds on the teaching and learning of Diplomas (QCA 2008c). The research argues that Diploma pedagogy should take account of the personal and social development of young people, including emotional development and the development of identity. Diplomas provide opportunities to do this because they are explicitly concerned to address attitudes and dispositions as well as knowledge and skills and they are intended to provide the means for 14- to 19-year-olds to explore and develop vocational identities. Second, the research proposed a synthesis of learning theories to make sense of Diploma teaching and learning:

1. an experiential dimension – learners engage in tasks and have experiences which they review and reflect upon to create knowledge which then informs further activity and experiences

2. a socio-cultural dimension – learners participate in groups, institutions and communities where they develop skills, beliefs, values and behaviour appropriate for participation

3. re-application or boundary crossing – learners are able to transfer or adapt skills, understanding and knowledge developed in one context to different contexts.

This multi-layered account of Diploma pedagogy makes it possible for us to recognise how a variety of pedagogic strategies can contribute to Diploma teaching and learning but at the same time warns us against becoming too dependent on one strategy or blurring what is meant by it. So for example, teachers are engineering experiential learning when they encourage students to plan, do and review activities. However, the plan/do/review process is associated with learning which is explicit and which is guided by teachers. Diploma learning should also include learning which comes from adapting to fit with clients or co-workers, for example on work experience. Such learning can result in long-term skills and attitude development which cannot easily be recognised but is nonetheless valuable. Furthermore, teachers will seek to find ways of helping students to re-apply what they have practised and learnt in one situation to different situations, perhaps through problem solving or role play exercises. A student may be asked to tackle an unfamiliar task or event or to adapt to work in different environments or with different teams.

The QCA (2009) has published a number of case studies that range over different Diplomas and different parts of England. The case studies illustrate the different ways that teachers have chosen to connect learning in classrooms, workplaces and specialised learning centres and co-ordinate the contributions of teachers, business representatives and others. The case studies illustrate that Diploma teaching and learning combine learning through review of first-hand experience and activity with learning through participation in work groups and the opportunity to apply or re-apply learning between varying contexts.

Some examples of Diploma teaching and learning

Advanced Diploma in information technology: Reading and central Berkshire consortium

> Learners explored the role of a multinational IT company in the development and application of new technologies. They investigated the requirements of local businesses and put forward new IT solutions.
>
> (QCA 2009, p. 29)

Advanced Diploma in society, health and development: Dewsbury consortium

> Learners reflected on their own decision making process for the care of the 0–5 age group and made comparisons with the procedures they had seen in a professional setting. Working with care professionals from a local hospital, they researched and produced an aftercare information document that was shared with patients.
>
> (QCA 2009, p. 35)

Elements of Diploma pedagogy

It follows from what has been said that Diploma pedagogy includes a lot of learning that goes on outside the classroom and that not all of it will involve teachers. As we have seen the Diploma promises a programme that is at once engaging for learners and which develops particular vocational skills and knowledge which can be re-applied in a *variety* of situations and contexts. Teachers will want to draw upon a range of different strategies to fulfil this promise. We can scope out what is involved in Diploma pedagogy by listing the different tasks that go in to teaching Diplomas:

1. identifying, selecting and gaining access to resources, contexts and personnel that support work-related teaching, including contributions from business representatives

2. working collaboratively with business representatives to plan, organise, teach, support and assess; sustaining and developing those relationships

3. designing, leading and supporting learning activities that match well with particular learner needs, awarding body requirements, resources and timetables, capabilities of staff and partners and with learning environments, resources and contexts

4. planning and managing programmes of learning including the sequential or iterative use of learning activities in different contexts with partners, effective and sustainable use of resources and also the planning and organising of assessment activities in appropriate contexts

5. reviewing with learners, teachers and others what has been learnt in order to plan for future individual and collective learning and to improve practice.

Strategies for Diploma pedagogy

Identifying and working with business

> Meeting inspirational people who make daily use of the knowledge contained in the curriculum can help raise aspirations, morale and attainment amongst the learners.
>
> (Harrison and Ota 2009, p. 5)

It will not be possible for 50 per cent of principal learning to be work-related without the extensive involvement of sector representatives – be they workers, employers or some kind of specialist intermediary. There is more than one way of making this happen but to get the most out of a finite local resource it is likely that Diploma teachers will want to co-ordinate and share partnership work. Some teachers, particularly when Diplomas were first introduced, have had to work in isolation, setting up visits, partnership projects and placements for their own Diploma classes. However, this kind of partnership is difficult to sustain over time, particularly if student numbers grow, so many consortia have chosen to create specialist link roles or to commission brokers to engage and manage business contributions.

Even if teachers are working collaboratively with other teachers and business representatives they will still need a capability for partnership. Like any other aspect of teaching this capability improves through experience and reflection. That said, teachers can draw on the experience of other teachers and published guidance. For example, those working in employer engagement have found that it pays to meet employers on their own premises, to take the trouble to brief and debrief, and to help employers to develop their capacity to contribute over time.

Teachers have to remember that employers may not be particularly effective at communicating with large groups of students – though, of course, some are! Experience suggests that the most valuable contribution that employers can make may not always be the most obvious; for example, students often value interactions with employers as much because employers are in a unique position to endorse embryonic vocational identities and to add credibility to learning activities as because of what employers know. The Diploma curriculum requires that students develop an understanding of the role of practitioners at work; this is not something that can be taught through a book. Learning about how practitioners act in open-ended situations and how they take account of wider social or normative issues involves dialogue with practitioners and evaluation of their practice. Teaching becomes strained if the classroom teacher is constantly having to simulate the practitioner.

It is not surprising that many teachers find that they are good at partnership work and enjoy it. Like other teaching, partnership work involves the building of trust, gaining of commitment and facilitating of contributions – the same skills that teachers develop in the classroom. On the other hand, partnership work gives teachers the opportunity to develop their capacity to negotiate rather than to direct and to collaborate rather than instruct. Ongoing communication with those working in the sector can help teachers to update their own knowledge of how things are done in the sector and renew their sense of themselves as practitioners. Research into practical learning reveals that if their vocational teachers can communicate a sense of their own professional or vocational identity this is highly effective in engaging and motivating students (Silver and Forrest 2008).

Mentoring is particularly appropriate in connection with Diplomas and work-related learning because it supports relationships between learners, teachers and workers that are both cognitive and affective. The mentoring relationship, like the teaching relationship, implies the existence of a zone of proximate development between what someone can do alone and what they can do with the help of another. Whereas the student is relatively passive in relation to the classroom teacher, the mentee is relatively active in relation to the mentor: setting goals, initiating activities, asking questions, seeking responses. Diploma teachers and students will find mentors who are employed within their sector particularly useful. Practitioner mentors can model the ways of thinking and talking about work that are current, and they are able to confirm or expose assumptions and demonstrate the affective standards that go with work tasks and roles.

Mentoring represents an opportunity for sector representatives to develop a more extended and personal relationship with learners and/or teachers. E-mentoring has helped to reduce the time burden of mentoring, though blended models where occasional face-to-face contacts are sustained by more frequent electronic contact are particularly effective (TDA and LLUK 2009, section 8).

Designing, leading and supporting learning activities: examples

Structuring learning through problem-solving briefs is a particularly appropriate pedagogy for Diploma teaching (TDA and LLUK 2009, section 7). Where learning is part of problem solving it naturally engenders the personalisation that comes with learner decision making and actions. Problems can be drawn from the relevant sector, which adds authenticity and relevance. The framing and articulation of problems is a 'teaching activity' that employers are well qualified to perform. Problem solving also has the advantage that it can support the re-application or transfer of knowledge from one situation to another. Problem solving is identified as one of the personal, learning and thinking skills that must be embedded in Diplomas.

Problem-solving learning is essentially open-ended in the sense that learners have some discretion about which solutions they will pursue and consequently individual learning experiences are likely to vary. However, the design of the problem, the teacher facilitation, the employer contributions and resourcing will all need to be planned if the activity is to generate identified Diploma learning outcomes and the students are to be able to solve the problems successfully. Teachers should not be excessively 'perfectionist' about work-related learning. For example, problem-solving exercises based on a realistic (rather than a real) situation may be an optimal way of teaching some learning outcomes.

Teachers can structure problem solving in a variety of ways:

- breaking down problem solving into stages: understanding the scenario, generating alternative approaches, evaluating or comparing solutions, presenting solutions;

- exploring different roles: client, consultant, decision maker, researcher, communicator, roles within organisations, stakeholders;

- tools for problem solving: using planning and research tools and methods, selecting conceptual and technical tools or information sources to help solve problems, applying conceptual or technical tools or general rules, reviewing and evaluating solutions.

Problem-solving briefs can be designed so that a complementary package of learning outcomes is addressed: for example, in the Environment and Land-based

Diploma, capabilities (e.g. know how to deal with pollution and waste from environmental systems) can be combined with understanding (e.g. understand current and relevant legislation to protect the environment) so that learners experience one outcome as the means to another. In this way learners can see the point of mastering information and have the means to judge its adequacy in relation to particular tasks. Selected functional and personal, learning and thinking skills can also be included in the brief (TDA and LLUK 2009, section 7.5).

Planning and managing programmes of learning

Diplomas are unitised qualifications and the units are likely to be taught by different teachers, perhaps in different places, over the life of a programme. Planning sequences of teaching and learning over time gives teachers an opportunity to:

1. make efficient use of business inputs; for example a visit might be used to frame several weeks of learning, rather than a single activity

2. link together separate learning activities and experiences so that they form part of a related whole; this will make it easier for learners to re-apply and review their learning over time

3. devise teaching and learning activities that address multiple learning outcomes so that the content demanded by awarding bodies can be covered in an efficient manner

4. develop the challenge and/or modify the amount of support or 'scaffolding' provided for learners so that, over time, they can develop their skills and deepen their understanding

5. co-ordinate the use of resources, equipment and personnel so that they are available when needed

6. make records of programmes of learning which can be shared with other practitioners and can be reviewed and developed in partnership with others, including business representatives.

Exemplar published programmes of study (TDA and LLUK 2009, section 6) or those supplied by colleagues or through Diploma line practitioner networks (LSIS 2010) can be excellent aids for planning. One big decision is whether to teach principal learning in a linear, unit-by-unit fashion or to devise programmes of learning activities that jointly address two or more units simultaneously. Evidently both strategies are possible and have their merits. A unit-by-unit approach has the advantage of spreading the production, control and submission of assessment evidence. It is simpler for learners and for teachers new to Diplomas to identify each learning activity with a single unit. Diplomas are already regarded by many as over-complex. On the other hand, unit-by-unit teaching and learning can be repetitive and time-consuming and it may obscure the way that knowledge, skills and understanding are used together in relevant work situations. It may work against making best use of business contributions since it ignores those inputs that correspond to units that are programmed for 'next term'. Some Diploma teachers have started with a linear approach but have progressed to some combined unit work as they have gone on.

Assessment for and of learning

Productively combining assessment and teaching is a key teaching capability; however, assessment has tended to have a low profile in work-related learning. With Diplomas, work-related learning takes the form of a qualification, and assessment takes on considerable importance. Some regard this as a problem, believing that teaching and learning will be distorted by the requirement to produce specified assessment evidence. However, universities and employers have signalled a readiness to recognise the credential value of Diplomas and it is reasonable to hope that the quality of external and internal assessment will improve with experience.

Teachers will need to be able to design assessment tasks that meet the requirements of awarding bodies but also take advantage of local contexts and give opportunities for learners to apply what they have learnt. Teachers will want to develop learners' abilities to self-assess and peer-assess and to plan for future learning, for example through the use of Individual Learning Plans.

Teachers and lecturers who are fluent with the assessment foci (and the Personal Learning and Thinking Skills and the Functional Skills requirements) are able to deliver on several assessment foci per learning session and are making faster progress through the material.

(Harrison and Ota 2009, p. 7)

Assessment for learning implies that teachers are able to give useful written and oral feedback, and co-ordinate learning challenge and feedback so that success can be recognised and motivation enhanced.

Reviewing with learners, teachers and others

For many, teaching Diplomas represents a significant change in practice. It is natural for teachers to review new teaching and learning activities. The introduction of Diplomas has led to the commissioning of extensive professional development opportunities (for example, through the Specialist Schools and Academies Trust and the Learning and Skills Improvement Service) that helps teachers to review and develop their teaching. Research into the development of Diploma pedagogy reveals two particular areas of need (Stanley 2009). On the one hand, there were many teachers (most likely to be found in schools) who lacked up-to-date knowledge of working practices in relation to their Diploma sectors. On the other hand, there were trainers and lecturers (most likely to be found in training centres and colleges) who lacked pedagogic skills such as motivating learners or assessment for learning.

The collaborative groups which have been set up locally to plan and deliver lines of learning will be concerned to review outcomes and the effectiveness of planning and programmes. It should be expected that new programmes and processes will not be got right first time around and that teachers and other contributors will keep learning. Unless delivery teams are self-critical they will not look out for alternatives or consider how their own practice might be improved. Some practitioners may find that their involvement in Diplomas provides them with an opportunity for action research, perhaps as part of a postgraduate diploma or an MA.

Discussion questions

1. How would you seek to persuade an employer to give his or her time to help to teach a particular Diploma?

2. Students taking Diplomas could receive their entire work-related learning through their Diploma programmes; what would be the advantages and disadvantages of such an approach?

3. All Diploma students are entitled to 10 days' work experience. How might Diploma work experience differ from 'normal' work experience?

Tasks

1. Identify a local organisation which is likely to provide support for a Diploma line of your choice in your own school or college. Which activities, departments or roles in that organisation would be worth investigating in order to try to develop work-related learning opportunities for your Diploma students?

2. Consider what tools and processes a team of teachers could use to evaluate the effectiveness of their Diploma teaching over a term.

Selected resources

http://www.diploma-support.org/ offers extensive support for Diploma teachers including practitioner networks, practitioner handbooks for each line of learning, assessment guidance, videos, professional development tools and access to bespoke training.

The TDA and LLUK have jointly carried out research into skills needs for Diploma teachers and published 'Training and Development Guidance' (2008). This sets out the skills, knowledge and attributes required of Diploma teachers in terms of six elements:

- personalised learning
- assessment
- generic learning skills
- information, advice and guidance
- working collaboratively
- developing reflective practice.

These elements are broken down into more detailed specification of what teachers should understand and be able to do, which, for example, make specific demands in terms of developing Individual Learning Plans, getting involved in research and using virtual networks.

The guidance can be downloaded from http://www.lluk.org/documents/081021-D-SM-Final-PDG-Design.pdf

Involving Business in Diploma Lessons: A guide for teachers (LLUK) can be downloaded from http://www.lluk.org/2947.htm or ordered on CD-ROM.

A video report on early Diploma experience (2009) can be found at http://www.teachers.tv/videos/diplomas-a-progress-report

The main awarding organisations offer extensive support for Diplomas including detailed handbooks, training events, operations packs, free consultancy and assessor training. See http://www.edexcel.com/, http://www.diplomainfo.org.uk/ and http://www.ocr.org.uk/

Note

1. Domain assessors take the lead role in assessment when a Diploma is delivered by a team of teachers.

References

Harrison, M. and Ota, C. (2009) *A Practical Guide to Effective Curriculum Planning and Delivery for the 14–19 Diploma in Engineering*. Available HTTP: <http://www.diploma-support.org/node/49132> (accessed 5 May 2010).

Hyland, T. and Winch, C. (2007) *A Guide to Vocational Education and Training: The Essential FE Toolkit Series*. London: Continuum.

LSIS (2009) *Practitioner Guide to the Diploma*. London: LSIS.

LSIS (2010) *Diploma Support Communities*. Available HTTP: <http://www.diploma-support.org/communities/forums/> (accessed 8 June 2010).

Ofsted (2009) *Implementation of 14–19 Reforms, Including the Introduction of Diplomas*. Available HTTP: <http://www.ofsted.gov.uk/content/download/7001/71839/file/Implementation%20of%2014-19%20reforms%20an%20evaluation%20of%20progress%20(PDF%20format).pdf> (accessed 16 September 2009).

QCA (2008a) *The Diploma: An Overview of the Qualification*. London: QCA.

QCA (2008b) *Design for Success: Consortia Planning*. London: QCA.

QCA (2008c) *The Diploma and Its Pedagogy*. Available HTTP: <http://www2.warwick.ac.uk/fac/soc/cei/research/archive/> (accessed 19 January 2010).

QCA (2009) *Applied Learning Case Studies*. London: QCA.

Silver, R. and Forrest, W. (2008) 'Learning to become one of us', in Kehoe, D. (ed.) *Practice Makes Perfect: The Importance of Practical Learning*. London: Social Market Foundation.

Stanley, J. (2009) *What Do Diploma Practitioners Say about Pedagogy?* Unpublished. London: QCA.

TDA and LLUK (Teaching Development Agency and Lifelong Learning UK) (2009) *Involving Business in Diploma Lessons: A Guide for Teachers*. Available HTTP: <http://www.lluk.org/2947.htm> (accessed 27 May 2010).

7

Generic skills

Trisha Fettes

This chapter provides a brief developmental history of generic skills, primarily in England, and their place in work-related learning, and discussion of approaches to teaching and learning generic skills.

Background to generic skills

Generic skills have been an element of education policy and practice in the UK for over 30 years, although variously labelled, for example transferable skills, common skills, core skills, key skills, essential skills, employability skills, enterprise skills, functional skills and personal, learning and thinking skills (PLTS). Internationally, many curricula have also incorporated competencies that include generic skills (Huddleston and Fettes 2000; Rychen *et al.* 2003).

Generic skills differ from other skills, for example specialist, technical and practical skills that are subject-specific or sector-related. They are the general skills that are commonly found across different sector and subject contexts that enable learners to be effective in managing their own learning, performance, work tasks and relationships with others.

Although the transferability of generic skills from one context to another has been contested (e.g. by Hyland and Johnson 1998; Boreham and Canning 2008) in terms of lacking empirical evidence to support such claims, these general skills have been consistently highlighted in policy documents and surveys as vital to success at work and lifelong learning.

Generic skills and work-related learning

Generic skills have long been seen as an important part of work-related learning, especially with regard to employability. For example, in a consultation document on ways to improve employability through the 14–16 curriculum, a specific objective was included: 'to help young people develop communication, number and information technology skills, and wider skills such as team working and managing their own learning' (DfEE 1996, p. 5).

A report drawing on findings from a review reiterated the underlying aims of work-related learning as including the development of 'key skills and broader personal aptitudes' and 'the ability to make conscious applications of knowledge, understanding and skills' (DCSF 2007, p. 8). *Career, Work-Related Learning and Enterprise 11–19: A Framework to Support Economic Wellbeing* (QCA 2008a) encompassed the need for young people to 'recognise, develop and apply their skills for enterprise and employability' in a minimum of two work-related activities, and have at least 'one discussion about the skills they have developed' (p. 20).

Through this provision it was expected that learners would be able to:

- understand and demonstrate the main qualities, attitudes and skills needed to enter and thrive in the working world
- evaluate the usefulness of a range of skills for gaining and sustaining employment and self-employment . . .
- apply their functional skills and personal, learning and thinking skills.

(QCA 2008a, p. 20)

Employer-led organisations have been a key driver in promoting generic skills, both in calling for action to address the basic skills deficit they perceived in school leavers and in highlighting the need for the development of wider skills and attitudes to prepare young people for the world of work. For example, since publication of *Towards a Skills Revolution* (CBI 1989), and a parallel report by the Trades Union Congress, *Skills 2000* (TUC 1989), the Confederation of British Industry has emphasised consistently (e.g. CBI 1993, 2006, 2007) the importance of a range of generic skills:

In an era when basic skills and competencies play an ever more vital part in the battle to remain competitive in the global economy, work experience offers an outstanding opportunity to help young people understand why these matter and to gain a taste of using them in the real world . . . The importance of the competencies will vary from organisation to organisation, but generic skills such as application of numeracy, communication and literacy, and teamworking are exactly that – generic. They are relevant to virtually every job and sector.

(CBI 2007, p. 5)

The CBI suggested that work experience was an opportunity for employers, students and schools to work together in putting centre-stage attributes, skills and knowledge that make up employability.

The National Skills Task Force (2000) also suggested that, with the changing nature of work, there was an increased demand for higher levels of generic skills: the 'six key skills and additional transferable skills that employers may need over time' (p. 23). However, although there have been similar skill listings, there has been no one agreed definition of employability skills. The UK Commission for Employment and Skills (UKCES 2009) drew on the most widely used lists of generic skills to produce its own definition:

We take employability skills to be the skills almost everyone needs to do almost any job. They are the skills that must be present to enable an individual to use the more specific knowledge and technical skills that their particular workplaces will require

... A foundation of Positive Approach ... [supporting the] three functional skills ... exercised in the context of four personal skills: self-management ... ; thinking and solving problems ... ; working together and communicating ... ; understanding the business.

(UKCES 2009, pp. 10–11)

The policy background to generic skills

The idea is not new that some skills are common and fundamental to successful performance in a wide range of settings and potentially transferable between these settings. For example, in the late 1970s the Further Education Unit developed the notion of a core skills curriculum for vocational students (FEU 1979). City & Guilds and the RSA (Royal Society of Arts) have offered various certification schemes since the early 1980s to assess general skills at different levels. In 1985, core skills were introduced within Youth Training Schemes (YTS) to provide unemployed school leavers with a broad preparation for the world of work. The Certificate of Pre-Vocational Education (CPVE), also introduced in 1985, included groups of skills in core areas.[1] From 1986, the Business and Technician Education Council (BTEC) employed a framework of common skills[2] to integrate curriculum design across all its First, National and Higher National qualifications.

In 1989, core skills were already offered in Scotland through Workplace Assessed Core Skills Units. However, for England, Wales and Northern Ireland, it was a speech by Kenneth Baker, Secretary of State for Education, at the annual conference of the Association of Colleges of Further and Higher Education, 15 February 1989, which marked a significant policy landmark. The proposal for the development of a set of core skills[3] for 16- to 19-year-olds (DfE et al. 1991) reflected a perceived need to prepare young people for an increasingly competitive and changing world, make the academic curriculum more relevant to life and work, and broaden the vocational curriculum.

Table 7.1 charts key policy developments relating to generic skills from 1989 to 2010: for example, the development of core skill units in GNVQs (DfE et al. 1991), the change of name to key skills following the Dearing Review (1996) and the availability of a key skills qualification as part of the Curriculum 2000 initiative, to the point at which a further change in government policy for England led to reconfiguring key skills as functional skills qualifications and the development of a framework of personal, learning and thinking skills (PLTS).

The White Paper *14–19 Education and Skills* (DfES 2005) highlighted the broader role of functional skills and PLTS in improving young people's employability as well as learning. This fitted with the vision for 2020 that included more personalised learning and the need to work towards a society in which all children and young people leave school with 'functional skills in English and mathematics, understanding how to learn, think creatively, take risks and handle change' (Teaching and Learning in 2020 Review Group, December 2006, p. 5).

Functional skills, the 'essential elements of English, mathematics and ICT that individuals need to enable them to engage successfully as citizens and progress to further learning and employment' (DCSF 2010, p. 2) were embedded across the relevant

TABLE 7.1 Key dates in generic skills policy development and implementation, 1989–2010

1989–1994	1995–1996	1997–1999	2000–2005	2006–2010
TUC (1989) and CBI (1989, 1993) promote core skills as outcome of all learning, including A/AS Levels Government policy intention (1989) to develop a set of core skills for 16- to 19-year-olds included in White Paper: *Education and Training for the 21st Century* (DfE et al. 1991) Collaborative work to develop a framework of core skills, leading to the publication of core skills units by NCVQ Communication, application of number and IT made mandatory in GNVQs. Units included in some NVQs. Core skills units required in new Modern Apprenticeships	Core skills included in National Education and Training Targets (NACETT 1995) Review of GNVQs (Capey 1995) and NVQs (Beaumont 1995): support for core skills, but delivery and assessment problems Review of all 16–19 qualifications (Dearing 1996) leading to rebranding of core skills as key skills and revised units Drive to include in all publicly funded post-16 education and training Redesign of key skills assessment model Generic skills included in National Curriculum, and Part one GNVQ The core skill unit in IT approved for use in Key Stage 4 from September 1996	Consultation about the future of post-16 qualifications (QCA 1998) showing strong and continued support for the promotion of key skills Development and piloting of a new qualification that recorded the level achieved in each of the first three core skills; and funding mechanisms that encouraged key skills teaching, supported by inspection and the UCAS profile and tariff	Roll-out of new key skills qualification as part of Curriculum 2000 with the expectation that individuals without A*–C in English, mathematics and IT acquire relevant key skills qualification(s) at level 2 2003, reconsideration of the status of the wider key skills 2004, revised standards Tests removed from the Key Skills qualifications in Wales from September 2004 White Paper, *14–19 Education and Skills* (DfES 2005) leading to functional skills qualifications (to replace key skills) and a framework of personal, learning and thinking skills (PLTS), 11–19, for England December 2005, review of current skills qualifications in Northern Ireland	2008, new Workplace Assessed Core Skills Units in Scotland 2007–2010 pilot of functional skills September 2010, functional skills qualifications available to all learners All Foundation learning programmes include functional skills within progression pathways All Diploma qualifications require PLTS to be embedded and achievement of all three functional skills at Level 1 (Foundation), or Level 2 (Higher or Advanced Diploma) September 2010, implementation of Essential Skills Wales

curriculum programmes of study and GCSE subject criteria. They were made mandatory in Diplomas (at Level 1 for the Foundation Diploma and at Level 2 for the Higher and Advanced Diplomas), included in Foundation Learning and intended to be delivered as part of Apprenticeship frameworks. From September 2010, functional skills were also made available to young people and adults as stand-alone qualifications at Entry Level (1, 2 and 3), Level 1 and Level 2.

The Personal, Learning and Thinking Skills Framework (QCDA n.d.), drawing upon previous work, included six groups of skills: independent enquirer, self-manager, effective participator, team worker, creative thinker, reflective learner. Each group was made distinctive, but interconnected, with a focus statement and a set of outcome statements indicative of associated skills, behaviours and personal qualities. There was recognition that skills from more than one group could be applied in a single activity (see Figure 7.1).

While Scotland retained its focus on core skills, offering a framework at Levels 2–6 of the Scottish Credit and Qualification Framework which defined core skills standards that could be used in different ways (Scottish Qualifications Authority 2008),[4] historically, England, Wales and Northern Ireland developed jointly their own core skills/key skills standards and qualifications. Differences in policy only emerged in 2004 when Wales dropped the external tests for key skills in favour of a portfolio of evidence. Subsequently, it was also decided not to implement functional skills in Wales, with the launch from September 2010 of a new suite of qualifications: Essential Skills Wales (DCELLS 2010).[5]

Plan what to do and how to go about producing the poster (Independent enquiry)

Review work, invite feedback from others on the poster and deal positively with praise and/or criticism, communicate learning in relevant ways (Reflective learner)

Produce a poster with images of work to extend understanding of a chosen sector

Generate and explore ideas for the poster, try out alternatives, follow ideas through (Creative thinker)

Organise self and resources, prioritising action in producing the poster (Self-manager) Evaluate images from different sources and consider influences on choice of images, take informed decisions (Independent enquirer)

The task could be organised as a group activity (Team worker) and/or as an opportunity for learners to explore particular concerns to them such as gender stereotyping (Effective participator skills).

FIGURE 7.1 Example 1: Opportunities for developing and applying personal, learning and thinking skills in a work-related task.

Rationale for generic skills

Generic skills are regarded as important because they are likely to retain their usefulness over the longer course of working life as the nature of work tasks and processes change, as well as in life more generally. In terms of employability, what appears to be wanted is the ability to put skills together in performance at work, but also to navigate career progression and to manage change:

> it is vital that young people can articulate the skills they possess in applications for jobs or courses, and during interviews. They must also be able to manage their skill development at work and during further studies.
>
> (QCA 2008b, p. 5)

Managing change involves being aware of the features of the particular context in which the skills are being applied, and the ability to adapt skills to new settings.

However, as some have argued (e.g. Brown 1997; Oates and Fettes 1998), it is misleading to imply that generic skills learnt in one setting can, by virtue of their commonality, be applied automatically to new settings. For 'knowledge generated and practised in one context to be put to work in new and different contexts', requires recontextualisation (Evans *et al.* 2009).[6]

There is evidence that 'transfer is unlikely to occur unless intentionally planned for in the way materials and contexts are structured' (Bennett *et al.* 2000, p. 18). Just adding generic skills on to the academic curriculum is insufficient in developing employability:

> it is necessary to bring elements of the world of work into the classroom, to confront students with situations and problems which resemble those they will eventually have to tackle, and to allow them to learn the necessary skills in work-like contexts.
>
> (Gibbs *et al.* 1994, p. 4)

Harkin and colleagues (2001) agree that generic skills are 'not free floating and automatically transferable to new situations' but should be 'developed *within* learning and work situations, not as add-on extras' (p. 29).

Compared with England, where qualifications have often driven the reform agenda, countries such as Denmark and Belgium, for example, have focused more on the learning process and 'securing learners' understanding of and ability to adapt skills and knowledge to the requirements of new, unfamiliar contexts' (Oates *et al.* 2002, p. 76). In England, the main focus has largely been on developing precision in the specification and assessment of skills, although the Personal, Learning and Thinking Skills framework did mark a departure from that approach in that it was not intended as a qualification, but designed for skills to be embedded in learning programmes or qualifications such as the Diploma. It necessarily requires more attention to be paid to the contexts in which these skills are developed.

Models of delivery

Over the years, there has been continual debate on the best ways of organising the teaching and learning of generic skills, with three main models being identified in the literature: discrete; embedded; and integrated.

Discrete generic skills development takes place in separately timetabled sessions or through dedicated teaching time or activities to ensure the skills are acquired. For work-related learning, examples include collapsed timetable days or workshops in which tasks are set by employers to develop skills such as problem-solving, teamwork or project-management skills (Figure 7.2).

The disadvantage of discrete sessions is that, without debriefing and effective follow-up, students may not recognise the skills they have used and go on to relate them to other parts of their learning programme.

In the embedded approach, the successful achievement of a sector or subject-specific activity may be dependent on having certain generic skills, but the activity's learning objectives take precedence, with relevant generic skills deemed to have been covered through achievement of the required outcomes from the activity. In Diplomas, for example, learning activities are designed to focus on particular aspects of principal learning. Whilst organising and carrying out these work-related tasks, students may demonstrate certain personal, learning and thinking skills written into the assessment criteria for the unit where relevant to the subject or sector.

However, although embedding can ensure relevance of generic skills, the danger is that they can become so sector- or subject-specific that they lose their visibility and potential for transfer (Pumphrey and Slater 2002). By contrast, an integrated approach makes explicit to learners both the learning objectives for generic skills to be acquired

Enterprise challenges feature in many work-related learning programmes, often linked to Enterprise Week, in which collapsed timetable days or a series of discrete sessions are used for students to undertake their challenge.

The challenge is set by employers, with students being given a brief, or real problem to tackle, and resources that are authentic to the workplace.

Students work in teams to:

- plan their activity, for example to design, produce, market and sell a product, provide a service or solve a real problem
- carry out tasks and meet their individual responsibilities
- reflect on and review their progress
- make a presentation to an invited audience outlining the processes and outcomes of their activity.

Skills developed in other areas of the curriculum can be brought together in application to the challenge tasks.

FIGURE 7.2 Enterprise challenge.

within the context of a learning activity and their relevance to tasks and problems being tackled. Hodgkinson and Wright (1999) suggest that an integrated approach is more likely to motivate learners and enable them to manage the process of their own learning. By showing how generic skills relate to particular tasks, problems and situations, learners can be supported in developing strategies for employing them in other contexts, including learning how to read a situation from a skills perspective (Figure 7.3).

In practice, however, the terms are sometimes used interchangeably and the distinction between discrete, embedded and integrated models may not be clear cut. Hodgkinson (1996), for example, suggests that the different approaches can be considered as a continuum with discrete development of skills at one end and embedded at the other or blended in combination.

Schools often use a combination of models. For example, evaluation of the first year of delivering Diplomas (Lynch *et al.* 2010) found that centres were intending to 'embed personal, learning and thinking skills in general teaching, such as in the principal learning units or project' (p. 38). However, for functional skills the most common approach was for these skills to be 'taught discretely . . . by specialist English, mathematics and Information Technology teachers', although there was also 'recognition of the benefits of mapping the skills to principal learning, so learners understood the relevance and could apply the skills' (p. 3). Pre-16, 'some centres had "discrete" sessions called "functional skills" within GCSE classes'; others 'embedded the skills into GCSEs in a more "hidden way"' (p. 36).

Evaluation of enterprise education Pathfinders found that enterprise, involving the development of skills such as teamwork, problem solving and learning to learn, and project management skills, was delivered through one or more of the following approaches: 'discrete activities; time-tabled lessons; extra-curricular provision; . . . alternative curriculum days with suspension of the timetable'; and/or 'embedded in work-related learning, vocational courses, PSHE and/or other subjects' (CEI 2006, p. 23).

An 11–16 school believes that generic skill development is vital for preparing young people for work and adult life and that enterprise should be more than five stand-alone days for Year 11 pupils. It takes the strategic decision to focus on enterprise skills and integrate their development across the curriculum. There is a policy for work-related learning, of which enterprise is part, and an annual audit is conducted of how enterprise fits into every subject. The definition of enterprise is in every classroom and posters are displayed around the school on the skills and attitudes required to be enterprising.

Enterprise skills are included in schemes of work and are part of lesson objectives. Teachers are encouraged in their lessons to make it clear to students when they are developing a particular skill and how it relates to a work-related context associated with their subject. Students are encouraged to reflect on their skills development and regularly review with their teachers the skills they have developed, both in and out of school. These skills are recorded and then summarised at the end of the year in a 'skills passport' that complements the qualifications they have achieved.

FIGURE 7.3 Example of integrated practice.

Teaching and learning generic skills

The teaching and learning of generic skills requires sufficient time for students to 'learn, practise, consolidate, review and apply their skills in different learning environments', and for teachers to think about:

> the specific learning experiences to be provided . . . the teaching approaches and methods that promote and support the learning, practice and application of skills . . . [and] the sequencing of generic skills learning.
>
> (QCA 2008b, p. 13)

Examples of interventions include teachers highlighting within subject teaching 'how a particular key skill is applied in an employment context related to their subject'; 'modelling the effective application of key skills' or using video clips for this purpose; 'using a problem-based approach to learning to encourage students to think for themselves'; building in opportunities for collaborative tasks in which students 'discuss their ideas . . . and learn from each other'; and involving employers in discussions about skills and activities that 'enrich the learning of key skills' (QCA 2001, pp. 7–9).

A coherent approach to generic skills involves systematically planning and reviewing learning activities across the whole curriculum, including experiences outside the classroom. Planning activity 'makes clear to learners and those who facilitate their learning: the different skills to be developed; why they are important; the many opportunities for their development, application and recognition' (QCA 2008c, p. 8).

Purposeful discussion is an essential part of the planning and reviewing process in helping students to:

> become familiar with and actively use the skills 'language' as part of their career portfolio and academic work; and explicitly make connections between different areas of their study, work and other experiences through their own skill development.
>
> (Fettes *et al.* 2006, p. 342)

Skills development can be maximised through the experiential learning cycle used to structure work-related activities: opportunities for students to participate in a work-related learning activity (experience), think about and discuss their experience (reflection), draw out lessons learnt (generalisation) and apply the lessons learnt in new situations or activities (application) (QCA 2005, p. 2; see Figure 7.4).

In summary, effective skills development for employability is likely to be:

- based on real workplace practice, through work placements or other close contact with employers, and involving input from people outside the mainstream learning environment
- experiential, with diverse opportunities to put principles into practice in realistic situations, to make mistakes, and to observe and learn from colleagues

Experience: As part of a visit to a local company students engage in an 'I-spy' task devised by apprentices. Each team is given a different department to visit and has to record where and how listed skills are being demonstrated by employees in that department. Team members are encouraged to ask questions of employees about the skills they use.

Reflection: On return to the training room the company training manager asks questions to prompt students to think about the different work processes they observed and what they have learnt about skills.

Generalisation: Teams share their findings and are encouraged to compare and contrast the skills observed in the respective departments, and to draw conclusions on those skills which are commonly used in the business and those which are specific to specialist areas of work.

Application: On return to school, students design a card game for younger students in which they have to match the skills with work tasks observed on the visit.

FIGURE 7.4 Work visit.

- personal, with trainers/teachers willing and able to engage with learners, challenging behaviour and helping them to reflect
- serious, with real consequences for success or failure built in
- reflective: offering frequent opportunities (and challenges) to look back on what one has achieved and seek to generalise it.

(UKCES 2009, p. 57)

Assessment and recording of generic skills in work-related learning

There is at the time of writing no statutory requirement for summative assessment or certification of work-related learning. However, work-related activities offer good opportunities for formative assessment:

> Schools should ensure that students are able to reflect upon their work-related experiences, to identify their learning in a formative way. Reflection and review are essential parts of learning from experience. It is important that students can recognise and articulate what they have learnt, especially to employers.

(QCA 2003, p. 12)

Some outcomes of work-related learning, including generic skills, are 'likely to be assessed as part of GCSEs/GCEs, Diplomas and other qualifications' and 'local certification' may be offered as 'recognition of successful participation in work-related activities' (QCA 2008a, p. 7), such as enterprise or work experience. The functional skills qualifications offer opportunities to formally assess some generic skills, with assessment designed to 'provide realistic contexts, scenarios and problems; specify tasks that are relevant to the context; require applications of knowledge, skills and understanding for a purpose; require problem solving; assess process skills and the outcome of their application in different contexts' (DfE 2011).

Recording can support the development and formative assessment of generic skills by focusing the attention of learners and facilitators on skills: providing a record of skills demonstrated at particular points in a learning programme; prompting reflection and providing a basis for planning further skill development; and showing progress over time.

Recording of PLTS could be situated within the process by which learners develop individual learning plans (ILPs) or an equivalent personal and careers planning system. In this case, the recording of PLTS will be integrated with activities such as evaluating achievement, exploring and supporting progression options, setting goals, and generating formal ways of communicating achievements and goals (such as through CVs and standard applications).

(QCA 2008b, p. 12)

Progression

It is known that:

poor functional skills are associated with higher unemployment, lower earnings, poorer chances of career progression and social exclusion. They also inhibit the ability of employees to contribute to business performance.

(CBI 2006, p. 4)

Progression in generic skills is related to factors such as the complexity and familiarity of the context (task, problem or situation) in which the skill is being used, the technical demand of the content that is being applied and the level of independence demonstrated in completing tasks and tackling problems. It is not just a question of learning a skill in the classroom; it is necessary to develop progressive capability and responsibility in applying that skill in activities of increasing complexity in a range of situations.

The Performance and Innovation Unit suggests that, to 'participate and progress in the future workplace', individuals need to have not only the basic skills, but the ability to be 'autonomous, self-motivated learners; in future, knowing how to improve one's own learning and performance will be more important than ever before' (PIU 2001, p. 56).

Selected issues

The review of evidence on best practice in teaching and assessing employability skills (UKCES 2008) concluded that:

One of the key barriers in relation to promoting employability-relevant skills . . . especially in the formal education system, is related to teacher/practitioner skills, knowledge and confidence. This is unsurprising where practitioners have not worked outside of the educational sector and/or where their own professional training and development has not included employability skills and relevant pedagogical practice . . . [or] relevant work experience . . . is out of date . . . This can lead to teachers and practitioners lacking first hand knowledge and awareness of employer-needs and the teaching approaches which best suit the learning of these skills.

(UKCES 2008, p. 128)

Opportunities for staff development are critical to the successful teaching and learning of generic skills. For example, evaluation of the Introduction of the Key Skills Qualification (CEI 2001) clearly showed that:

where there are skilled staff with positive attitudes to key skills and the ability to show their value (e.g. by acting as role models, highlighting the relevance of key skills to main programmes and their importance to employability and the requirements of higher education – not just focusing on the recruitment/admissions stage), this has a positive impact on the motivation and performance of students.

(CEI 2001, p. 43)

In considering approaches to professional development, 'it is important not to discount the evidence of what works for learners in relation to teachers' own training needs' (UKCES 2008, p. 128). For example, action research projects can be a powerful learning tool in exploring the teaching and learning of generic skills, in mirroring processes associated with generic skills in improving own learning and performance, providing momentum to professional development and prompting teachers to look at their practice from a new perspective (Figure 7.5).

Activities in which teachers can learn about generic skills through observing sessions run by more experienced colleagues, or through engaging in tasks that encourage them to apply and reflect on generic skills, can also be helpful, provided there is opportunity for debriefing and follow-up (Figure 7.6).

As part of professional development through the Key Skills Support Programme (funded by the DfES and managed by the LSDA, 2002–2003), a group of teachers from different schools and colleges chose to engage in action research projects, each supported by a mentor from higher education. The objectives were to model experiential learning processes, and gain insights into effective teaching and learning strategies that promoted effective skill development. Some projects involved workplace observations and developing activities for learners that contextualised generic skills in real work tasks.

A formal review took place mid-point during which the teachers presented a poster about their research for the purpose of prompting critical reflection, highlighting key points they wished to share with others, inviting constructive feedback from colleagues and engaging in critical professional debate about skills. At the end of the project, the teachers gave a presentation of their findings and reflections on their own learning and performance to a wider audience (Fettes 2003).

FIGURE 7.5 Action research: strategies for enhancing the teaching and learning of the wider key skills.

A series of 15-minute, generic, active learning tasks were designed for PGCE students from different subject areas to develop their awareness of the six personal, learning and thinking skills (PLTS). Skills in self-management were needed for successful completion of the session as a whole. Students worked in small groups to tackle the following tasks on a carousel basis:

- an opinion finder, asking questions of each other about issues relating to the teaching and learning of PLTS, before sharing findings and drawing conclusions (Independent enquirer)

- work as a team to make a cube from one sheet of card and illustrate a different PLT skill on each side (Team worker)

- design a logo with strap line to market PLTS to pupils (Creative thinker)

- on sticky notes each write an issue of concern about developing PLTS with pupils, put on a flip chart and review issues with others; agree one to take forward and consider practical steps for addressing it (Effective participator).

Each group also gained experience of observing others to assess the application of PLTS and map skills against the activity, and reviewed activities and their own learning (Reflective learner). Students wrote a letter to themselves noting what they had learnt and how they might apply their learning; the sealed letter was given to their tutor for posting back to them later to encourage further reflection.

FIGURE 7.6 Session to develop awareness of PLTS.

Through experience of developing and applying generic skills for themselves, teachers are more likely to gain understanding of methods that would work with their students.

Discussion questions

1. In what ways, if any, can generic skills contribute to employability?
2. Is it really necessary to *teach* generic skills?

Tasks

1. Task A: use the template (Figure 7.7) to describe (in the centre box) an example of a work-related activity, for example a workplace visit or an enterprise task. In the outer boxes, record two or more generic skills of particular relevance to successful participation in your chosen activity.

2. Task B: this time use the template to record (in the centre box) a particular generic skill, such as teamwork or functional mathematics. Identify (in the outer boxes) two or more work-related activities that would offer opportunities to develop this skill.

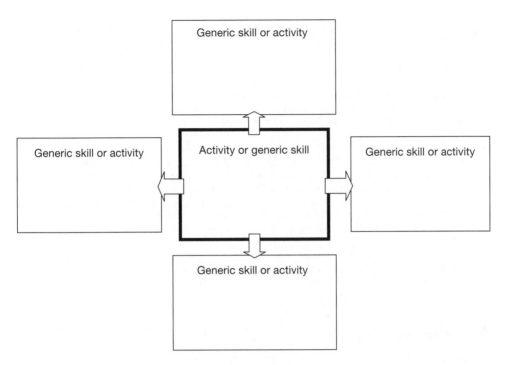

FIGURE 7.7 Generic skills map.

The template can be used in planning or reviewing lessons, either independently or with colleagues, to stimulate thinking and discussion about generic skills. It can also be used in a similar way with learners; for example, in helping them to identify the skills they will need/have used for a particular work-related activity, or to identify the different contexts in which a specific skill could be/has been used. For instance, in debriefing for work experience, learners could be encouraged to describe a particular task they enjoyed and the skills they applied to it, and then display their individual maps for discussion about ways generic skills can be useful and adapted to a variety of tasks in different settings.

3. Devise a lesson plan that aims to help students recognise the importance and relevance of generic skills to work-related and other aspects of a particular subject within the curriculum or programme area.

Selected resources

http://education.gov.uk/schools/teachingandlearning/qualifications/functionalskills (further details about functional skills)

http://www.fssupport.org/ and http://www.fssupport.org/resources (Functional Skills Support Programme and resources)

http://curriculum.qcda.gov.uk/key-stages-3-and-4/skills/plts/index.aspx (further details about personal, learning and thinking skills)

https://orderline.qcda.gov.uk/gempdf/1847219160.PDF (generic skills in Diploma learning)

Notes

1. CPVE core areas: communication and social skills; applied numeracy; problem solving; science, technology and IT; social, industrial and economic awareness.
2. BTEC: self-development skills; communication and working effectively with others; information, quantitative and numerical skills; practical skills.
3. The proposed set of core skills included communication, numeracy, personal relations, familiarity with technology, especially IT, and familiarity with changing working and social context, especially foreign languages.
4. Scotland's core skills can be offered as dedicated units, embedded within another unit or course (naturally occurring or deliberately written in) or through signposting opportunities in unit/course delivery. A catalogue details units and courses that have an embedded core skill or core skill component(s), with achievement of the unit or course resulting in automatic certification.
5. The Essential Skills include Communication, Application of Number and ICT, at Entry level through to Level 4. New standards for Working with Others, Improving Own Learning, and Performance and Problem Solving are planned to be accredited for delivery from September 2012.
6. Consideration of 'the programme design environment (content recontextualisation); the teaching and facilitating environment (pedagogic recontextualisation); the workplace (workplace recontextualisation); the learners making sense of the whole (learner recontextualisation)' (Evans *et al.* 2009, p. 12).

References

Beaumont, G. (1995) *Review of 100 NVQs and SVQs*. London: NCVQ.

Bennett, N., Dunne, E. and Carré, C. (2000) *Skills Development in Higher Education and Employment*. Buckingham: SRHE.

Boreham, N. and Canning, R. (2008) 'School and work: meeting employers' expectations with core skills', in Bryce, T.G.K. and Humes, W.M. (eds) *Scottish Education, Third Edition: Beyond Devolution*, Edinburgh: Edinburgh University Press. Available HTTP: <http://hdl.handle.net/1893/1140> (accessed 19 January 2011).

Brown, A. (1997) *Development of Key Skills across Contexts and over Time*. Paper presented at a Higher Education for Capability Conference on Key Skills in Higher Education: Identification, delivery and assessment, Senate House, University of London, 21 April.

Capey, J. (1995) *GNVQ Assessment Review*. London: NCVQ.

CBI (Confederation of British Industry) (1989) *Towards a Skills Revolution: A Youth Charter, Report of the CBI's Vocational Education and Training Task Force*. London: CBI.

CBI (1993) *Routes for Success, Careership: A Strategy for All 16–19 Year Old Learning*. London: CBI.

CBI (2006) *Working on the Three Rs: Employers' Priorities for Functional Skills in Maths and English*. London: CBI.

CBI (2007) *Time Well Spent: Embedding Employability in Work Experience*. London: CBI.

CEI (Centre for Education and Industry) (2001) *Evaluation of the Introduction of the Key Skills Qualification*. London: QCA.

CEI (2006) *National Evaluation of Enterprise Pathfinder Projects, March 2004–December 2005*. London: DfES.

DCELLS (Department for Children, Education, Lifelong Learning and Skills) (2010) *Essential Skills Wales*. Cardiff: Welsh Assembly Government.

DCSF (Department for Children, Schools and Families) (2007) *Building the Best, a Review of Work-Related Learning*. London: DCSF.

DCSF (2010) *Functional Skills: A Guide*. London: DCSF.

Dearing, R. (1996) *Review of Qualifications for 16–19 Year Olds*. London: SCAA.

DfE (Department for Education) (2011) *Functional Skills General Article*. Available HTTP: <http://education.gov.uk/schools/teachingandlearning/qualifications/functionalskills/a0064058/functional-skills> (accessed 28 January 2011).

Department for Education, Employment Department and Welsh Office (1991) *Education and Training for the 21st Century*. London: HMSO.

DfEE (Department for Education and Employment) (1996) *Equipping Young People for Working Life: A Consultative Document on Improving Employability through the 14–16 Curriculum*. London: DfEE.

DfES (Department for Education and Skills) (2005) *14–19 Education and Skills*. London: DfES.

Evans, K., Guile, D. and Harris, J. (2009) *Putting Knowledge to Work: Integrating Work-Based and Subject-Based Knowledge in Intermediate Level Qualifications and Workforce Upskilling – The Exemplars*. London: WLE Centre, Institute of Education.

Fettes, T. (2003) *Evaluation of Findings from Action Research on the 'Wider' Key Skills*. London: LSDA.

Fettes, T., Gillespie, J. and Hodgkinson, L. (2006) 'Undergraduate skills development through discussion and self-assessment', in Rust, C. (ed.) *Improving Student Learning through Assessment, Proceedings of the 2005 13th International Symposium*. Oxford: Oxford Centre for Staff and Learning Development.

FEU (Further Education Unit) (1979) *A Basis for Choice*. London: FEU.

Gibbs, G., Rust, C., Jenkins, A. and Jaques, D. (1994) *Developing Students' Transferable Skills*. Oxford: Oxford Centre for Staff Development.

Harkin, J., Turner, G. and Dawn, T. (2001) *Teaching Young Adults: A Handbook for Teachers in Post-compulsory Education*. London: RoutledgeFalmer.

Hodgkinson, L. (1996) *Changing the Higher Education Curriculum*. Sheffield: DfEE.

Hodgkinson, L. and Wright, C. (1999) *Evaluating the Effect of Key Skills in the Higher Education Curriculum*. Milton Keynes: Open University.

Huddleston, P. and Fettes, T. (2000) *Vocationalism within General Education: An International Perspective*. London: QCA.

Hyland, T. and Johnson, S. (1998) 'Of cabbages and key skills: exploding the mythology of core transferable skills in post-school education', *Journal of Further and Higher Education*, 22 (2): 163–172.

Lynch, S., McCone, T., Wade, P., Featherstone, G., Evans, K., Golden, S. (National Foundation for Educational Research) and Haynes, G. (University of Exeter) (2010) *National Evaluation of Diplomas: The First Year of Delivery*. London: DCSF.

NACETT (National Advisory Council for Education and Training Targets) (1995) *Report on Progress towards the National Targets*. London: NACETT.

National Skills Task Force (2000) *Skills for All: Proposals for a National Skills Agenda, Final Report*. London: DfEE.

Oates, T. and Fettes, T. (1998) *Key Skills Strategy Paper*. London: QCA.

Oates, T., Bresciani, P. and Clematide, B. (2002) 'Qualifications, competences and learning environments for the future: analyses of the development of three parallel approaches', in Kamarainen, P., Attwell, G. and Brown, A. (eds) *Transformation of Learning in Education and Training: Key Qualifications Revisited*. Luxembourg: CEDEFOP reference series, 37. Available: HTTP: <http://eric.ed.gov/PDFS/ED469800.pdf> (accessed 27 January 2011).

PIU (Performance and Innovation Unit) (2001) *In Demand: Adult Skills in the 21st Century*. London: PIU, Cabinet Office.

Pumphrey, J. and Slater, J. (2002) *An Assessment of Generic Skills Needs*. Nottingham: Council for Administration.

QCA (Qualifications and Curriculum Authority) (1998) *Qualifying for Success: Report on the Consultation about the Future of Post-16 Qualifications*. London: QCA.

QCA (2001) *Key Skills for Developing Employability*. London: QCA.

QCA (2003) *Work-Related Learning for All at Key Stage 4: Guidance for Implementing the Statutory Requirement from 2004*. London: QCA.

QCA (2005) *Work-Related Learning at Key Stage 4, Maximising Learning from Work-Related Experiences*. London: QCA.

QCA (2008a) *Career, Work-Related Learning and Enterprise 11–19: A Framework to Support Economic Wellbeing*. London: QCA.

QCA (2008b) *Guidelines on Recording Personal, Learning and Thinking Skills in the Diploma*. London: QCA.

QCA (2008c) *Generic Skills in Diploma Learning*. London: QCA.

QCDA (Qualifications and Curriculum Development Agency) (n.d.) *Personal, Learning and Thinking Skills*. Available HTTP: <http://curriculum.qcda.gov.uk/key-stages-3-and-4/skills/plts/index.aspx> (accessed 2 July 2010).

Rychen, D.S., Dalganik, L.H., McLaughlin, M.E. (eds) (2003) *Definition and Selection of Key Competences, Contributions to the Second DeSeCo Symposium*, Geneva, Switzerland, 11–13 February 2002. Neuchâtel: Swiss Federal Statistical Office. Available HTTP: <http://www.oecd.org/dataoecd/48/20/41529505.pdf> (accessed 27 January 2011).

Scottish Qualifications Authority (2008) *Core Skills Framework: An Introduction*. Glasgow: SQA.

Teaching and Learning in 2020 Review Group (2006) *2020 Vision*. London: DfES.

TUC (Trades Union Congress) (1989) *Skills 2000*. London: TUC.

UKCES (UK Commission for Employment and Skills) (2008) *Employability Project, Review of Evidence of Best Practice in Teaching and Assessing Employability Skills*. London: UKCES.

UKCES (2009) *The Employability Challenge Full Report*. London: UKCES.

8

Careers education, advice and guidance

Marian Morris

The role and place of careers education and guidance in the curriculum has been in a state of flux for many years. In some schools and colleges, a coherent, integrated, well-planned careers education and guidance programme has long been central to the support system available to young people. It has had senior leadership support and has been designed and taught by subject specialists to ensure that young people have the skills, information and knowledge to make decisions about their learning pathways and make effective transitions into post-16 and post-18 learning and employment. In others, however, lip service has been paid to the statutory duty [introduced in 1997 as part of the Education (Schools) Act (Great Britain Statutes 1997)] to provide an impartial careers education and guidance programme. In such institutions, it has largely been a Cinderella subject, delivered, for instance, as a 'bolt-on' element of an (often overcrowded) personal, social, health and economic (PSHE) education programme, by staff without any training in the area and often without any particular interest in the subject (Morris *et al.* 1995; McCrone *et al.* 2009).

This latter approach to careers education and guidance is no longer tenable. Significant changes, both in the context in which the subject is delivered and in the statutory duties placed on educational institutions, mean that an impartial programme of careers education and information, advice and guidance (IAG) is now recognised as an essential part of the curriculum, with a *guarantee* for all pupils enshrined in the 2009 schools White Paper (Great Britain Parliament 2009). This guarantee states that that 'all secondary school pupils will have access to high-quality careers education and information, advice and guidance so they can make informed choices about learning, work and lifestyles and are well supported during transitions' (DCSF 2009a, p. 35). It is accompanied, for the first time, by *statutory guidance* on careers education and information, advice and guidance (IAG).[1] Alongside this, the provisions of the Apprenticeships, Skills, Children and Learning Act (Great Britain Statutes 2009), which came into operation in September 2010, require all schools to ensure that their programme of careers education includes information on 16–18 education or training options and apprenticeships. All teachers (and those co-ordinating careers education and IAG) are expected to 'understand the implications of the Government's programme of reforms to 14–19 education, in particular the raising of the age of participation in learning and reforms to the qualifications framework' (DCSF 2009b, p. 3).

So what are careers education and IAG exactly? What has led to the recent changes in policy and the development of the pupil guarantee? What are the implications of these changes for practitioners in schools and colleges? In order to understand the current position of careers education and IAG in schools and colleges, one needs to look both at how it is now defined and at the various functions it has played under different policy agendas.

The purpose of careers education and IAG

Research by Callanan and colleagues, in one of the pieces of research that informed the statutory guidance on careers education and IAG, concluded that:

> Information, Advice and Guidance (IAG) and other forms of support were found to be critical to young people's educational careers at three key points: in selecting Key Stage 4 options, during Key Stage 4 where disengagement or underachievement occur; [sic] and in selecting post-16 destinations.
>
> (Callanan *et al.* 2009, p. 4)

In publishing its statutory guidance, the Department for Children, Schools and Families (DCSF) also highlighted the importance of careers education and IAG in preventing disengagement during Key Stage 3, supporting transition to work or further learning at 16 (Morris *et al.* 1999a,b) and providing a gateway to personalised learning (Hargreaves 2005).

It is important to recognise the four different elements encompassed in the term 'careers education and IAG', however, since these have quite distinct meanings and, traditionally, have been delivered by different groups of professionals. In an updated version of the *Better Practice* guide (Donaghue *et al.* 2008), Donaghue summarised the scope of each of these elements, differentiating between careers education (a planned, progressive programme of learning activities) and the other elements of careers education and IAG, as in Figure 8.1.

These definitions characterise careers education as a form of skill and knowledge development, rather than simply as a source of career information; they show how careers guidance serves personal development and is more than a means of matching people to local, regional or national skills' needs. More recently, the *Ways and Choices* resource, published to support statutory guidance, has taken the role of careers education further, suggesting that the benefits of a well-planned programme for young people are:

- to make career enhancing decisions about their immediate options in learning, work and leisure; and knowing how to make plans, applications and personal transitions
- to develop and practise the self-help skills they need to progress their own career plans and development, including making discerning use of careers information, advice and guidance

---

Careers education

The provision of a planned, progressive programme of learning activities that helps young people to:

- learn about the structures, systems and factors that guide, shape and influence people's careers prospects and career development

- explore how these could affect their future choices, why they need to consider them when making their own career decisions and plans and how they can do so

- develop and practise the self-help skills they need to progress their own career plans and development, including making discerning use of careers information, advice and guidance.

Careers information

The provision of accurate, up-to-date and objective information on opportunities, progression routes, choices, where to find help and advice, and how to access it.

Careers advice

The provision of advice through activities that help young people to gather, understand and interpret information and apply it to their own situation.

Careers guidance

The provision of impartial guidance and specialist support to help young people understand themselves and their needs, confront barriers, resolve conflicts, develop new perspectives and make progress.

(Donaghue *et al.* 2008, p. 2)

FIGURE 8.1 Careers education and IAG.

- acquiring personal understanding and skills for their long-term career happiness and wellbeing including self-reliance and autonomy, self-awareness and self-acceptance, narrative powers (the ability to tell their own story), resilience and a positive attitude to change.

(VT Group, the Association for Careers Education and Guidance and Youth Access 2010)

Traditionally, the school has been acknowledged as the main locus for the provision of careers education. The source of wider IAG provision (particularly careers guidance and counselling) has generally been seen as the role of the careers professionals, who work outside the school, but in some form of partnership with it. The extent to which either schools or external careers professionals have engaged with their various roles – and with each other – has fluctuated significantly over the past 30 years. There are a number of lessons that need to be learned from the past to ensure that it is possible to capitalise on the current statutory status of careers education and IAG in order to meet the needs of young people and of the economy as a whole.

To begin with, careers education has suffered consistently from a lack of understanding over its primary purpose and its place in the wider work-related curriculum. Too often, in the past, it was seen as essential only for those pupils who would leave school at 16 and who had no plans to stay in learning beyond compulsory education. As a result, it has lacked status and, in many cases, senior leadership support. During the 1980s, for instance, careers education and guidance had to compete for limited timetable space with other non-statutory elements of the national curriculum. Where senior leaders were not convinced of the value of careers education and guidance for the development of their whole school (and not just for some pupils), programmes remained short, content was inadequate and delivery fell to non-specialist staff with availability on their timetable (Morris *et al.* 1995).

The introduction of new qualification routes (such as the General National Vocational Qualifications, GNVQs) and increased opportunities for young people to follow programmes that enabled them to mix academic and vocational courses, placed greater importance on young people receiving independent, realistic, and up-to-date information and advice. Unfortunately, some schools continued to see non-statutory careers education as of limited significance for the majority of pupils. In some schools, this situation has remained unchanged to the present day, despite the introduction, in 1997, of a statutory requirement to deliver some form of careers education programme to all pupils at Key Stage 4 (Blenkinsop *et al.* 2006; McCrone *et al.* 2009). Other schools have embraced a much broader vision for careers education and guidance (CEG). It has been seen, variously, as a means of enhancing student self-esteem or motivation, a means of promoting life-long learning and reducing pre- or post-16 disengagement, a means of creating curriculum relevance, or an agent of change, leading to significant refocusing of the school curriculum or organisational strategy (Morris *et al.* 2000). In such schools, the careers education and guidance programmes were often more coherent and central to school development planning.

Second, the development of effective programmes of careers education and guidance was sometimes constrained by a lack of institutional engagement with guidance professionals. In the late 1980s and early 1990s, links with the careers service[2] ranged from an interdependent partnership, in which the linked careers adviser contributed to the careers education programme (a minority of schools), to contact solely for the purpose of providing a guidance interview for pupils. While the majority of schools fell somewhere between these two points (Morris *et al.* 1995), the level of interaction between schools and careers service staff varied even within individual local authorities. A number of policy and practice initiatives served to change this level of interaction, although not always in a positive way. The Careers Library Initiative in the mid-1990s, for example, enabled schools to update their (often redundant) careers libraries and provide access to accurate, up-to-date and objective information. This often led to the forging of improved relationships with careers service staff (by now based in 51 independent companies).[3]

In a number of cases, however, these improved links were damaged during the focusing agenda of the late 1990s that preceded the advent of the Connexions Service in 2001.4 The perceived withdrawal of 'blanket interviewing' for all Year 11 students,[5] in order to focus on activities for the students deemed hardest to reach, was seen by some head teachers as a signal that careers education and guidance was not essential for all pupils (Morris *et al*. 2001). Most recently, the Connexions Service has come back under local authority control, signalling further changes in school and careers service interaction.

Third, the advent of internet and online resources has revolutionised information searching and retrieval and has blurred the boundaries between the work of school practitioners and the work of careers professionals. Although information technology has improved access, research suggests that young people still need the support of careers professionals to mediate and guide them through the materials (Morris *et al*. 1999a,b; McCrone *et al*. 2005; Blenkinsop *et al*. 2006). More recently, there has been a further blurring of professional boundaries, with non-teachers, some of whom have professional guidance qualifications, taking on the careers subject leadership role in schools. In a national survey of careers leaders in schools undertaken in 2008, nearly one quarter of all respondents came from a non-education background (McCrone *et al*. 2009). Although this has led to more flexible staffing arrangements in schools, the research found that it has also meant that there has been a growing separation between those designing and those teaching careers education programmes.

Finally, the political status of careers education and IAG and its perceived role in relation to the skill economy and the development of individuals has varied significantly. Over the years, four main arguments for careers education and IAG can be identified (Stoney 1997; Morris *et al*. 2000). These include broad *economic* arguments, concerned with making schooling more relevant to adult and working life, with promoting effective progression from compulsory education, and with deploying the potential workforce to maximum advantage and with minimum inefficiency. During the 1990s, for example, two Competitiveness White Papers, *Helping Business to Win* (Great Britain Parliament 1994) and *Forging Ahead* (Great Britain Parliament 1995), redefined and extended the role of careers education and guidance as a major contributory factor in meeting the skill needs of industry in an age of global competition.

Alongside these demand-side arguments, a number of supply-side arguments emerged more forcefully in the late-1990s, with the *educational* argument (concerned with developing flexible and career-related competencies amongst individuals) receiving strong expression in the government's White Paper *Excellence in Schools* (Great Britain Parliament 1997). This identified careers education and guidance as a significant element of government strategy for promoting higher educational standards, alongside its support for links between schools and the business community and the extension of work-related learning.

During the late 1990s, a number of schools and guidance practitioners also recognised arguments around *social justice* (with careers education and IAG seen as central to promoting entitlement and equality and optimising young people's life choices) and *values* (with careers education and guidance seen as central to developing responsible, self-reliant and enterprising young citizens). Yet it was not until the amendments published in the Education and Skills Act (2008) that the statutory requirement for schools to provide impartial careers education and guidance (introduced originally in 1997) was extended to ensure the provision of information and advice that 'promotes the best interest of pupils and does not seek to promote the interests of the school' (section 43-45), giving policy emphasis to the social justice argument.

These developments, in particular the statutory guidance and the pupil guarantee, provide evidence of the then government's commitment to strengthening careers education and IAG in schools and colleges. The subsequent introduction of Diplomas and the planned increase in the age of compulsory participation in learning to 18 create additional choices for young people, which the careers service will be expected to support. So what is the current state of careers education and IAG in schools and colleges in relation to the needs of young people and what impact will the new statutory guidance have on existing practice? In particular, what are the implications of the new pupil guarantee for practice in the classroom?

The organisation of careers education and IAG in schools

The government's statutory guidance on impartial careers education (DCSF 2009c) assumes that, in most secondary schools, it is provided within programmes of personal, social, health and economic education (PSHEE), is embedded within the wider curriculum and, according to the then DSCF, 'is closely connected to the delivery of the statutory requirement for work-related learning at Key Stage 4' (DCSF 2009c, p. 7). It has been some years since a comprehensive and representative survey of how (and by whom) careers education is delivered in schools was undertaken (Morris 2004). Nonetheless, research and inspection findings suggest that careers education and IAG are not yet provided to a uniformly high standard across schools or colleges. As outlined in previous sections, the reasons for this are partly structural, partly historical and partly political.

Currently, within any one institution, responsibility for organising the careers education and IAG programme might be the duty of a qualified teacher (75 per cent of the respondents to a survey of careers leaders in schools in 2009 were teachers) or a higher-level teaching assistant. In a growing number of schools, however, this role has been given to someone employed by the school but with a background in industry, or someone with a guidance qualification, who may have previously worked in an external careers service (McCrone et al. 2009). Not all of these non-teaching staff will be qualified to degree level (15 per cent of the 2009 survey respondents fell into this category), which means that the careers education element of the programme may be planned (or even delivered) by someone without a teaching qualification. Amongst careers co-ordinators, the proportion with a specific careers education or guidance qualification appears to be lower towards the end of the first decade of the twenty-first century than it was in the past (McCrone et al. 2009).

Furthermore, the involvement of senior leaders in directing or co-ordinating the careers education and IAG programme currently may be relatively limited (only 15 per cent of the respondents to the 2009 survey of careers co-ordinators were senior leaders). Further, just over one third of the careers co-ordinators responding to the 2009 survey had been in post for more than five years, with the majority having two years or less of experience in the field of careers education and IAG.

If schools follow the government's statutory guidance correctly, however, many of these patterns will change. Headteachers now have a responsibility to raise the status of careers education and IAG and to improve the knowledge and skill levels, not only of those staff co-ordinating or leading the subject, but of all staff in the school. They have been given the task of ensuring that careers education and IAG becomes central to the work of the school and is taken seriously by all staff, including the governing body. The DCSF guidance sets out a 12-point checklist (summarised in Figure 8.2), emphasising the need for communicating the importance of careers education and IAG to all staff and for putting in place the supportive mechanisms that are essential to ensure the provision of a comprehensive and impartial careers education and guidance programme.

The formulation of this guidance suggests that the educational and social justice arguments for careers education and IAG ran alongside the economic arguments in the thinking of the then government. At the time of writing (2010) the statutory elements of the guidance still stand but it is not yet clear which argument will dominate the thinking of the new administration. The imminent raising of the Participation Age, however, brings into sharp relief the need to ensure that all young people are fully informed and prepared to participate in education or training up to age 18.

Teaching and learning in careers education and IAG in schools

The statutory guidance summarised above provides an outline for the organisation and operation of careers education and IAG in schools and acknowledges the need to follow principles of impartiality, to challenge stereotyping and to provide a work-related context. One intention of this guidance is to ensure that schools are best placed to provide the support that young people need to make the decisions that are right for them. In detailed qualitative research conducted with 165 young people across 14 schools between February 2005 and February 2006, Blenkinsop and colleagues (2006) found that the quality of young people's careers-related decisions varied not only according to their own individual approach to (and skills in) decision making, but also according to context (including the curriculum offer and existing support mechanisms in school) and the ways in which information and advice were mediated. Young people who appeared to make the most rational, thought-through decisions at transition points and remained content with those decisions, were based, on the whole, in schools that had effective curriculum management, student support and leadership and high (but attainable) staff expectations. They concluded:

> student-centred schools[6] with comprehensive advice, guidance and support strategies in place have the best potential to develop effective decision-making mindsets amongst their students (whatever their socio-economic or academic circumstances), which in turn, may help them make effective decisions. Where such strategies were lacking, young people either appeared to make ineffective decisions, or there was evidence of a range of 'positive' and 'negative' decision-makers (which suggests that the support may have been working for some students, but not for all).
>
> (Blenkinsop *et al.* 2006, p. 93)

1. Review delivery of careers education in school with reference to the principles of impartial careers education and learning pathways.

2. Appoint a senior member of staff to the leadership role for careers education and IAG and consider combining this role with responsibility for creating, managing and developing the school's relationships with business.

3. Provide the responsible senior leader with the autonomy and appropriate resources and agree clear objectives with measurable targets for improvement as part of a careers education and IAG development plan linked to the school improvement plan.

4. Ensure that any 'careers leader' or 'careers co-ordinator' to whom responsibilities are further devolved has the skills and knowledge, and is allocated sufficient time, to undertake their duties effectively.

5. Ensure that *all* staff understand the school's statutory responsibilities and receive the training and support that they need, particularly those teaching careers education and those providing personal tutoring.

6. Provide parents and carers with information about the services available to help young people make effective learning and career decisions, including the contribution that personal tutoring might make.

7. Encourage teachers to enhance their teaching by providing a work-related context for pupils' learning.

8. Consider whether, and how, emphasis should be placed on experiential learning to inform pupil's understanding of learning and work opportunities, exploiting synergies across the careers education, work-related learning, enterprise and financial capability elements of the 'Economic Wellbeing and Financial Capability' strand of PSHE education.

9. Ensure that information about school courses on the 14–19 Prospectus is updated at key points during the academic year. Collaborate with local partners to pilot and introduce the Common Application Process (CAP) for Year 11 pupils to ensure it is fully online by 2011.

10. Ensure that careers education provision is effective in challenging all forms of stereotyping, opening up access to work-related learning for disabled young people and promoting access to higher education, particularly from groups that are currently under-represented.

11. Ensure that learners receive the support they need to gain a suitable place in learning under the September Guarantee.

12. Conduct regular internal reviews (engaging at least one governor) of the quality of careers provision and develop a plan to address weaknesses. Encourage the Governing Body to discuss IAG and pupil destinations at least once a year.

FIGURE 8.2 Effective careers education/IAG: 12-point checklist (summarised). Source: DCSF (2009c).

Alongside this need to provide appropriate structures and support, however, is the need to focus on the individual; to enhance their skills and self-awareness and to ensure that they are best placed to make decisions. By age 13, some young people may have already made relatively stable decisions about their future career path, even though these may reflect a narrow view of available pathways. Others remain confused or uncertain at age 16 and beyond and find it difficult to make what to them may feel like life-changing decisions. The challenge will be to enable young people, at whatever their starting point, to become open and willing to explore potential options. As Gottfredson (1981) argued, there is a natural tendency amongst adolescents to move towards what they deem to be 'realistic' in terms of career aspirations, even when there is evidence to suggest that other options might be open to them.

At present, there is no single prevailing pedagogy for careers education and IAG. To some extent this reflects the varying status and emphasis on the subject in the past. Although theoretical and empirical research has led to the development of over 70 different models of learning styles (see Coffield *et al.* 2004), most of the theoretical work on adolescent decision making (a key focus of careers education and IAG) has drawn on conceptual understanding derived from work with adults. There is now a growing body of European and American research in this field, which has begun to influence programme planning in careers education and IAG.

In the past, the curriculum was dominated by three theoretical models (identified in Payne 2003), each of which led to a particular pedagogical approach to careers education and guidance:

- *Economic* models, in which young people are assumed to be motivated to maximise their economic and social outcomes. These models led to an action-planning approach (widespread in the 1990s) in which the provision of access to comprehensive information dominated the thinking of careers education and IAG providers.

- Models based on the concept of *pragmatic rationality*, in which it is recognised that few young people approach decision making in the planned and context-free way assumed in the economic model. These models led to suggested modifications of the action planning approach, which acknowledged that young people were operating in a particular context, that their career decisions might be opportunistic (based on contacts and experiences, for example) and that decision making would not follow a particular timetable (Hodkinson and Sparkes 1993).

- *Structuralist* models, in which young people's decisions are thought to be circumscribed, often unconsciously, by institutional, economic or cultural constraints. These led to classroom practices that challenged young people's internalised expectations and assumptions about their career path. This model of thinking is also evident in many of the policies that emerged at the start of the twenty-first century, linked to raising young people's aspirations and widening participation in higher education.

More recently, a growing understanding of the importance of *self-efficacy* (the belief that one has the power to produce effects by one's actions in decision making) has prompted a much greater focus on developing the skills young people need to make the best use of the information, advice and guidance available to them (Bandura *et al.* 2001). As a result, there is a recognition that those providing careers education are not simply imparters of subject knowledge (about curriculum and learning pathways or employment opportunities, for example) but instead need to focus on the development of pupils' skills.

It is accepted that they need to encourage young people to develop the ability to make decisions, rather than emphasise the decisions themselves. In doing this, it is expected that they will make use of interactive strategies and experiential learning techniques, using information technology (IT) as appropriate. Finally, it is anticipated that they will place an emphasis on the careers-related learning needs of their students, drawing on concepts of personalised learning.

For those developing or teaching careers education and IAG programmes this means ensuring that they:

- develop an understanding of the careers-related learning needs and preferences of their students
- provide comprehensive and impartial information on learning pathways and work opportunities through a variety of different media
- provide a work-related context for activities
- challenge stereotyping
- provide opportunities for experiential learning and tailored support.

Designing a programme

Even though it was not a statutory curriculum area in the past, there is a wealth of online and other resources available to those developing teaching and learning activities for careers education and IAG in schools. In order to meet the needs of your pupils, however, you will want to develop your own tailored and coherent programme that allows pupil progression, but also acknowledges that pupils come with very different mindsets. A valuable starting point would be to use the concept of *personalised learning*. In *Better Practice*, Donaghue and colleagues (2008) suggest that the most valuable help in planning a careers education programme is to get to know young people as individuals.

> What are their achievements, dreams and expectations? How do they see themselves? What can they do? What interests them? What are their backgrounds? What is going on in their lives? What are their values, attitudes and beliefs in relation to living, learning and earning? Who influences them? What help do they need from the careers programme?
>
> (Donaghue *et al.* 2008)

In exploring young people's decision making at 14 and 16, Blenkinsop and colleagues (2006) drew on and adapted some work on pupil educational mindsets by a market research company, SHM (2006). These mindsets (Figure 8.3), based on an analysis of young people's attitudes to the future, tolerance of risk and theories of

- Decided planners: those with a clear idea of what they want to do and a plan of how to achieve it (though their plans may be not always be realistic).

- Comfort seekers: those with no clear picture of their future plans but who choose what is familiar at the time of making choices.

- The short-term conformists: those who think about the next step in the system, but without any clear plan for the future.

- The confident aspirationals: confident, optimistic individuals who think that hard work and ambition will help them succeed, but may nonetheless have no clear picture of where they are going.

- Long-term planners: those who have a clearly defined progression plan through education, but may not necessarily be sure about the field in which they wish to work.

- Indecisive worriers: those who are overly anxious about their future and find it difficult to make career options.

- Defeated copers: those who will accept whatever opportunities (or lack of opportunities) that they face.

- Unrealistic dreamers: those who believe they will succeed, but have done little research into their potential careers and rely on luck rather than planning and work.

FIGURE 8.3 Examples of educational mindsets.

success, led to the identification of different approaches that young people take to decision making and recognition of the need to adapt careers education programmes to suit different strategies for seeking information, advice and guidance.

Discussion questions

1. Blenkinsop and colleagues (2006) found that mindsets were not always stable and tended to change over time and at or after transition points. How do you think a consideration of pupil mindsets might help you in planning a careers education programme?

2. The young people in your class may be optimistic or pessimistic about their future. They may be willing to take risks and look for new challenges or they may want to stay with something that is familiar. How could you set about finding out about the mindsets of the young people in your class?

3. For some young people, teachers and other professionals will play an important part in decision making about the future. For others, families or friends may appear to be more important. How would you work with other teachers to identify the people (or activities) that appear to have the biggest influence on the decisions that young people in your school make about their future?

Tasks

When planning a programme or working with others in teaching it, it is worth considering ways in which careers education lessons could provide opportunities for consulting with and listening to learners. Think about how careers education lessons could be used:

1. to encourage young people to access different sources of information. What strategies might work to prompt the 'comfort seekers' or the 'defeated copers' (who tend to make decisions in similar ways) to look beyond their friends or families for advice?

2. to ensure there is sufficient challenge and variety in the programme. How could you best encourage the 'decided planners' to reflect on their chosen options or help the 'confident aspirationals' to engage with course or labour market information?

3. to provide time for targeted one-to-one discussions with young people (and/ or their parents/carers). How would you make sure that the 'comfort seekers', 'indecisive worriers' or 'defeated copers' are provided with the type of support and encouragement they need to develop greater confidence in their ability to make choices and decisions?

4. to ensure access to real-world or work-related opportunities. How can you make best use of business or other links to enable 'comfort seekers' to become more familiar with a wider range of opportunities, to reassure 'indecisive worriers' or to help 'unrealistic dreamers' or 'confident aspirationals' engage with the world outside school or college?

5. to ensure access to a varied range of information sources. How can you encourage those 'defeated copers' or 'comfort seekers' who display a lack of interest in career progression to engage with information and support?

6. to build in activities to encourage self-assessment. How could 'confident aspirationals' be helped to make the best use of their ambitions?

Resources

Cegnet (http://www.cegnet.co.uk), the website of the careers education and IAG support programme, funded by the DfE and run by the Association of Careers Education and Guidance (ACEG), provides the most comprehensive source of resources at present. They have been published alongside the statutory guidance, to help teachers design their curriculum and plan their careers education lessons to fulfil the needs of the pupil guarantee. They include:

- a framework of learning outcomes for young people aged 7–19
- Fact Cards about post-16 pathways
- DVDs for use with young people in classrooms and parents and carers in post-16 option events

- a set of 20 interactive lessons for use by teachers and others working with young people from Key Stage 3 (age 13+) to post-16.

The site also offers access to schemes of work for Key Stages 3 and 4 and post-16 and resources to challenge stereotyping.

Numerous publishing companies provide materials for careers education and IAG programmes, including the widely used and adapted Real Game series for students from Key Stage 2 to post-16 students (http://www.realgame.co.uk/content/1144243980.086/).

The Training and Development Agency for Schools website includes material to support career-related learning in English, history and modern foreign languages and to support continuing professional development for teachers engaged in careers education and IAG (http://www.tda.gov.uk/teacher/developing-career/iag-and-14-19.aspx).

Notes

1. The DfES introduced a non-statutory framework for careers education and guidance in 2003 (Department for Education and Skills 2003).
2. Careers services at that time were located in the local education authority, of which there were around 130.
3. Following the Trade Union and Employment Right Act (1993), careers services left local authority control in 1994, and reformed as a smaller set of privately managed companies, with the expectation of a stronger prevailing business ethic and the expansion of services.
4. In 2001 the careers service became the Connexions Service, in response to ideas set out in the Social Exclusion Unit's report *Bridging the Gap* (Social Exclusion Unit 1999) and the White Paper *Learning to Succeed* (Great Britain Parliament 1999) and the role of careers adviser was replaced by that of the Personal Adviser, whose role included advice and guidance on issues as diverse as housing, health and employment, as well as careers guidance.
5. A guidance interview for all Year 11 pupils, carried out by a careers adviser from the careers service, was one legacy of the concept of careers education and guidance for all introduced by the Employment Department's Technical Vocational and Education Initiative (TVEI) in the early 1990s. This idea was also enshrined in subsequent initiatives such as the National Record of Achievement (NRA), Urban Compacts, Youth Credits and Progress File.
6. The term 'student-centred school' arises from the work of Foskett and colleagues (2004), in which they identified a range of different cultures including a school/image-focused culture emphasising ethos and leadership; a student-centred culture oriented towards supporting student decision making; a functional/administrative culture focused on operational management procedures; and a strategic/policy orientation that was responsive to external policies and motivated by the wish to optimise opportunities and entitlements.

References

Bandura, A., Barbaranelli, C., Caprar, G.V. and Pastorelli, C. (2001) 'Self-efficacy beliefs as shapers of children's aspirations and career trajectories', *Child Development*, 72 (1): 187–206.

Blenkinsop, S., McCrone, T., Wade, P. and Morris, M. (2006) *How Do Young People Make Choices at 14 and 16?* DfES Research Report 773. London: DfES.

Callanan, M., Kinsella, R., Graham, J., Turczuk, O. and Finch, S. (2009) *Pupils with Declining Attainment at Key Stages 3 and 4: Profiles, Experiences and Impacts of Underachievement and Disengagement*. DCSF Research Report 086. Available HTTP: <https://www.education.gov.uk/publications/RSG/publicationDetail/Page1/DCSF-RR086> (accessed 11 May 2011).

Coffield, F., Moseley, D., Hall, E. and Ecclestone, K. (2004) *Should We Be Using Learning Styles? What Research Has to Say to Practice*. London: LSRC.

DCSF (Department for Children, Schools and Families) (2009a) *Your Child, Your Schools, Our Future: Building a 21st Century Schools System – The Pupil Guarantee*. Available HTTP: <https://www.education.gov.uk/publications/eOrderingDownload/21st_Century_Schools.pdf> (accessed 11 May 2011).

DCSF (2009b) *Impartial Careers Education: Briefing for All Staff in Schools and Pupil Referral Units/Short Stay Schools*. Available HTTP: <https://www.education.gov.uk/publications/eOrderingDownload/00978-2009DOM-EN.pdf> (accessed 11 May 2011).

DCSF (2009c) *Statutory Guidance: Impartial Careers Education*. Available HTTP: <http://publications.dcsf.gov.uk/default.aspx?PageFunction=productdetails&PageMode=publications&ProductId=DCSF-00978-2009&> (accessed 16 December 2010).

Department for Education and Skills (2003) *Careers Education and Guidance in England: A National Framework 11–19: Guidance on Curriculum, Examinations and Assessment*. London: DfES.

Donaghue, J. (ed.) with Barnes, A. and Wright, K. (2008) *Better Practice: A Guide to Delivering Effective Career Learning 11–19*. Fareham: VT Lifeskills. Available HTTP: <http://www.cegnet.net/content/default.asp?PageId=2388> (accessed 11 May 2011).

Foskett, N.H., Dyke, M. and Maringe, F. (2004) *The Influence of the School in the Decision to Participate in Learning Post-16*. London: DfES.

Gottfredson, L.S. (1981) 'Circumscription and compromise: a developmental theory of career aspiration', *Journal of Counselling Psychology*, Monograph, 28: 545–579.

Great Britain Parliament. House of Commons (1994) *Competitiveness: Helping Business to Win*. Cm 2563. London: The Stationery Office.

Great Britain Parliament. House of Commons. (1995) *Competitiveness: Forging Ahead*. Cm 2867. London: The Stationery Office. Available HTTP: <http://www.archive.official-documents.co.uk/document/dti/dti-comp/dti-comp.htm> (accessed 16 December 2010).

Great Britain Parliament. House of Commons (1997) *Excellence in Schools*. Cm 3681. London: The Stationery Office.

Great Britain Parliament. House of Commons (1999) *Learning to Succeed: A New Framework for Post-16 Learning*. Cm 4392. London: The Stationery Office.

Great Britain Parliament. House of Commons (2009) *Your Child, Your Schools, Our Future: Building a 21st Century Schools System*. Cm 7588. London: The Stationery Office. Available HTTP: <http://www.official-documents.gov.uk/document/cm75/7588/7588.asp> (accessed 11 May 2011).

Great Britain Statutes (1997) *Education (Schools) Act 1997*. London: The Stationery Office. Available HTTP: <http://www.opsi.gov.uk/acts/acts1997/ukpga_19970059_en_1> (accessed 16 December 2010).

Great Britain Statutes (2009) *Apprenticeships, Skills, Children and Learning Act 2009*. London: The Stationery Office. Available HTTP: <http://www.opsi.gov.uk/acts/acts2009/ukpga_20090022_en_1> (accessed 16 December 2010).

Hargreaves, D. (2005) *Personalising Learning – 4: Curriculum and Advice & Guidance*. London: Specialist Schools Trust.

Hodkinson, P. and Sparkes, A.C. (1993) 'Young people's career choices and careers guidance action planning: a case-study of Training Credits in action', *British Journal of Guidance and Counselling*, 21 (3): 246–261.

McCrone, T., Morris, M. and Walker, M. (2005) *Pupil Choices at Key Stage 3: Literature Review*. DfES Research Report RW68. Available HTTP: <https://www.education.gov.uk/publications/standard/publicationdetail/page1/RW68> (accessed 11 May 2011).

McCrone, T., Marshall, H., White, K., Reed, F., Morris, M., Andrews, D. and Barnes, A. (2009) *Careers Coordinators in Schools*. DCSF Research Report 171. London: DCSF. Available HTTP: <https://www.education.gov.uk/publications/eOrderingDownload/DCSF-RR171.pdf > (accessed11 May 2011).

Morris, M. (2004) *Advice and Guidance in Schools: Report Prepared for the National Audit Office*. London: National Audit Office.

Morris, M., Simkin, C. and Stoney, S. (1995) *The Role of the Careers Service in Careers Education and Guidance in Schools*. QADU/RD7. Sheffield: DFEE.

Morris, M., Golden, S. and Lines, A. (1999a) *The Impact of Careers Education and Guidance on Transition at 16*. RD 21. Sheffield: DfEE.

Morris, M., Lines, A. and Golden, S. (1999b) *The Impact of Careers Education and Guidance on Young People in Years 9 and 10: A Follow Up Study*. RD 20. Sheffield: DfEE.

Morris, M., Rudd, P., Nelson, J. and Davies, D. (2000) *The Contribution of Careers Education and Guidance to School Effectiveness in 'Partnership' Schools*. DfEE Research Report 198. London: DfEE.

Morris, M., Rickinson, M. and Davies, D. (2001) *The Delivery of Careers Education and Guidance in Schools*. DfES Research Report 296. London: DfES.

Payne, J. (2003) *Choice at the End of Compulsory Schooling: A Research Review*. DfES Research Report 414. London: DfES.

SHM (2006) *Mindset Profiles: Segmenting Decision-Makers at Ages 14 and 16*. DCSF Research Report RW67. London: DfES.

Social Exclusion Unit (1999) *Bridging the Gap*. Cm 4405. London: The Stationery Office.

Stoney, S. (1997) *DfEE Working Paper*. Unpublished.

VT Group, the Association for Careers Education and Guidance and Youth Access (2010) *Ways and Choices Classroom Resources*. Available HTTP: <http://www.cegnet.info/files/CEGNET0001/resources/Lesson%20Guide_4_VT.pdf> (accessed 11 May 2011).

9

Other work-related learning activities

Prue Huddleston

Introduction

This book has attempted to provide an overview of the rationale, history, policy context and current provision of work-related learning within English schools as we enter a new decade, when new challenges are set for both the economy and education, as well as the interrelationship between the two. Preceding chapters have focused upon some of the more familiar and ubiquitous types of activity, for example work experience. This chapter offers a summary of other less well-known, or perhaps less considered, manifestations of work-related learning, including the role of employers in such processes and activities.

In drawing these accounts together it is important to reflect upon the starting point for this book, namely that work-related learning is described as 'learning through', 'learning for', and 'learning about' work (DCSF 2009, p. 6). A closer examination of this statement should remind us that work-related learning comprises not just the activity in which the student engages but also the process of that engagement and, most importantly, the knowledge, understanding and skills that are acquired as a result. Given this, particular activities may be considered as distinctly work-related, for example working in a team to solve a problem, or making a presentation to one's peers, but would also be applicable to a range of other learning situations which are not necessarily connected with workplaces, for example playing sport or taking part in a drama production. Both these activities are also undertaken by professionals in workplaces.

What is being suggested is that there are pedagogical approaches that are seen as 'active' or 'applied' which are associated with work-related learning but which could also apply to more traditional subject teaching. Just because a subject is given an 'academic' label does not require it to be taught in a didactic manner. A recent history lesson observed in an inner city comprehensive school on the subject of the murder of

Thomas à Becket involved pupils taking part in a 'crime scene investigation' (complete with blue and white police tape) in which they were required to assess the evidence supplied by witnesses, some of doubtful reliability, read accounts of the event, of varying provenance, and draw conclusions. This lesson produced an interested response from pupils and was characterised by an active engagement with the subject matter and the activity. Was it work-related, or just plain good teaching?

Having discussed the pedagogical possibilities, let us turn to the activities associated with work-related learning. It is reasonable to state that some types of activity are only possible with the active input of those who come from the world beyond school, volunteers as well as the employed and self-employed. I have not said, deliberately, the 'world of work' since schools and colleges are themselves workplaces; we often ignore the rich work-related learning possibilities available within the context of the school or college.

Examples of other work-related learning activities are given below, together with some reflections and good practice points. As you read through them you might wish to refer to Chapter 3 and consider how far any of these activities take place in your school or college, and the extent to which this represents a coherent programme of work-related learning. In addition to the activities, what pedagogical approaches are being adopted?

The activities covered in detail in earlier chapters of this book – namely work experience; enterprise education; careers education and guidance – are not repeated here, but in making your assessment regarding the coherent approach you should bear these in mind within the totality of the offering. Some of the activities may be interlinked; for example a visit to an employer's premises may yield opportunities for future work experience places. It is helpful to try and think of work-related learning as a holistic cross-curriculum approach suitable for all learners.

Curriculum-linked workplace visits

Such visits (see Figure 9.1) are jointly planned by schools/colleges and businesses to allow students access to real business environments with planned learning outcomes directly related to students' programmes of study. What students learn from the visit should be directly incorporated into students' learning in the classroom or workshop.

Talks by visiting speakers from outside school/college

This is usually quite a straightforward activity to arrange, either by an individual teacher/lecturer or through a brokerage organisation which might have particular contacts (see Figure 9.2). Where a sector-specific speaker is required, it is possible to approach one of the sector organisations, which often have lists of members who are prepared to speak in schools, for example on careers in their sector. The engineering sector is particularly strong in this regard. For speakers and activities involving science, technology, engineering and mathematics, STEMNET (see stemnet.org.uk/content/ambassadors) is a useful starting point.

Year 10 students visited a local theme park within the West Midlands as part of their GCSE Applied Leisure and Tourism programme. They were asked to focus on the marketing function of the theme park, including the ways in which it advertised its products and services, its target market, potential competitors, promotional offers and areas for further development. The visit included a tour of the site, a talk by the marketing manager, followed by a question and answer session, lunch in one of the food outlets and a free ride on one of the attractions. Material collected during the visit contributed to the students' portfolio tasks for internal assessment.

Good practice points

- There was a clear brief for the visit.
- The company was well prepared with an appropriate day of activity and dedicated and knowledgeable personnel to host the visit.
- The visit was clearly linked to the students' programme of study.
- There were identified learning outcomes, which related to compulsory coursework assessment.

Reflection

- Are there similar sites within driving distance of your school/college that might provide a useful context for a visit? If not a theme park, then perhaps a museum or leisure centre?
- Why do you think the theme park is willing to dedicate resource to this type of school visit?

FIGURE 9.1 Example: visit to theme park.

World of work events

These may cover a wide variety of activities, for example business people running challenges in schools/colleges or on business premises, business simulations, careers-focused days, which may be sector-specific or involve representatives from different sectors (see Figure 9.3). Often, the timetable will be suspended for a day so that the activity can be sustained and thus simulate a more realistic business environment. Students are usually expected to work in teams and to deadlines and provide solutions to challenges, or problems, set by the business visitors, for example build a bridge from card, paper clips, straws and so on. The Army also provides some interesting challenges for schools/colleges.

Mentoring

Mentoring is a widespread activity across many schools, partly in response to initiatives such as 'Aim Higher', which have focused on raising aspiration and achievement

A Year 12 A Level business studies class attended a talk given by a former student of the school describing how he had set up and run a successful bar/café in a city centre location. He outlined the ways in which he had developed the business idea, produced a business plan, sourced finance and finally opened and continued to trade. The talk came to life when the students visited the bar in the following week. Students were able to draw on the experience when completing coursework on *Starting a Business.*

Good practice points

- The bar owner was a near contemporary of the student group and thus provided a strong role model.

- He knew the school and the business studies teacher well and was comfortable with speaking in the environment.

- The example of a bar/café was accessible for Year 12 students – more so than a large corporation.

- The speaker was well briefed by the teacher and the content of his talk was clearly aligned with the topics being covered in A Level.

- The business studies teacher maintains excellent networks of former students and also with other small businesses in the area.

Reflection

- Does your school/college keep a list of former students and what they are doing; is there an alumni association which could provide speakers, role models, mentors for current pupils?

- Why do you think that the engineering sector is so keen to engage with education?

FIGURE 9.2 Example: talk by former pupil about starting a business.

in relation to higher education. Mentoring is now well established for a range of purposes, not just those associated with widening participation but also those addressing issues of inclusion, provision of role models and subject-specific support, for example with reading.

Not all mentoring is carried out by business people; other examples include peer mentoring, in which older students mentor younger members of the school; student mentoring, in which higher education students mentor students in local schools; and volunteer mentoring, carried out by members of the community. Whatever the programme, the purposes of mentoring are to provide one-to-one support and encouragement to students, encourage target setting and review progress in a non-judgemental way. Mentors also function as role models.

In the case of mentoring by business people, this may involve employers running company-wide programmes for their employees and developing links with particular schools; or an education–business partnership may recruit mentors from a range

A brokerage organisation working within the 'Square Mile' with large financial services providers and law firms organises a range of world of work events for schools in inner London boroughs. One of these – 'City for a Day' – involves students visiting one of the large corporations in the City of London, where they are invited to interview staff about their jobs. Following a talk and video presentation about the City, students are allowed time to prepare questions for a group of staff from the companies about careers in the City, the types of jobs they are doing, what it is like working in the City and the qualifications they needed for the job. The students are entertained to lunch in one of the board rooms as part of the session and shown some areas of the head offices.

Good practice points

- The use of a respected brokerage organisation reduces the burden on participating companies since all the publicity, recruitment and organisation of the events is carried out by the broker.

- The programme is of a consistent standard.

- There is an excellent relationship between participating companies and the brokerage organisation.

- There is a clear menu of opportunities offered to schools, so that schools know precisely what is entailed and what learning outcomes are intended.

- The offering is reviewed regularly with schools and has been subject to external evaluation (Huddleston and Muir 2008).

Reflection

- Are you aware of any world of work activities organised by your local education–business partnership, or by any other broker in your area?

- Are these types of activities age-/stage-specific, or could they be adapted across the age range?

- Consider the advantages and disadvantages of 'buying in' the services of a brokerage organisation to recruit businesses to be involved in this type of activity.

- Consider the advantages and disadvantages of buying an 'off the shelf' activity from a supplier of world-related learning activities for schools.

FIGURE 9.3 Example: City for a Day.

of local companies. Running effective mentoring programmes is a time-consuming operation and for this reason a company may prefer to sign up to an existing programme or mentoring network rather than run a scheme itself.

There is a significant literature on mentoring (Miller 1998) and it can take a variety of forms, for example on a one-to-one basis, in a group, electronically, or sometimes a combination of methods. Whatever its nature, research indicates (Miller 1998) that there are some fundamental principles that need to be in place for successful mentoring to occur. These include:

- appropriate matching of mentor to mentee

- clear definition of roles and responsibilities of all parties (mentors, mentees, teachers, employers, scheme co-ordinators, senior management teams)

- an agreed understanding at the outset of the time commitment, the expected frequency of meetings, the importance of continuity and reliability

- all necessary safeguarding issues addressed and Criminal Records Bureau checks completed

- parental permission obtained

- appropriate locations sought for mentoring activities

- agreed focus and targets for mentoring; examples include to improve attendance; to provide an insight into jobs in particular sectors; to support subject work; to provide role models.

From the perspective of an employee, engaging in mentoring can bring a range of benefits, including developing self-confidence; improving communication skills; gaining access to potential recruits; sharing a particular subject interest or enthusiasm; 'giving something back'. Some companies will recognise and reward this type of community engagement through their corporate social responsibility department.

Mock interviews

The purpose of mock interviews conducted by business people (see Figure 9.4) is to bring a realistic dimension into job application, recruitment and selection (either as part of a course or as preparation for work experience, part-time or full-time employment, or university entrance). The experience is particularly valuable when the visiting business person has recruitment and selection as part of his or her job role. However, any business representative will be able to provide insights into his or her own experience of applying for jobs and subsequent interviews. If the volunteer is a young employee the messages will be particularly immediate, since he or she may only recently have joined the company. Those company employees with responsibility for recruiting and selecting school/college leavers will be especially well placed to bring a real-life dimension to the mock interviews.

Workshops and master classes

These involve experts from outside school leading discussions and/or giving talks or lectures, either in school/college or on their own premises, about specific topics or about the realities of a particular sector or workplace. The opportunities afforded by modern technology have resulted in larger numbers of students being able to access 'guru' lectures through video-conferencing or professionally produced DVDs. An example is provided by the Career Academy (Finance) programme in which young sixth formers, studying business and participating in the Career Academy programme (www.careeracademies.org.uk), are able to access video 'master classes' given by leading business experts on subjects such as marketing. A similar example is provided

An international finance company offers eight work experience places per year to a local school; there is significant competition for the places amongst students, who see them as highly desirable, not least because of their city location.

The company's education liaison manager discusses with departments how many places can be offered and the nature of the placements, including a job description and person specification. These are then circulated to the participating school and students are invited to apply using a bespoke application form and asked to include a CV. Applications are reviewed and students invited for interview at the company headquarters; a selection is made and feedback provided to all candidates.

Good practice points

- The exercise exposes young people to the realities of the workplace.

- The importance of personal presentation, both written and spoken, is emphasised as an important 'life skill', not just for job applications.

- The company takes its involvement seriously by thinking about potential work placements which have learning potential.

- Employers and students have the opportunity to plan the work experience in advance and to get to know each other.

FIGURE 9.4 Example: applying for work experience vacancies.

by recent work of the designer Jasper Conran who, in association with the Design Museum, has produced a DVD for schools on the design process in which he sets students a business/design task. Clearly, this could not have been achieved without the use of digital technology.

Reflection

- Can you think of potential opportunities for using workshops and master classes within your school/college?

- Could you link with other schools/colleges in your area to extend such opportunities?

- If you do not have access to sufficient workshops/practical areas within your school/college to provide learners with a realistic insight into work in a particular sector, you might like to direct them to http://www.icould.com, which provides careers information and insights into a wide range of jobs for both teachers and young people.

Work shadowing

Here learners will have the opportunity of observing staff in real working environments and talking to them about their organisations and job roles in a more detailed way than is possible for the younger learner within the traditional work experience placement. It is particularly helpful when the intended learning outcome is more career-focused. It is often more suitable for post-16 students than for pre-16 since it may allow access to environments unsuitable for the younger learner, for example if there are confidentiality issues or if senior staff are involved. The length of the experience is important since it may appear that the young person is 'hanging around' rather than learning anything. Two or three days is probably the optimum time.

Such placements need to be handled with care and require clear explanations of the purpose of the experience for the young person and for the company. A planned programme of observation is essential so that the young person can gain an holistic view of the organisation, or of a particular job role. Clearance may need to be gained from third parties, for example if a student is to be taken into meetings with outside agencies or customers.

Such experiences may have a career orientation, particularly in the professions, and act as a 'taster' for intended job roles. Entrance to some higher education courses, for example veterinary science, education and medicine, may require evidence from an applicant of experience of the field of study. Work shadowing could provide such evidence.

Practical experience, 'live projects'

These may be provided by employers or by sector-representative bodies and include short job-specific tasks and other hands-on experiences which allow opportunities for students to practise what they have learned in the classroom, for example working with particular materials on a design problem, or developing a guide for visitors to a tourist venue (Figure 9.5).

Industry days

Here teams of students may take part in business games, challenges, competitions and work simulations to resolve business-related problems, using role-playing, teamwork, decision-making and problem-solving skills. This is an activity suitable across the whole age and ability range, provided the problems and tasks set are appropriate. This type of activity is very similar to, or may be described as, an enterprise day (see Chapter 5). The involvement of business people on the day gives an added dimension of authenticity, particularly if they can be used as judges. Sometimes these days may involve competition between students from different schools/colleges.

Good practice points

- Do not underestimate the complexity of organising such large-scale events.
- Ensure that the locations and facilities are adequate for a whole year group, or groups from different schools, including those with special educational needs.
- Brief all teachers about the day: its rationale, the intended learning outcomes, its relevance for their subject area, their anticipated role in it.

An English Heritage castle attraction in the West Midlands set a practical task for a group of sixth-form students to review its gift shop and catering facilities and to identify ways in which it could improve the revenue from both these outlets. The activity involved a briefing from the site manager, a tour of the facilities, lunch in the barn restaurant and a discussion of initial ideas. Following the visit students drew up proposals for improving the profitability of both business activities. The students involved were studying A Level history and A Level business.

Good practice points

■ Teachers visited the site before the visit to identify learning opportunities which met the needs of the organisation as well as the needs of students.

■ The visit provided a cultural dimension for the students since none of them had visited a heritage site previously.

■ The task was realistic and manageable and was taken seriously by the site manager.

■ The site manager gained access to a 'challenging' consumer segment, namely young people, who currently do not constitute a sufficiently large, and necessary, segment of its customer profile.

■ Gaining the views of young people in this way was cheaper than employing an external consultancy organisation.

FIGURE 9.5 Example: English Heritage castle attraction.

■ Ensure that adequate time is built in for visiting business people, including breaks and 'catch up' sessions; confirm their understanding of what will be happening and their intended role.

■ Allow sufficient time for an appropriate debriefing of the event, from all perspectives, and confirm learning outcomes.

■ Hold a review meeting after the event and collect feedback to inform future planning.

Conclusions

This chapter has attempted to provide an overview of the range of work-related learning activities in which schools and colleges engage, but it is by no means exhaustive. It is clear that many of them overlap, and that some may provide opportunities for others; for example work experience placements for students may highlight opportunities for teacher placements, or other teacher development opportunities, such as writing materials. There are also opportunities from which businesses can benefit, for example, free consultancy, access to actual or potential markets, staff development experiences.

In Chapter 3 we discussed the challenges of providing a coherent work-related learning offer across the whole school for all students. Given the range of possible activities and experiences highlighted in this chapter, it is clear that ensuring coherence and progression across such a diverse range, often delivered by different people, subject departments and external organisations, is challenging. Decisions will need to be made at whole school level about the shared responsibilities for, and the distribution and timing of, work-related learning activities. However, it may be that decisions are devolved to departmental or individual practitioner level, or simply to a coalition of the willing.

In educational terms this is not ideal; unless such activity has clear educational aims and learning outcomes its merit has to be questioned. Adopting a laissez-faire approach in such matters can lead to confusion, overlap, lack of coherence and progression, or simply nothing happening at all. The role of the school work-related learning co-ordinator is crucial in bringing consistency and sharing good practice.

The foregoing examples have demonstrated that in terms of contexts and content work-related learning can provide rich and diverse opportunities for learning. They can also help us to think more deeply about the ways in which we teach, the ways in which young people learn and the ways in which we can learn together and with partners from beyond school. As practitioners you will want to consider what you are doing, what the educational aims are and what learning gains are being achieved. You may have some work to do with your colleagues as well.

References

DCSF (2009) *The Work-Related Learning Guide*, 2nd edn. London: DCSF.

Huddleston, P. and Muir, F. (2008) *Evaluation of the Brokerage Citylink Schools' Programme*. Coventry: CEI.

Miller, A. (1998) *Business and Community Mentoring in Schools*. DfEE Research Report No. 43. London: DfEE.

10

Conclusions

Julian Stanley

The first part of this book sought to describe the general features of work-related learning and to offer a framework within which all varieties of work-related learning can be understood. On this account, work-related learning is conceptualised as learning which is hybrid between classroom learning and learning in workplaces. Table 1.1 identifies eight dimensions according to which we can understand and compare any kind of work-related learning: purpose, content, environment, teacher, resources, conditions, tasks and learning processes.

In Chapter 1 it was argued that this provides a more comprehensive analysis than the conventional account which distinguishes only three strands: learning *for* work, *about* work and *through* work. Furthermore, this refinement helps us to make sense of the way that a multiplicity of purposes are advanced and debated as reasons for providing work-related learning.

Quite different types of work-related learning such as careers education and guidance and work experience can be analysed in terms of these dimensions: they may, for example, share some purposes (such as learning more about particular jobs) but not others, such as personal development; they may well differ in terms of where they take place and who does the teaching. Understanding these overlaps better can help us to understand whether we should see different kinds of work-related learning as contributing towards the same goal or whether they might form part of a single planned experience which generates distinctive learning outcomes. Both are possible!

Whilst the conceptual framework sketched in Chapter 1 provides a tool for analysis, the chapter by chapter account in this book appears to tell a different story. In reality, it would appear there are different histories for different types of work-related learning, different legislation, guidance and funding, and different agencies and specialists who are concerned to champion, develop and deliver different kinds of work-related learning. In practice many teachers and students understand different kinds of work-related learning as quite distinctive practices – with different purposes and experiences. This perception is supported by the fact that different kinds of work-related learning are driven by different institutions and different networks and professional associations.

It could be argued that this is just a matter of perspective – or rather a matter of vantage point. From the distance, all kinds of work-related learning have a family connection but, as you zoom in, you can distinguish the different priorities, ways of doing things and languages associated with the different strands. It is difficult to dispute this state of affairs and some readers of this book may be interested only in particular chapters! However, by reflecting on the connections and crossing places between the strands we may be able to improve understanding and generate some proposals for developing practice. In the rest of this chapter, I will explore the unity of work-related learning in three fields: policy, organisational integration, and teaching and learning.

Policy

Policy is critical to educational practice. Setting new policies may not necessarily bring about changes in practice at school level, but, given the authority and accountability that the state has assumed, educational activities that are not backed by policy are likely to be neglected. If we read across the chapters in this book we can discern some common preoccupations shared by policy makers working in different governments and agencies over the last 30-odd years.

Policy makers have been concerned to change the curriculum so that it worked better in terms of equipping young people with the capabilities and knowledge that they were thought to need to cope with short-, medium- and long-term economic change. Policy makers have wanted increased economic growth and improved economic and social opportunities for all, particularly those perceived as disadvantaged; they have sought to make education the engine of growth and social mobility – an ambition which has encouraged changes in the curriculum. Time and again, policy makers reformed and amended the curriculum in the light of broader economic and social objectives.

However, the liberal view, that education should always be concerned with the development of the individual as much as social or economic goals, has continued to inform policy – although its visibility and influence have fluctuated. This philosophy has also been important in the development of work-related learning. It has lent support for the argument that the curriculum should allow for diversity and choice in terms of content and pathways, that the first-hand experience of individual learners should shape the way that learning is organised, that students should develop a critical knowledge of work and the economy, and that individual decision taking and the development and achievement of personal goals should inform teaching and learning.

These policy beliefs and concerns have been transmitted from one minister to another and from one agency to its successors. They have become part of the landscape – so extensively shared as to be almost invisible. Taken together they encourage the development of work-related learning and even provide it with an overarching purpose. As detailed in Chapter 2, work-related learning has become important because it is believed to make education a more effective tool to secure salient economic and social goals: full employment, economic growth, increased social mobility, efficient transition into employment, management and privatisation of risk, the integration of the UK into a globalised economy, current and future technological change and so on. At the same time, work-related learning does accommodate the liberal aspiration of an education that prioritises individual development. Reviewing the chapters on enterprise education, careers education and work experience, for example, we can see how their development has taken account of liberal aspirations – at least to some degree.

So long as work-related learning appeared to be able to reconcile the reforms that were deemed necessary to achieve economic and social goals with the preservation of a liberal education, which has continued to be a touchstone for much of the teaching profession, it offered a particularly attractive policy lever. Under Labour governments from 1997 to 2010 this approach became increasingly explicit and energetic. The Every Child Matters objectives, which developed in the aftermath of the Victoria Climbié enquiry, used a concept of work-related learning as part of a larger vision of what the public sector would aim to provide for young people:

- be healthy
- stay safe
- enjoy and achieve
- make a positive contribution
- achieve economic wellbeing (DCSF 2003).

This vision situated traditional educational goals within a broader set of goals for wellbeing and it encouraged the development of work-related learning as a way in which these goals might be achieved. This vision influenced the revision of the national curriculum that took place in the 2000s, leading to a new subject area, Personal, Social, Health and Economic Education, emerging as an entitlement in 2008. As documented in Chapter 3, this subject area provided a systematic and comprehensive set of learning objectives ranging across careers, enterprise and financial capability; it listed four common concepts (career, capability, risk, economic understanding) and four sets of key processes (self-development, exploration, enterprise, financial capability), going on to list the range of topics that might be addressed within this subject.

The curriculum statement provided in Qualifications and Curriculum Authority (QCA)'s programme of study for Economic Wellbeing and Financial Capability provides a high-water mark for the development of policy on work-related learning. It supplied a systematic and unified account of a work-related learning curriculum, which enjoyed recognition as part of the national curriculum and was intended to become statutory by 2011. Were this policy to remain in force, these curriculum documents could be expected to influence training, guidance, planning, teaching, review and inspection so that the diverse traditions of practice in the different strands of work-related learning became more connected.

As things have turned out, this seems unlikely to be the case. It is too early to say what the coalition government elected in 2010 will do to the national curriculum; however, it has already signalled that the curriculum should be slimmed down and there should be a renewed focus on traditional subjects. This implies that a comprehensive Economic Wellbeing and Financial Capability programme of study is unlikely to become statutory. It seems improbable that, in the short term at least, there will be a policy to integrate the several work-related learning practices or to seek to get teachers, students or inspectors to look at them as all part of the same thing. This is not to say that policy may not provide encouragement and even resources for particular elements of work-related learning; for example, it has been announced that an All Party Parliamentary Group supporting personal finance education is to be formed (pfeg, 2010).

Organisational integration

The other way in which the different strands of work-related learning can combine is when a single organisation takes responsibility for the delivery of all or many of them and when an organisation decides to make links between the different strands. However, it is part of the character of work-related learning that it tends to be delivered by partnerships of organisations rather than by single organisations.

Schools

In one sense, the provision of work-related learning can never be entirely unified or continuous. Work-related learning is bound to be distributed across different subjects because it represents the aspiration to make connections between subject learning and work. It is essential for work-related learning that schools and colleges work with businesses and work organisations, since learning directly from workers is a key feature of work-related learning. It would be very limiting to try to deliver work-related learning entirely within a conventional school timetable since this would rule out activities, such as learning in the workplace, trading in a market place and interacting with workers, that form part of the repertoire of work-related learning activity.

However, many schools and colleges have sought to find ways of connecting together their provision of work-related learning. They have done this, in part, to achieve greater organisational efficiency but also because they think that the educational goals of work-related learning are advanced if students and teachers can understand how different elements of work-related learning connect. Many schools will have a member of the senior leadership team who takes responsibility for all or most of the work-related learning strands: work experience, careers education, education–business links. Schools often appoint a work-related learning co-ordinator, whose role is to develop work-related learning across the institution, to raise awareness, support colleagues, arrange continuing professional development (CPD), track and plan work-related learning across subjects, events and years, and evaluate and audit delivery.

A school may even have a team – for example a careers specialist, a work experience administrator, a co-ordinator and a senior leader – that comes together to develop new ideas and review practice. Schools where work-related learning is relatively well integrated are likely to have an overall policy which sets out the purposes and scope of work-related learning in that institution and how it is understood. Work-related learning elements will be identified in the school's development plan.

This kind of integration at institutional level helps teachers to get things done: some activities and events can be exploited so that they yield more learning; things that work can be replicated, practices that do not work so well are more likely to be reviewed and improved or replaced; repetition of learning can be identified and removed; innovation is encouraged when teachers feel that it is recognised and approved of by the whole organisation – in particular by the leadership. If teachers are developing this more connected understanding, then it is more likely that the learning they lead will allow connections to be made for students. Students will, for example, be helped to draw upon their work experience placements as part of their career development and personal development curricula – as well as seeing it as an opportunity to develop employability skills.

Links with employers will be used to support a wide range of learning, for example the development of aspirations and vocational learning, as well as for practice interviews. It will always be the case that some connections are fortuitous and initial partnership work may be limited to a particular activity. However, over time partners develop trust and respect for one another and they find that they can do more and more together.

A store manager will perhaps give some time to a Year 11 Careers Day because her store is new to the town and she wants to establish good relations with the community. Over time, as she gets to know teachers in a school and comes to understand their aims she may be ready to encourage her staff to become mentors or she may become a school governor or get involved in enterprise projects. In other words, schools and their partners all stand to gain when connections are made between the different parts of work-related learning both because scarce resources and time can be conserved and because when partners can make connections between projects it helps to build trust and this facilitates further partnership.

The ongoing development of the Business and Enterprise College specialism, supported by the Specialist Schools and Academies Trust, has encouraged schools with this specialism to look for ways of extending enterprise education so that it is not just an area of excellence in their curriculum but a defining feature of their institutional culture and an engine for their continued improvement. A common strategy has been to identify a set of 'enterprise skills' which are agreed to represent the general qualities that it wants its students to develop. These skills are generic skills; they are often very similar to the personal, learning and thinking skills that were defined by QCA and discussed in Chapter 7. However, any Business and Enterprise Specialist College can choose its own particular formulation and these can reflect the school's context, history or other specialisms.

These skills can then be taught and learnt collectively. All teachers can be asked to include these 'enterprise skills' in their lesson plans, school leaders will then expect to see these skills taught and developed during observations.[1] Students expect to have these skills recognised and accredited, lesson by lesson. Usually, these schools track and tally up the achievements of students in terms of these skills using some kind of database, which can be linked to a rewards system such as Vivo Miles (https://vivo-miles.com/), through which learners can convert their accumulated stock of skills into material rewards or charitable donations.

In this way, a set of 'enterprise skills' is identified as desirable for teachers and students. The pursuit and achievement of these skills serve to engage students in learning generally and to encourage teachers to attend to learning outcomes beyond their particular subject learning goals. This kind of 'embedding' may not fit with the culture of every school; however, it does demonstrate that elements of work-related learning can be generalised across the curriculum and serve as a strategy to improve student engagement and prioritise particular kinds of learning.

Providers

Another way in which the work-related learning strands can be integrated is when those organisations that support or provide work-related learning services are able to unite authority, expertise or guidance in a number of strands. In the past, a connected-up approach was provided at national level by the QCA. This supported the development and review of work experience, careers education and other aspects of work-related learning. Although it was by no means the only organisation that was able to influence the development of strands like enterprise education and financial capability, it did seek to show the connections between them and produced a series of reviews and framework documents that aimed to make clear the connections (such as QCA 2008a).

At a local level, education–business link organisations (EBLOs) have developed the capability to support schools in delivering a wide range of work-related learning. Business links are critical to many different kinds of work-related learning; local EBLOs have been able to build up relationships and systems so that they can meet the particular needs of schools by matching them to employers or gatekeepers who can supply the required input. They have become specialists in the recruitment of employers, communicating with and rewarding them – acting as their 'way-finders' in the educational world. Alongside this key function, EBLOs have developed sufficient knowledge and expertise in work-related learning so that they are able to represent educational interests to business and vice versa. Very often, EBLOs develop educational resources and services which address particular work-related learning strands: enterprise education, financial capability and so on. In some cases, EBLOs are multi-service agencies which hold contracts to deliver a variety of work-related learning services, for example careers education, work experience, STEM activities (Science, Technology, Engineering and Mathematics enrichment activities).

An organisation which is supporting a number of work-related learning strands is likely to find ways in which it can internally share resources and expertise. Those who work as brokers and service providers in these organisations are likely to see connections between the different kinds of work-related learning that they have been commissioned to supply – even if the commissions come from different budgets and different agencies.

However, at this point it is uncertain whether local EBLOs will be able to offer a 'one-stop shop' for work-related learning brokerage and services in the future. Cuts in public spending, announced in autumn 2010, mean that they are likely to lose their core funding. In the future, their capacity to survive will depend on their ability to compete with other providers to offer services to local schools and colleges.

Practice: teaching and learning

The different kinds of work-related learning can also be said to share a number of styles of teaching and learning. In the past work-related learning has been promoted as a 'student-centred' alternative to a didactic or 'teacher-centred' pedagogy. Work-related learning has been identified as being 'practical', 'active' or 'experiential' as opposed to 'theoretical', 'passive' or 'transmitted'. Not all of these terms have stood the test of time; some, such as 'experiential learning', have enjoyed critical attention by scholars, whilst others have remained the property of teachers and trainers. What is important here is whether there are processes of teaching and learning which have application from one strand of work-related learning to another and from work-related learning to other kinds of teaching and learning.

Work-related learning raises questions for teaching and learning because it demands a change of focus from the established academic curriculum to work. The manner in which learning goes on at work provides an alternative model which can be used to complement, challenge and extend established traditions of academic teaching and learning. We can explore this challenge in terms of the eight dimensions identified above: purpose, content, environment, teacher, resources, conditions, tasks and learning processes. Most of these dimensions are aspects of teaching and learning; all of them have implications for teaching and learning.

Purpose

Work-related learning adds to the purposes of learning. In addition to the mastery of subject knowledge and the achievement of qualifications it brings a set of purposes associated with transition into employment, with performance, resilience and success in work and other goals that relate to the overall performance of the economy. The character of these purposes implies that conventional pedagogies that are closely associated with *educational* progression are unlikely to be wholly adequate or appropriate.

If work-related learning focuses on different goals then it seems appropriate that these goals will be signalled to learners and teachers in distinctive ways. Conventional academic achievement is rewarded with grades, marks or qualifications. However, learners undertaking work experience placements may be working to achieve a strong reference as an outcome whereas students competing in an enterprise competition may enjoy a share of the profits.

Content

The knowledge, understanding and skills that are targeted by work-related learning range from task- or organisation-specific skills to much broader subject-related material, drawn, for example, from business studies or sociology. For the latter, conventional subject pedagogies, such as questioning groups of students or asking them to find answers to questions by reading texts, are likely to be appropriate. However, when the topics are action- or decision-related and highly contextualised, then the pedagogy is likely to become more action-orientated: practice rather than discourse or text becomes the object around which learning turns.

In addition to knowledge and understanding, work-related learning calls for other learning outcomes: skills, attitudes, behaviours, capabilities, dispositions and aspirations associated with work in general or with particular jobs, vocations or professions. This kind of content implies distinctive kinds of teaching and learning: demonstration, practice, imitation, development and trying things out. These may complement, or even partially replace, conventional pedagogies, for example the transmission, recording, analysis, communication and evaluation of information.

Students may learn about the working life of an individual or research a local company. In this case, what is wanted is not (usually) an 'objective' or scientific description, but a personal and subjective account – because this is the perspective that is sought. Work-related learning may be highly personal to the learner, as in the case of the guidance element of careers education. In this last case, an appropriate pedagogy must be personalised and impartial – because the intended knowledge and outcomes are personal.

Environment

Work-related learning draws attention to work as an environment for learning and, by making us aware of our assumptions about learning environments, to the importance of environment as a factor in all learning. In the workplace, learning is affected by relationships with other workers, supervisors, customers and equipment. Because schools and colleges are places designed for learning, we tend to take it for granted that they are the best kinds of environment for learning, but research into work-related learning has demonstrated that student learning can be stimulated by other kinds of environment. The 'adult' environment of a work placement can transform the disposition of young people to learn; performing a calculation in a workshop can carry a different meaning from what it would in the classroom.

An awareness of the importance of 'work environments' is now widespread in education. Many newly built secondary schools contain spaces that echo the open-plan offices of modern service-sector companies; investment in Diplomas and other vocational provision is leading to the development of specialist workshops and training centres that have a work-like character. Not only can work-related learning offer alternative environments for selected students, but it can also help to inform the way that 'mainstream' learning environments are organised.

Teachers

Work-related learning complements the teaching force because it recognises that workers, employers, entrepreneurs, volunteers and so on can, if the circumstances are right, help students to learn. Evaluations of work-related learning show that workers, employers, entrepreneurs and volunteers can be effective as facilitators of learning. If a student advances her skills on work placement because her supervisor shows her how to complete a task and then praises her for doing it well, or if a student seeks to shine at a mock interview with a volunteer, it is likely that learning has been accelerated because the student perceives the value of learning from that non-teacher. This is supported by what we know about the social character of learning: that social relationships exercise influence upon our behaviour and thought.

When it comes to acquiring skills and dispositions relating to work, access to workers and employers other than teachers is essential. This may occur informally through family and friends or through part-time work experiences. However, some young people may not have timely access to workers and employers informally or these informal experiences may be restricted in some way, perhaps limiting the aspirations of young people with respect to their gender or social class. There is robust evidence that mentoring, for example, can extend the aspirations of young people and thereby compensate for differential access to social capital (Taskforce on Education and Employment 2010).

As schools develop their experience of working with non-teachers, they are finding more and more ways to harness their contributions. Some secondary schools are now looking to develop strategies to enhance the role that parents play in educational activities.

Resources

Work-related learning implies that young people have opportunities to learn not only from specialised educational resources but also from resources used at work. This implies access to tools and equipment that are used in workplaces, whether they are standard, such as software packages, or specialist, such as the machines used in particular industries. In point of fact, schools in the UK spend a good deal of time training young people how to use the various Microsoft Office applications – a set of skills which has now become virtually essential to employment.

Enterprise education has experimented successfully with schemes that let young people take control of small amounts of capital (see Chapter 5). Learning of this kind is 'resource-based' in the sense that the students are asked to plan and take action in response to the resource, which in turn helps them to understand the resource better and to learn, through collaboration and experience, how to use that resource more effectively.

Although work-related learning continues to involve learning directly from authentic work resources, the mainstreaming of work-related learning has led to the production of specialist educational resources which are intended to support work-related learning: games, simulations, computer software, websites, activities, DVDs and so forth. Cohort after cohort of students have been inspired by simple but effective resources, such as the Real Game.[2]

The power of these educational resources to stimulate and engage students and teachers reminds us that the power of work-related learning is not simply making connections with the 'real world' but rather the creation of some kind of connection to the real world which stimulates worthwhile student learning. That real connection may be mediated by a learning resource, a video or a teacher; however, it may still prove sufficient to engage and excite.

Conditions

The conditions of work are a feature of the work environment; they affect the way that we work. By conditions I am thinking of the organisation of work tasks in time, in space and in relationship to other people. The conditions of work affect the way that learning in the workplace happens. Those involved in teamwork can benefit from collaboration; those involved in project work will be able to transfer experiences between projects and so forth. The learning of those working with customers or outdoors will be affected by their working conditions.

Work-related learning provides opportunities to introduce work-like conditions into the school curriculum and then to exploit their potential to support distinctive ways of learning. Challenges, simulations, enterprise models, mentoring relationships and work placements all provide distinctive learning conditions which offer opportunities to focus on particular skills or knowledge (see Chapters 5 and 9). As schools become more confident about using distinctive conditions, such as an enterprise or a business challenge model, they find that they can use them in a greater variety of curriculum areas and with a wider range of different partners.

Tasks

Work-related learning reminds us that education is expected to prepare us to perform tasks at work and that we can learn a great deal from planning, performing and reviewing our performance. Where learning activities are designed to look and feel like 'work tasks', this signals to learners and teachers the potential value and application of what they can learn. Tasks can be designed to provide opportunities for the development of particular skills, such as problem solving or planning, or dispositions such as creativity or a 'can do attitude'.

Task-based learning tends to favour a more facilitative approach to teaching, because, once the task is agreed, the teacher takes on a supportive rather than a principal role in the activity. This empowers the learner, though it can also increase the risk of failure. This implies that task-based work-related learning can help learners to develop autonomy and encourage creativity, but that support will be needed to encourage learners to take on extra freedom and manage risk.

A focus on tasks also draws attention to the embodied character of learning, that is to the way in which our perceptions, physical actions and thinking are connected together. Researchers have investigated the ways in which practice and observation mutually reinforce one another in the development of craft and sports skills and they have suggested that repetition and sustained engagement are vital to skill development (Sennett 2009). Attaching learning to goal-orientated tasks and asking learners to take responsibility for particular tasks which form part of a larger project are pedagogies that help learners to take ownership of their learning and so commit the time and interest that is necessary if they are to fully benefit from involvement.

These are approaches that are well established in enterprise education, business challenges, work experience and vocational education. However, there is scope to extend them to other parts of work-related learning and more broadly across the curriculum.

Learning processes

Chapter 6 of this book explored different theories of how students learn on vocational programmes and 14–19 Diplomas in particular. Drawing upon wider research, Chapter 6 proposed that an adequate account of Diploma pedagogy should synthesise a number of different theories of learning and teaching:

- experiential theories – learners engage in tasks and have experiences which they review and reflect upon to create knowledge which then informs further activity and experiences

- socio-cultural theories – learners participate in groups, institutions and communities where they develop skills, beliefs, values and behaviour appropriate for participation
- re-application or boundary crossing – learners are able to transfer or adapt skills, understanding and knowledge developed in one context to different contexts.

These theories of learning are not unique to work-related learning; however, they are particularly pertinent if we are trying to understand how work-related learning can take place and how it might be designed to succeed. Hands-on experience, for example through simulations and work placements, is vital to work-related learning, because it supports engagement, skills development, review and reflection. However, students also learn from others, both by interacting with them and by sharing beliefs and knowledge. The development of attitudes and aspirations can be powerfully influenced by social learning such as teamwork, competitive challenges, interviews, mentoring and work experience.

Experiential and socio-cultural learning are particularly prominent in work-related learning; their distinctiveness is part of the case for work-related learning. Work as a context lends itself to experiential and socio-cultural learning, but it is not the only context that does and these pedagogies are not restricted to work-related learning.

Re-application or transfer refers to the capability of re-applying what has been learnt in one context to another (see Chapter 8). Much work-related learning is heavily contextualised: students are taught how to tackle particular tasks or address problems arising in certain types of organisation or how to collaborate in particular groups. If the value of what has been learnt is to be maximised then students should learn how to successfully re-apply their learning to alternative contexts. Research into the transfer of learning suggests that this kind of re-application is not automatic: students need to have the opportunity to explore contrasting contexts and to try out knowledge transfer and review what happens (QCA 2008b).

It is a strength of work-related learning that it recognises the particular context of learning and makes a virtue out of these particularities. A school that I visited in Kent recently was working hard to exploit the learning potential of local streets (through an 'adopt a street' campaign) and its rural environment (it had a number of enterprise projects associated with plant growing and rural businesses).

However, through involvement in many such projects, students were expected to develop general 'enterprise skills' which could be routinely deployed in any subject, in pretty much any lesson and beyond the school in entrepreneurial activities.

Summary

To summarise, work-related learning is indeed a collection of distinctive educational practices. Over the last 30 years, many of these practices have been favoured by policy and supported by funding so that their status and take-up have grown; work experience is the outstanding example. At both policy and institutional level, there have been some moves to integrate these different practices – both to make better sense of them and for practical, delivery purposes. However, with the radical change in educational policy that has been promised by the new government elected in 2010, it seems that there will no longer be any encouragement from the state for the integration of work-related learning. Indeed it seems likely that there will be less encouragement and funding for certain types of work-related learning.

Nevertheless, if we look at the different kinds of activities that constitute work-related learning and we analyse them, we find that they share family characteristics, to a greater or lesser degree, and that they can all be understood within the same framework. Furthermore, we can see that work-related learning has developed a range of pedagogies, drawing on features of work or workplace learning, and that these pedagogies have been tested and refined so that they can be widely used in schools and colleges. These pedagogies are, at this time, the greatest legacy of work-related learning: it is up to practitioners to decide how they take these pedagogies forward and what goals they may try to use them for.

Notes

1. See the Toot Hill School case study in Chapter 5.
2. http://www.realgame.co.uk/ – currently an online resource, the Real Game has been available in different formats for many years.

References

DCSF (2003) *Every Child Matters: Change for Children.*. Available HTTP: <http://www.dcsf.gov.uk/everychildmatters/_download/?id=2675> (accessed 20 December 2010).

pfeg (2010) *Autumn Newsletter*. London: pfeg.

QCA (2008a) *Career, Work-Related Learning and Enterprise 11–19: A Framework to Support Economic Wellbeing*. London: QCA.

QCA (2008b) *The Diploma and Its Pedagogy*. London: QCA. Available HTTP: <http://www2.warwick.ac.uk/fac/soc/cei/research/archive/> (accessed 20 December 2010).

Sennett, R. (2009) *The Craftsman*. London: Penguin.

Taskforce on Education and Employment (2010) *What Is To Be Gained?* Available HTTP: <http://www.educationandemployers.org/> (accessed 20 December 2010).

Index